CONTRACT FARMING & LAND TENANCY

in Indian Agriculture

Thank you for choosing a SAGE product!
If you have any comment, observation or feedback,
I would like to personally hear from you.

Please write to me at contactceo@sagepub.in

Vivek Mehra, Managing Director and CEO, SAGE India.

Bulk Sales

SAGE India offers special discounts
for purchase of books in bulk.
We also make available special imprints
and excerpts from our books on demand.

For orders and enquiries, write to us at

Marketing Department
SAGE Publications India Pvt Ltd
B1/I-1, Mohan Cooperative Industrial Area
Mathura Road, Post Bag 7
New Delhi 110044, India

E-mail us at marketing@sagepub.in

Subscribe to our mailing list
Write to marketing@sagepub.in

This book is also available as an e-book.

CONTRACT FARMING & LAND TENANCY
in Indian Agriculture

Parmod Kumar
Manjunatha A. V.
Suman K. Sourav

Los Angeles | London | New Delhi
Singapore | Washington DC | Melbourne

First published in 2021 by

SAGE Publications India Pvt Ltd
B1/I-1 Mohan Cooperative Industrial Area
Mathura Road, New Delhi 110 044, India
www.sagepub.in

SAGE Publications Inc
2455 Teller Road
Thousand Oaks, California 91320, USA

SAGE Publications Ltd
1 Oliver's Yard, 55 City Road
London EC1Y 1SP, United Kingdom

SAGE Publications Asia-Pacific Pte Ltd
18 Cross Street #10-10/11/12
China Square Central
Singapore 048423

Published by Vivek Mehra for SAGE Publications India Pvt Ltd. Typeset in 10.5/13 pt Bembo by AG Infographics, Delhi.

Library of Congress Control Number: 2020951165

ISBN: 978-93-5388-626-4 (HB)

SAGE Team: Rajesh Dey, Ankit Verma, Shivani A. Damle and Kanika Mathur

Contents

List of Illustrations

TABLES

FIGURES

ANNEXURES

List of Abbreviations

ACC	Appachi Cotton Company
ACE	Agriculture Centre of Excellence
AP	Andhra Pradesh
APMC	Agricultural Produce Market Committee
ATA	Agricultural Tenancies Act
CAP	Common Agricultural Policy
CCI	Cotton Corporation of India
CF	Contract farming
CGG	Community grower group
e-NAM	e-National Agriculture Market
ESI	Employees' State Insurance
EU	European Union
FAO	Food and Agriculture Organization
FCI	Food Corporation of India
FPCs	Farmer producer companies
FPO	Farmer Producer Organizations
FSC	Farmer service centre
FYM	Farm yard manure
FYP	Five-Year Plan
GCA	Gross cropped area
HLL	Hindustan Lever Limited
IDRC	International Development Research Centre
KSHDA	Karnataka State Horticulture Development Agency
KLRA	Karnataka Land Reforms Act
LECs	Loan eligibility cards
MP	Madhya Pradesh
MSP	Minimum support price
MSSL	Mahindra Shublabh Services Limited
NIA	Net irrigated area
NITI	National Institution for Transforming India

NMS	New member states
NOA	Net operated area
NSSO	National Sample Survey Office
NWRS	Negotiable Warehouse Receipt System
OBC	Other Backward Class
PAFC	Punjab Agro Foodgrains Corporation
PF	Provident fund
PMFBY	Pradhan Mantri Fasal Bima Yojana
RTC	Record of Rights, Tenancy and Crop Information
SC	Scheduled Castes
SHG	Self-help group
SPS	Single Payment Scheme
SSA	Sub-Saharan Africa
ST	Scheduled Tribes
TN	Tamil Nadu
UP	Uttar Pradesh
UT	Union Territory

Foreword

Indian agriculture is dominated by marginal and tiny land holdings. More than two-thirds of operational land holdings operate on less than 1 ha area and 86 per cent operate on less than 2 ha area. These farmers suffer from several disadvantages. Low-scale, poor bargaining power in input and output market, low capacity to invest in farming, missing opportunities for future growth and low level of income despite higher productivity per unit of land are cited as main concerns of smallholders. Low level of economic returns to meet family expenditure, inability to repay loans and the inability to absorb price and production shocks often push many such farmers into distress. The options to escape hardships of this kind of situation are (a) expand farm business by leasing-in land from other fellow farmers (b) exit farming if better income avenues are available and earn rent on own land by leasing it out (c) have contract with some agribusiness firm to grow high-value crops which enable access to modern technology, capital, knowledge and sharing of price risk. These options can be appropriately used if there is a transparent and liberal regulatory environment for land leasing and contract farming (CF). Such regulatory environment is beneficial for all categories of farmers, agribusiness firms, agro-processors, exporters and organized retailers which in turn can give boost to farm economy, total economy as well as employment. It is thus imperative to examine all aspects of land lease and CF in the country.

The central government has attempted to bring significant policy reforms in agriculture in the wake of the challenges of COVID-19 pandemic. These reforms are: Amendments to Essential Commodities Act of 1955, a central trading law to liberalize sale/purchase of farm produce without any kind of restrictions and farming agreement on price assurance and farm services. The third reform is aimed at promoting

CF by addressing limitations of the existing state-level CF acts and regulations. Besides these, National Institution for Transforming India (NITI) Aayog has been trying to pursue States to enact land-lease law using the format of Model Agricultural Land Leasing Act prepared by the NITI Aayog as a model.

Various experts are of the view that these policy reforms would prove biggest game changer for agriculture and farmers in the long run. They have the potential to transform Indian agriculture in ways that are currently not realized. If reforms introduced are successful in attracting agribusiness firms towards agriculture, the possibilities are immense. A single firm can contract with hundreds of farmers and consolidate their activities in one go, enabling them with economies of scale, thus solving India's biggest policy challenge. Through CF, corporate sector will have an incentive to invest in agricultural infrastructure for storage and food processing and other agro-based industries, thus creating backward and forward market linkages. CF will also help bringing crop diversification and shift focus of Indian agriculture towards high-value production like fruits and vegetables, animal and fishery products. There are other positive changes CF will usher in. It is because of these reasons that the Government of India took initiatives in the direction of formulating Model Agricultural Land Leasing Act and came with an Ordinance on The Farmers (Empowerment and Protection) Agreement on Price Assurance and Farm Service Ordinance on15 June 2020, to enhance farmer's income and farm viability.

This book has important messages and lessons for promoting land-lease law and CF. It systematically analyses CF in the broader frame-work of existing land and lease market system. It is an empirical study based on a large sample of farmers in four states of the country and it examines equity, efficiency and sustainability issues in alternate land arrangements. The authors very ably captured and narrated ground-level experience relating to the choice of farmers for CF, reasons for reluctance to enter into formal land-lease arrangements and sub-optimal outcome under existing arrangements. This study seeks to understand the principle key determinants that drive contractual/lease relationships through many examples in the country. The authors elicit and present views of farmers on CF under different settings, which are crucial for promotion of CF in the country. The book further provides insights on experience of CF and various types of informal and oral land leasing as well as land sharing institutional arrangements. I hope the book will help in better appreciation of benefits of enacting agricultural land-lease law and spread of CF in the country.

Professor Ramesh Chand
Member, NITI Aayog, Government of India
Yojana Bhawan, New Delhi

Preface

CF in developing countries is a debatable subject. Proponents of CF advocate that it is a key strategy for rural transformation based on a dynamic partnership between smallholder and companies. It provides opportunities to both the parties to benefit from modern technology, marketing facilities and other services to increase their income. The contract often involves provision of seed, fertilizer, technical assistance, credit and guaranteed price at harvest. This form of vertical coordination between grower and company solves a number of constraints related to small-farm productivity, price risk and access to inputs, credit and information. Farmers may learn some skill set such as record keeping, efficient use of farm resources, improved methods of applying chemicals and fertilizers, understanding the importance of quality and desirable crop characteristics and demands of export market.

The opponents of CF say that agribusiness firms use contracts to take advantage of cheap labour and transfer production risk to farmers. They also believe that companies will prefer medium and large-size farmers to procure raw material thus exacerbating rural inequality among farmers. Some critics observe that the history of contracting is 'replete with company manipulation and abrogation of contracts' and peasants are self-exploited, working more intensively and extensively (including their children and other non-paid household labour) on their own farm. The relation between agribusiness firms and farmers are similar to slave owners and slaves. Contracting firms also brings tension between the family members (especially between heads of household and their wives and children) of the contracting households. This results in neglecting fields which are brought under contract production.

CF in India is happening because of pre-requisite of good quality, time-bound and economic raw materials. It does not matter whether the agribusiness firm is operating in domestic or international market.

As per the Land Ceiling Act in India, agribusiness firms are forbidden to purchase agricultural land and cultivate them for their requirements of raw material. Also, this is not a viable option most of the time. Some parts of India (especially northern part) are still based on monoculture of wheat and paddy crop which accounts for more than 60 per cent of GCA and has resulted in decline of ground-water table, ecological degradation and over-capitalization of the farm sector. Agriculture is the driver of growth for the farming community. Therefore, the economic condition of majority of farmers, especially marginal and small, cannot be improved unless there is diversification in their cropping pattern and in the technology of production. CF is being promoted in India to achieve the diversification of crop production by promoting high-value crops, lowering cost of production with better extension and raising incomes by assured market, and higher prices for the produce.

Another concern of improving economic condition of marginal and small farmer is land rental restrictions in India. Some studies revealed that with elimination of restrictions on land rental market, 40–70 per cent of efficient producers will get the land. Land leasing is a subject matter of states in India. Every state regulates their land leasing act by themselves. In case of marginal and small farmers, they rent the land based on crop-yield sharing basis, whereas medium and large farmers rent land on cash-rent lease contracts. In both the cases productivity of the rented land is lower by 8–13 per cent than the owned land. The reason behind this is the land is not rented for a long period because of the tenancy acts which restrict to rent the land for longer period and the cultivator is not sure whether he/she will get the same land next time or not. Therefore, there is no incentive for the cultivator to make heavy investment.

India has satisfactorily achieved higher production and food security. However, it needs critical attention on post-harvest and marketing of agricultural produce with a major concern to increase farmer's income and farm viability. Still, 22.5 per cent of the country's farmers are living below poverty line. According to 'Situation Assessment Survey of Agricultural households, 2013' report, the average monthly income of the agricultural household at all-India level was ₹6,426 against the average monthly consumption expenditure of ₹6,223. In view of this situation, the government has committed itself to double the farmers' income by the year 2022 through adoption of targeted policies and multipronged schemes and programmes.

It is well known that Indian agriculture is dominated by a large number of small and marginal farmers which constitute 85 per cent of the total land holdings in the country. The average size of the land holding is as low as 1.1 ha. Land division and fragmentation is still continuing because of separation of family members. Therefore, pooling of land resources to achieve efficient scale of operation and marketing stages has been felt necessary. The NITI Aayog has drafted and circulated a Model Land Leasing Act to all the states and union territories (UTs). In addition to that, the union finance minister announced government's commitment to prepare a Model Contract Farming Act during budget speech of 2017–2018. The Ministry of Agriculture and Farmers' Welfare has constituted a committee to draft a Model Contract Farming Act under the chairmanship of Dr Ashok Dalwai. The committee has prepared a draft Act that has been put in public for seeking suggestions for possible further improvements.

Keeping in mind the objectives of this study, a cross-sectional study has been done from four states; two states, namely, Punjab and Haryana from North India and other two states, namely, Karnataka and AP (including Telangana) from South India. The book is compilation of this study that gives a detailed assessment of CF and land tenancy situations in these four states. Some interesting inferences are drawn across different farm sizes in contract and land tenancy farming system. Some pros and cons of CF have been observed which will provide guidelines in the finalization of the draft Model Contract Farming Act. We are sure that this book will help to formulate a strong policy in favour of stakeholders involved in CF and land tenancy in India. The book shall be a useful reference for agriculture and other academic universities and institutions, students and academic researchers.

Acknowledgements

This book is an outcome of a study titled *Contract Farming, Land Leasing and Land Sharing in India: Prospects and Challenges*. The study was entrusted by the Department of Agriculture, Cooperation and Farmers Welfare, Ministry of Agriculture and Farmers Welfare, Government of India, New Delhi.

The study enables to understand CF and land tenancy institutions and their impact on farming communities. The results and policy suggestions provide insights in policy fine-tuning and bringing in improvements in the recently amended CF and land leasing acts. Data has been collected from Punjab, Haryana, Karnataka and Unified AP (including Telangana) for carrying out this study. In the aggregate, 500 farm households, comprising 400 farmers belonging to the category of contract farmers, land-leasing farmers and share-cropping farmers and 100 farmers from the control group not belonging to any of the above-mentioned categories were selected in each state.

Authors thank the Crop Division of the Ministry of Agriculture and Farmers Welfare for the strong support for carrying out the study. Authors sincerely thank the officials of the ministry for their support and inputs—especially to Dr S.K. Malhotra, MOA, and Dr A.P. Singh, NITI Aayog—which has helped in successful completion of the task. Thanks are also due to the officials of the Crop Division of the Ministry for their cooperation. Thanks also to concerned officials of the agriculture and horticulture departments of the respective states for their cooperation in all respects.

Authors would like to thank Professor M.G. Chandrakanth, Director, Institute for Social and Economic Change, for his support and encouragement. Thanks also to Soujanya C.K., who was involved in all stages of the study and Dr P. Thippaiah for his brief engagements in this project. The foremost thanks to farmers and other stakeholders in the four states who provided detailed information during the course of survey work of this study. Without their cooperation, this study could not have taken this shape. Thanks are also due to the company officials for providing detailed list of farmers engaged in CF and also providing other necessary information regarding the company questionnaires. The list is too long to be spelt out individually.

Thanks to partner organizations, Sirtazi Support, Lucknow, and Livelihoods and Natural Resource Management Institute, Hyderabad, for carrying out the primary survey across the selected states.

Last but not least, we would like to thank our colleagues Dr I. Maruthi and Dr K.B. Ramappa for the motivation. The secretarial assistance by Mr Vijay N. Malave and Mr Mutthuraja of Agricultural Development and Rural Transformation Centre are gratefully acknowledged.

Chapter 1

Contract Farming and Land Tenancy in India
An Introduction

Contract farming (CF) is an agreement between farmers and agribusiness firms or a local processing unit or a multinational company for the production and supply of agricultural products under forward agreements, usually at pre-determined prices. The contract is thereby a commitment by a seller/farmer to supply an agricultural commodity of a particular quality, at a particular time, in requisite amount and at a pre-agreed price to the buyer. The success of the contract requires a long-term commitment from both the parties (Eaton & Shepherd, 2001). There are certain characteristics that contracting companies take into consideration for selecting crops.—These are perishability, bulkiness, type of crops, whether the crop is processable or not, variation in quality, familiarity of crop/s and so on (Paty, 2005).

CF provides a way of organizing agricultural production in which producers are obliged to supply certain amount of produce with specific quality at decided time and place to agro-industrial enterprises. These enterprises also make provision for supplying key resources such as credits, inputs and extension services to the producers to strengthen the contract agreement. The intensity of contractual agreement varies according to the commitment of the binding parties in which enterprises agree to supply inputs and services and producers commit recommended production practices, inputs and product grades.

Minot (1986) classifies contracts into the following three non-mutually exclusive categories:

- **Market specification:** These contracts are a kind of pre-harvest agreements in which buyers and producers are bound to specific terms and conditions which governs the sale of the produce. Generally, conditions in this contract specify price, quality and timing.
- **Resource provision:** In conjunction with marketing arrangements, the buyer agrees to supply selected inputs, extension or credit, technical advice covering production practices and land preparation, along with standardizing the quality of the crop. These conditions directly shape and regulate the production and labour process of the grower.
- **Production management:** Contracts bind the farmer to follow a particular production method, input regimes and harvesting specifications, usually in exchange for a marketing agreement or resource provision.

The relevance of each type of contract varies from product to product and from time to time (Fulton & Clark, 1996; Hill & Ingersent, 1982; Key & Runsten, 1999). Whereas the first type is generally referred to as a marketing contract, the second and third types belong to the category of production contracts (Ayako & Glover, 1989; Little & Watts, 1994; Scott, 1984). The risk involved in production and marketing both to the buyer and the seller also varies in the above three types of contracts.

In its various forms, CF permits firms to improve the production technology and act as a linking channel in the missing market without having their own land of production (Runsten & Key, 1996). With effective management, CF can be a triggering agent to develop market and transfer technological knowledge and skills to producers which are mutually beneficial to the farmers and contracting agencies. It is indeed true that CF is characterized by its various forms of contractual agreement which not only varies with the type of products contracted, but also varies with how those products will be produced (Jackson & Cheater, 1994). The approach has already been successful in the

West, especially for perishables like fruits and vegetables, poultry, dairy products, prawns and fish. In the developing countries also, CF is becoming an increasingly popular means of product supply where the land tenure rules or the political realities would not permit such large-scale farming.[1]

It is important to recognize that restructuring of the agricultural system in the form of CF has been an outcome of wider changes in market environment in the industry and trade sectors. These changes at the macro level also induce micro changes where number of producers start practising CF which has great potential to change the entire production structure and relations in the traditional ways of agriculture. CF is also seen as a part of internationalization process in the agricultural sector which comprises three different dimensions such as globalization of production, capital and trade. All these three dimensions are intervened through strategies followed by contracting agencies in input supply and production decisions, supply of capital and finance and global sourcing of agro-products (Singh, 2002).

VARIOUS MODELS OF CF

Global

1. The centralized model: Centralized model is a vertical coordination where the sponsor purchases the crop from farmers and processes and markets the produce (Mansur et al., 2009). The contracts under this model are often associated with large farms because of large volumes required to make processing a success of produce (Bijman, 2008). The agribusiness firms buy the produce from large number of smallholders under strict quality control conditions and in predetermined quantities. The model usually involves the provision of extensive technical support, inputs and close control of the production process. The centralized scheme is generally associated with tobacco, cotton, sugar cane and

---

[1] CF has spread rapidly in Africa over the last two decades, encouraged by structural adjustment programmes and shortages of foreign exchange in poor countries (See for e.g., Ayako and Glover, 1989; Glover, 1990; Little and Watts, 1994).

bananas and with tree crops such as coffee, tea, cocoa and rubber, but can also be used for poultry, pork and dairy production (Eaton & Shepherd, 2001). The examples in real world are (a) sugarcane production by CF in Thailand; (b) in Philippines, a vegetable-canning company followed this model to control diversion of farmers from growing crops and making extra-contractual sales (Eaton & Shepherd, 2001).

1. Thenucleus estate model: In this model, agribusiness owns the plantation adjacent to a processing plant. The estate is usually large which guarantees input to processing plant and sometimes relatively small which is used only for research and breeding purposes. This model is mainly used for tree crops. Usually, sponsors start with a pilot estate and after a trial period the technology and management techniques are disseminated to the farmers (sometimes they are called as 'satellite' growers). This model of CF is often applied in connection with resettlement or transmigration schemes for oil palm and other crops (Eaton & Shepherd, 2001; Mansur et al., 2009). For example, (a) Indonesia and Papua New Guinea used this model as resettlement and transmigration scheme for oil-palm growers and dairy farming (Eaton & Shepherd, 2001); (b) smallholders in Tabanan of Indonesia growing corn in contract with Denpasar company, Tobacco plantation throughout Indonesia and Japanese-ginger production in Kabupaten Bangli regency of Indonesia (Patrick, 2004); (c) hog, shrimp and broiler business in Thailand followed this model using large corporations (Sriboonchitta & Wiboonpongse, 2005).

2. The multipartite model: Governments, NGOs and service providers are involved between company and the farmers. They are also involved in dealing with farmer's organizations such as cooperatives as well as joint ventures between the government and the private sector. The third party (an NGO or the government) in a multipartite model plays an important role in dispute resolution and contract enforcement (Eaton & Shepherd, 2001; Mansur et al., 2009). For example, (a) in India Oil Palm CF in AP, Karnataka and other states the government is responsible for fixing up the prices and providing extension services to the farmers with the help of entrepreneurs.

These entrepreneurs through government are responsible for importing planting material, distribution of seedlings to farmers and arranging inputs. The processing units provide transportation facility to the farmer through the help of an agent (Dev & Rao, 2005); (b) in Mexico, Kenya, and West Africa, governments have actively invested in CF through joint ventures with the private sector. In China, government departments as well as township committees and, at times, foreign companies have jointly entered into contracts with village committees and, since the early 1980s, individual farmers (Eaton & Shepherd, 2001).

3. The informal model: This model is mainly characterized by informal contracts done between individual entrepreneurs or small companies and producers. The contracts are mainly done on seasonal basis. The crops grown under this model include fresh vegetables, watermelons and tropical fruits that require less processing. This model is different from above models for its limited resources for strong vertical co-ordination. Therefore, its success largely depends on the support/incentive provided by government or other service providers. The terms and conditions for the binding agreement is mainly limited to provision of seeds and basic fertilizer by sponsors and production of certain grades and quality products by the producers (Eaton & Shepherd, 2001; Mansur et al., 2009). A common example of the informal model is where the sponsor, after purchasing the crop, simply grades and packages it for resale to the retail trade. Supermarkets frequently purchase fresh produce through individual developers and, in some cases, directly from farmers (Eaton & Shepherd, 2001).

4. The intermediary model: This model involves intermediaries between producers and buyers. In this model, buyers are at the risk of losing control over quality, quantity and price because of their weak linkages with the farmers. On the other hand, farmers are also not safe from market uncertainties. This model is mostly found in South-East Asia (Eaton & Shepherd, 2001; Mansur et al., 2009). This model was seen operating in (a) in early 1990's firms in Sri Lanka encouraged by the government to participate in Gherkin production. In northern province of Thailand, farmers grow chrysanthemum and fresh vegetables

for the Chiangamai and Bangkok markets under verbal agreements with individual developers. Developers just provide credit at times for seeds, fertilizers and plastic sheets whereas technical assistance is given by the government. A snap-frozen industry in northern Thailand directly contracts out to middlemen or collectors who organize to grow soybeans, green beans and baby corn primarily for Japanese market (Eaton & Shepherd, 2001). (b) Ethiopia: africa JUICE Tiliba Share Company, a leading supplier of Fairtrade tropical fruit juice (passion fruit) for the European market. It is a hybrid of joint venture, nucleus and multipartite model. The company offers ownership opportunities to local smallholder farmers in Ethiopia by selling shares. The ownership will be structured as follows: africa JUICE (81%), Ethiopian Government (14%) and the local community (5%) (Melese, 2011). (c) Smallholders in Kabupaten Tabanan, Bali, growing paprika, tomato, lettuce, cabbage, celery, cauliflower and cut flowers under informal model of CF where agribusiness firm sub-contracts with the trader for the production of required crops (Patrick, 2004). (d) Gherkin Cultivation in Chittoor district of AP (Dev & Rao, 2005).

5. Partly informal models: It involves formal type of contract between farmers and middlemen (quota men) which includes written contract. The middlemen and processing companies have informal contract type. This type of model is found in Thailand for food processing companies and fresh vegetable firms. The middlemen will be responsible for collecting produce from the farmers for the company to meet certain granted quotas. The processing firms in turn supply seed materials to farmers through middlemen (Wiboonpongse & Sriboonchitta, 2008).

6. Harvest and pay: This form of CF is generally prevalent in the areas where farmers have very limited access or no access to the formal and informal credit institutions. So by seeing this opportunity, some local traders came up with credits to help smallholders to buy inputs (seeds and fertilizer) in return of smallholder promise to sell their produce only to them. The cost of credit gets settled at the time of product procurement when a negotiated price is determined by taking into account the cost of credit and spot-market price (Patrick, 2004).

Within India

The Bipartite Model

In this type of model, the contract agreement is between the company and the farmer where company supplies inputs to farmers and farmers, in turn, supply their produce to the company directly. There are only two parties involved in the contracting system. Farmer(s) contract with the company to supply specific produce at agreed price, quality and quantity. In return of that, company pays the agreed amount and inputs required in the production process. There are plenty of examples of bipartite model in India, for example, (a) the CF model followed by the Pepsi, HLL and Nijjer growers in Punjab were bipartite model. It is an agreement with the company and the farmer. The company supplied inputs to the farmers and procured the specified quantity. This model failed since there was hardly any incentive provided by the company and the entire risk was borne by the farmers while the company had the insurance against them. The contract gave the company right to refuse the produce and growers were penalized if they defaulted from their commitment (Singh, 2004).(b) Suguna Poultry Farm Ltd, in Tamil Nadu (TN), has emerged as one of the leading integrated broiler producers in the country with this type of CF. This kind of contractual arrangement has made the poultry producers free of worries about production and marketing of the poultry products. Currently, 90 per cent of the poultry production comes under this contractual agreement in TN (Gulati et al., 2008; Singh, 2004).(c) In Punjab, companies such as Chambal Agritech and AM Todd mainly procure under the bi-partite model of contract in which sponsors provide some inputs to the growers and buy-back their produce. However, sometimes sponsors are also seen to have tri-partite case of agreement in which they also provide credit along with buying the produce at farm gate. Frito Lay International (Pepsi) in Maharashtra worked through an intermediary called 'Hundekari', who builds up relations with the small growers by representing them as company agents and manages activities from registering farmers to buy-back the produce. In Karnataka, farmers themselves organize informal associations and manage operations like seed distribution and schedule of product delivery among themselves (Kaur & Singla, 2016; Singh, 2007).

Tripartite Model

This model incorporates industry, growers and financial institutions. Under this system, the industry supplies quality planting material at sub-sidized rate and assures Minimum Support Price (MSP) of the prevailing market price, whichever is higher. In tripartite model, an additional financial institution is involved to facilitate credit transfer. The company involved in this model gets credit from bank to buy inputs and supply them to the farmers and farmers pay for the inputs by supplying produce to the company. When company receives the amount by selling the farmer's produce, then they pay back to the bank. The end payment to the farmers (in some cases) are made after deducting the dues.

As an example, (a) this model was practised by Punjab Agro-Food Industries Corporation (PAFC), department of agriculture, Punjab. The model specified the fixed price and bonus to be paid by PAFC to the farmer for the produce type and quantity of seed to be supplied by the seed company at a particular price for given acreage, farmer's responsibility of delivering the quality produce at a specific place, the payment by PAFC within two days after delivery and; PAFC being the sole authorities in deciding weight of the produce and the only arbitrator in case the contract terms were dishonoured by any of the parties. The contract was signed by all three parties in the presence of two witnesses for the farmer (Singh, 2004). (b) State department of agriculture in TN has proposed contractual cotton cultivation programme in Thanjavur, Nagapattinam, Tiruvarur (coastal), Tirunelveli, Salem, Erode and Namakkal districts. In this model, financial and insurance agencies are involved in supplying credits to the growers and securing accidental loss of crops. Also, the choice of cotton and their quality parameters are decided in consultation with the TN Agricultural University and textile mills in the State through Southern India Mills' Association. Hindustan Lever Limited (HLL), Rallis and ICICI jointly promote CF in wheat in Madhya Pradesh (MP). In this contractual agreement, ICICI bank provides credit to farmers, Rallis supplies inputs and technical know-how and HLL buys back the produce at fixed price. By entering into such an agreement, all contracting parties derive benefits from this arrangement. Farmers get benefitted by having timely availability of inputs and technical know-how along with assured market for their produce. This supplements in improving the supply chain efficiency of the buyers (in this case-HLL). Rallis and ICICI get benefitted by having a fixed customer base for their products and services. This model has further scope of extension by incorporating insurance firms, warehouses and manufacturing agencies of machines and equipment (Gulati, 2008).

The Quadripartite Model

Sometimes, few companies such as agri-input companies, farm equipment companies, retailers, food companies, banks and agri-finance corporations jointly take venture to facilitate CF. The facilitating companies provide all the inputs, technical and financial support to all the registered farmers/producers for a specific crop and offer reasonable prices for the produce. The input companies tie-up with the banks and with buyers of produce to form a consortium. Therefore, the system formed with the interaction of such parties form a quadripartite model. Later, the quadripartite model had been modified by including local arthiya/commission agent/input dealer as a franchisee for the agri-facilitator and this system of interaction constitute six-partite model. The main objective of agribusiness facilitator in this model is to make strategies for sustained growth through partnership for sustainability and of course make money by helping others, including farmers. Their strategies involve aggregating inputs and linking credits with input supply, which is said to be agribusiness in the 21st century (Boehlje et al., 1995). A similar concept was proposed in 2001 by HLL chairman M.S. Banga as a farmer service centre (FSC) which can act as a focal point for credit suppliers, crop insurers, agri-input suppliers and food processors to buy-back from farmers and leasing of farm equipment and specialized grain transport and storage facilities (Banga, 2001).

In TN, similar kind of organizational structures were found under CF. However, one different kind of model, that is, 'private-community grower group-farmer model' was found. In this model, a private company undertakes CF on a profit-sharing basis with a community grower group (CGG) who have large acreage of farms. Farmers in the group are trained in-house in scientific organic farm management and certification. The CGG also follow fair trade practices wherein all sorts of extra costs are eliminated between producer and buyer. Middlemen are eliminated, child labour is banned, gender equality is taken care of and transparency is maintained in the trade. Product details are also recorded to trace the origin, nature and quantities of raw materials procured and their usage. Crops grown under this model of CF are banana, wheat, cotton, papaya, pineapple, basmati, mango, soybean, red gram, black gram, green gram, turmeric, grapes, chickpea, groundnut, sesame and cashew. Ion Enviro company has shown a successful example of this model.[2]

This system is similar to tripartite model barring the involvement of research institute. For example, (a) this type of model was being practised by Mahindra Shublabh Services Limited (MSSL) in Punjab and Rallis India in MP, Maharashtra, Haryana and Karnataka. The MSSL had an agreement with the government of Punjab for diversification. Company provided farmers with quality seeds, fertilizers, pesticides, farm equipment and extension services to raise yields. It also played a facilitating role to link farmers with processors and banks for market and credit respectively (Singh, 2004). Rallis India Company provided all inputs, technical support and finance to registered growers for a specific crop and facilitated the sale of produce at reasonable prices. The company followed a consortium approach. It tied-up with banks like ICICI and SBI and with buyers to provide credit. In addition, every farmer had accident insurance coverage (Singh, 2004). (b) In Kaithal in Haryana, for organic basmati rice, Agrocel supplied organic inputs certified by Skal and seed supplied by Picric and procured the entire basmati paddy from the farmers at the factory gate. Agrocel charges ₹500 from Picric as service charge for coordinating contract organic basmati production with the farmers (Singh, 2007).

Private-Community Grower Group-Farmer Model

Ion Environ undertakes CF with CGG having large acreage on a profit-sharing basis. Farmers are trained in-house in scientific organic farm management and certification. CGG are promoted through NGOs,

---

[2] http://www.agritech.tnau.ac.in/agricultural_marketing/agrimark_contract%20farming.html

self-help groups (SHGs) or registered associations. In the process, they bring to rural areas the best of organic processes and water management techniques, thereby educating and empowering farmers. Written and documentary accounts are recorded to trace the origin, nature and quantities of raw materials procured and their usage. The crops cultivated include banana, wheat, cotton, papaya, pineapple, basmati, mango, soybean, tur, black gram, green gram, turmeric, grapes, Bengal gram, groundnut, sesame and cashew (Gulati, 2008).

Grading House–SHG–Farmer Model

Appachi Cotton Company (ACC), the ginning and trading house in Pollachi under the name Integrated Cotton Cultivation, established backward and forward integration between the 'grower' (farmer) and the 'consumer' (textile units). Under this arrangement, farmers are largely benefitted through easy availability of inputs (good quality and door delivery), credits at an interest rate of 12 per cent per annum, extension services, supervision by experts in every alternate week and predefined selling option agreed with ACC. The key element in this contractual agreement is formation of farmers' SHGs (Gulati, 2008).

PREVAILING CF IN INDIA

Given above are different models of CF; one can sum up that CF is a kind of system in which production and supply of agricultural produce are done under forward contracts and the essence of such contracts are in the form of commitments made by the farmers/producers to provide an agricultural commodity of specific quality, at a time and a price and in the quantity required by the buyers (Singh, 2002). Contracting system in agriculture had started from the sugarcane sector operating under the cooperative structure in India. Later, the sugarcane industry became dependent on state government support and needed some political intervention. Similarly, dairy sector also flourished under the cooperative structure and millions of small farmers got benefitted through Operation Flood in 1970s. Later, private players also followed formation of cooperative structure and started contracting with dairy farmers to source liquid milk from them. Some other corporate firms from poultry industry, basmati rice mills, potato production also applied CF concept and became popular as well as successful. In early 1990s, some high-value crops such as tomato and chillies were brought under CF. Most recently, contracting in exotic vegetables such as baby corn, bell peppers, Jalapeños, gherkins, etc., have been started (Gulati et al., 2009).

DEMAND FOR CF IN CHANGING AGRICULTURAL SCENARIOS IN INDIA

In recent decades, it has been observed that due to high economic growth, rising per capita income, urbanization and more participation of women in labour force have enforced diversification in agricultural production in India. The dietary pattern of Indian people has shifted from food grains to high-value commodities such as fruits, vegetables, meat and fish products followed by increase in demand for processed and semi-processed products. This demand-driven production system is opening new opportunities in food retailing and processing. But it raises a major concern of linking different segments of production, value addition and marketing so that interests of various stakeholders are safeguarded. Therefore, it will be worthwhile to investigate into the nature and progress of CF in India (Gulati et al., 2009; Prasad et al., 2013; Punjabi, 2015; Singh & Ashokan, 2003).

STATUS OF LAND TENANCY (LEASING) IN INDIA

As per the legal status of land leasing, various regions of India are broadly grouped into five categories from legally banned to no legal ban on leasing-out/in land. In some states, leasing-out land is permissible for certain categories of landowners like disabled, widows, minors, defence personnel, etc. In some regions, tenant acquires the right to purchase the leased land from the owner within a specified period of tenancy. In tribal regions, transfer of tribal land to non-tribal land (even on lease basis) is only permitted by a competent authority. Haque (2012) believes that land leasing can be an important source of access to land and livelihood for rural poor, if the land lease market is activated by the process of legalization and liberalization.

At the time of independence, approximately 50 per cent of area was under zamindari system and other intermediary tenures. The remaining area was under Ryotwari system. Zamindari system was introduced by Cornwallis in 1793 through Permanent Settlement Act. It was introduced in the provinces of Bengal, Bihar, Orissa and Varanasi. Zamindars were recognized as middlemen between the tax collector and peasants. Being the owner of land, they were given rights to collect the rent from the peasants. Whatever the amount of rent collected from peasants was divided into 11 parts and 1 part was given to the zamindars. Whereas Ryotwari system was introduced by Thomas Munro in Madras, Bombay, some parts of Assam and Coorg provinces in 1820. In this system, ownership rights were handed over to the peasants and taxes were directly collected from peasants. The peasants had to pay 50 per cent of the produce in case of dry land and 60 per cent of produce in case of irrigated land as revenue to the Britishers.[3]

In the first few years after independence, most of the intermediary interests were abolished and whole country was brought under more or less the same kind of tenurial system. In Ryotwari system, it was supposed to be one of peasant proprietorship but in actual practice leasing-out land was common in Ryotwari areas. Similarly, in zamindari areas there had been sub-leasing. Most of the leases in these two areas were oral and terminable at will. Some legislative efforts were being made to provide a measure of security to the tenants even before independence. But after independence, the matter was seriously taken up and legislation was enacted to afford security of tenure to tenants, to provide fixation of fair rent and in some cases, for conferment of ownership rights on tenants. So, these measures which have been taken to safeguard tenant's rights constitute 'tenancy reform' (Appu, 1975).

EVOLUTION OF TENANCY REFORMS IN INDIA

Appu (1975) did an explorative review of evolution of tenancy reforms during first four Five-Year Plans (FYPs) in India after independence. There were several amendments made in the tenancy laws in one after another FYPs. After independence, the Indian National Congress

---

[3] http://www.clearias.com/land-revenue-systems-zamindari-ryotwari-mahalwari/

became the ruling party and recommended some agrarian reforms which said:

> All intermediaries between the tiller and the State should be eliminated and all middlemen should be replaced by non-profit taking agencies, such as cooperatives. Land should be held for use as a source of employment. The use of lands of those who are either non-cultivating landlords or otherwise unable for any period to exercise the right of cultivating them, must come to rest in the village cooperative community subject to the condition that the original lawful holder or his successor will be entitled to come back to the land for genuine cultivation.
>
> In the case of minors and the physically incapacitated persons, a share of the produce of the land should be given to them.
>
> The maximum size of holdings should be fixed. The surplus land over such a maximum should be acquired and placed at the disposal of the village cooperative. Small holdings should be consolidated, and steps taken to prevent further fragmentation (Dantwala, 1950).

Later on, these policies were redefined in more precise terms in the matter of land reforms. Therefore, the policy laid down in the First FYP (1951–1956) was that the large landowners were allowed to resume land for personal cultivation up to the ceiling limit within five years of duration and the surplus land over ceiling limit would be acquired permanently along with heritable rights by the tenants. Also, the rent of the land should not exceed the level of one-fourth to one-fifth of the gross produce. However, there were still some threat of resumption for personal cultivation hanging over the heads of tenants. So, this plan was not really effective to safeguard the rights of tenants (Appu, 1975).

In the Second FYP (1956–1961), it was recognized that the tenancy reforms implemented in the First FYP failed to confer any measure of security to the tenants. There was large-scale eviction of tenants under the guise of 'voluntary surrender'. The reason behind this was the ignorance on the part of the people of legislative provisions regarding security of tenure, possible lacunae in the law, inadequate land records and defective administrative arrangements. So, in this FYP these faulty aspects of reforms were diagnosed. The Second FYP also suggested that the produce rent should be paid in cash and the maximum rent should be fixed as the multiple of land revenue. Also, the tenants in non-resumable areas were enabled to purchase ownership rights by paying at a reasonable level and the purchase price (including land revenue) should not exceed 20 to 25 per cent of gross revenue (Appu, 1975).

As per the directives of central government, state government had to implement the reforms but the impact of tenancy legislation on the welfare of tenants was seen to be less, as expected. The reasons for this were that the state government failed to enact legislation for regulating the so-called 'voluntary surrender' and for defining 'personal cultivation'. So, in the Third FYP (1961–1966) a final goal was set to confer rights of ownership on as large number of tenants as possible. It was suggested that this could be achieved either by entitling ownership to states and transfer ownership rights to tenants or by declaring tenants as owners and requiring them to make payments in instalment (Appu, 1975).

During formulation of the Fourth FYP (1969–1974), it was realized that even after many years of implementation of tenancy reforms, the position of tenants-at-will continued to be extremely insecure. The plan said that:

> It has been observed that under the present arrangement of informal tenancy and share cropping, the landlord considers it unwise to invest in improving his land; likewise, the share-cropper or the tenant is either unable or reluctant to invest in inputs like fertilizers. The insecurity of tenancy has not only impeded the widespread adoption of the high-yielding varieties but in some cases led to social and agrarian tensions. In the present context, therefore, it is essential that a cultivating tenant or a sharecropper should have effective security of tenure of the land he cultivates and the existing tenancies declared non-resumable and permanent (Appu, 1975).

To create tenancy in future, the plan recommended that leasing-out should be permitted in the future,

> Only in special cases such as a person suffering from disability or in case a person joins the defence services. In such cases, the tenancy should be for a period of three years at a time subject to renewal unless the disability ceases. In case the person belongs to the defence services, it is recognized that he should be able to take possession of the tenanted land without any delay (Appu, 1975).

In the draft of Fifth FYP (1974–1978), a broad assessment of land reforms adopted since independence had been done and it stated that 'the laws for abolition of intermediary tenures have been implemented fairly efficiently whilst in the fields of tenancy reform and ceiling on holding, legislation has fallen short of the desired objectives and implementation of the enacted laws has been inadequate.' The concentration of landownership had been decreased very slightly. Share of landownership over 50 acres showed a relative decline and increase in the share of 20–50 acres landownership. However, with this shift of landownership, the poor peasant-tenant got evicted on a wide scale and became landless labourers or unrecorded sharecroppers who shifted from plot to plot. On the other hand, the relatively well to do peasants obtained ownership rights by purchase of land which they had formerly leased and improved their economic condition. Therefore, overall, the redistribution of land had taken place within the top 10–15 per cent of the agricultural population and the condition of peasants got worse with large-scale eviction. Hence in this FYP, land reforms continued with the previous policies of ceiling, redistribution of surplus land holding, elimination of middlemen, etc., with additional steps towards the consolidation of a record of rights for individual households in computerized form. Also, it was stressed on formation of people's committees in every village to finalize the disputes settled by Land Commission Act (Social Scientist, 1974).

In the Sixth FYP (1980–1985), the main strategy was to effectively implement the accepted policies of land reforms. The implementation of various elements of the policies had been taken up on a time-bound basis during the Sixth FYP. Following elements were considered while implementing the policies of land reforms.[4]

1. States without legislative provisions for conferment of ownership rights on all tenants except for specified exempted categories (defence personnel, minors, disabled, etc.) were directed to introduce appropriate legislative measures within a period of 1 year, that is, by 1981–1982.
2. Scheduled Tribes (ST) and Scheduled Castes (SC) were prioritized over redistribution of ceiling surplus land and the redistribution

---

[4] http://planningcommission.gov.in/plans/planrel/fiveyr/6th/6planch9.html

   programme was expected to be completed within a period of
   two years.
3. Compiling/updating of land records were programmed in a sys-
   tematic manner and phased to be completed within a period of five
   years, that is, 1980–1985.
4. All states were directed to run the programme of consolidation of
   land holdings and phased for completion in 10 years. The priority
   was given to the command areas of irrigation projects which should
   be completed in three to five years.
5. Allotment of land to landless for construction of houses was also
   programmed to be completed in this FYP.

Strict enforcement of land reforms continued in the Seventh FYP
(1985–1990). Despite rigorous attempts by the Union government
to consolidate ceiling surplus land, a sum total of 51.8 million ha had
been consolidated till the Sixth FYP. This consolidated area constitutes only 33 per cent of the total cropped area in the country. During
the Seventh FYP, land reforms were linked with different poverty
alleviation programmes including the Minimum Needs Programme.
Development of waste lands and marginal lands allotted under land
reform measures were prioritized in this FYP. Also, a periodical
updating of land records from the base of all land reform measures
have been emphasized. The rights of tenants and sharecroppers were
also planned to be recorded under the upgradation scheme.[5]

In the Eighth FYP (1992–1997), the factors came on the way of
realizing goals of land reform policy that had been addressed. Some
stepwise operations were designed to address the factors realizing goals
of land reforms. First, an environment was created to ensure that the
actual cultivators are made aware of their rights and enabled to claim
their benefits. Second, some steps should be taken to encourage early
detection of surplus lands. Third, whatever the land acquired as a surplus should be brought under profitable agronomic practices which
will meet the objectives of poverty alleviation and productivity
enhancement. Some necessary support of resources and modernization to the skills and capabilities of the lower-level, official machinery

---

[5] http://planningcommission.gov.in/plans/planrel/fiveyr/7th/vol2/7v2ch2.html

should be given to manage land records properly and help the evolution of an equitable agrarian order.[6]

In the Ninth FYP (1997–2002), the ingredients of land reform policy continued as the same as before but the focus shifted to a few critical areas. All efforts were made to detect and redistribute the ceiling surplus land and to enforce the ceiling laws stringently. The rights of tenants and sharecroppers were also emphasized to be recorded and ensuring security of their tenure. Leasing-in of land was proposed to be permissible within the ceiling limits. The poor people were also given access to wastelands and common property resources. Some amendments in the existing legislations of some states were required to ensure land rights of women with regard to inheritance of both lands owned as also under tenancy. Updating of land records were also seen as a necessary prerequisite of any effective land reform policy. As land reforms are state subject, so the states were persuaded to take up these necessary measures.[7]

The consecutive FYPs made consistent efforts on conferring ownership rights to the tenant and put emphasis on agrarian restructuring to make agriculture more efficient and produce greater 'output and employment'. In the beginning of the Tenth FYP (2002–2007), it was realized that the impacts of tenancy reforms are not satisfactory. Tenancy laws in the states are followed in different patterns. Several states such as UP, Bihar and Orissa have either completely banned tenancy or imposed some restrictive conditions which makes impossible to lease lands. On the other hand, it is observed that over 34 per cent of land in Bihar is operated under concealed tenancy. Therefore, changes in the agrarian economy over the last three decades indicate the policymakers to rethink on the tenancy laws. Agriculture has reached at the stage of commercial farming; some reverse tenancy is happening in the agrarian economy in which middle and large farmers are leasing land from small and marginal farmers.[8]

In several regions, the existing institutional arrangements (tenancy laws) lead landowners to keep the land fallow in fear of losing their

---

[6] http://planningcommission.gov.in/plans/planrel/fiveyr/8th/vol2/8v2ch2.htm
[7] http://planningcommission.gov.in/plans/planrel/fiveyr/9th/vol2/v2c2-1.htm
[8] Planning Commission of India, 10th Five Year Plan, Vol 2, page 301

ownership rights. On the other side, it restricts the poor people to lease-in land from landowners. So, this creates a gap in demand and supply of land in lease market which reduces the output and efficiency of agricultural land. In the Eleventh FYP (2007–2012), following reforms in the tenancy legislation were recommended:

Tenancy should be legalized in a 'limited' manner. It should provide security to the tenant for the contractual period, which could be long enough to encourage long-term investment by the tenant. It should also protect the rights to the land of the landowner so that he has an incentive to lease his land instead of keeping it fallow or underutilizing it. Long-term tenure arrangements should thus maximize agricultural production and increase the returns to both the parties: the landlord and the tenant.

Instead of prescribed rentals, which are violated in informal tenancies, an upper and lower bound of rents may be prescribed at the State level. If these bands are wide enough, this will do away with the need for illegal arrangements, ensure that the rents are determined by market forces within the prescribed band, and thus increase efficiency and cooperation of both the willing parties.

Legalizing of tenancy within the above framework will result in increasing the supply of land and will encourage all categories of rural households to participate in the lease market based upon resource endowment, education, employment prospects, prevailing wage levels, and the institutional backup available.

As agrarian conditions vary across the States, a one size fit all prescription cannot be advocated. In cases where the landlords are dominant and there is strong likelihood that interests of tenants may not be safeguarded, special clauses could be necessary.

Small landowners who would otherwise have to operate small uneconomic holdings should have the opportunity to legally lease-out land to other farmers with the assurance of being able to resume possession at the end of the stated period of tenancy.

The marginal and small landowners should be assisted with adequate institutional support and rural development schemes, so that they are not compelled to lease-out land to big farmers or corporate houses, thereby creating conditions for involuntary reverse tenancy. In the case of sharecroppers, they should have access to credit, once they enter into long-term contracts.[9]

---

[9] Planning commission of India, 11th Five Year Plan, Vol III, page 33

In the Twelfth FYP (2012–2017), tenancy laws are made to strengthen women farmers. It has been recommended that an assessment of all uncultivated arable land presently with the government should be done away with and long-term rights for group cultivation to the women farmers' group should be given. Women farmers are also facilitated for purchasing agricultural land in a group by providing a loan-cum-grant scheme with 50 per cent of the loan as a low-interest loan and the remaining 50 per cent as a grant. Financial support is also provided to women farmers/SHGs for group farming on leased or owned land along with credit subsidy, technology access and so on.[10]

SOME BRIEF DETAILS OF LAND REFORMS IN STUDY REGIONS

Punjab

In Punjab, there is no explicit ban on land leasing. However, section 16 of the Land Revenue Act, 1972 provides that the tenant of a big landowner is entitled to purchase his tenanted land if he has been in continuous possession of the land for a period of six years or the tenanted land does not come under reserved or ceiling area of the landowner or when the landowner is a disabled person, widow or unmarried woman or a person suffering from physical or mental disability and also the tenant must have land below ceiling. Also, a landowner within ceiling can evict a tenant, subject to the tenant being left with no less than five standard acres.

Haryana

Similar to Punjab, there is no explicit ban on land leasing. But there are other restrictive clauses in Haryana as in Punjab. However, the Haryana law does not allow for automatic purchase of land by tenants even if that land falls under ceiling surplus of areas of landowner. Such lands are vested to the government but tenants are given preference in the allotment of such lands. In Haryana, the minimum duration for leasing-in land is three years but less than six years.

---

[10] Planning commission of India, 12th Five Year Plan, Vol III, page 168

Andhra Pradesh

In Andhra Pradesh (AP) also, the leasing-in/leasing-out land is not explicitly banned. But terms and conditions of land are restrictive in nature. Whoever practises leasing of land after 1974 has to have it done in written form and should get the land registered for a minimum period of six years. At the time of resumption of land by the landowner, the tenant has to be left with no less than half of the area of land held by him during the lease period.

Karnataka

According to the Mysore Land Reforms Act, 1961 as amended with effect from 1 March 1974, leasing-out land is banned except by a soldier and a seaman.

CURRENT STATUS OF TENANCY LAWS IN DIFFERENT STATES OF INDIA

In the previous section, a review of changes in tenancy reforms at central level has been done. It has been seen that tenancy reforms evolved through abolishing intermediaries between tiller and state, conferring ownership rights to tenants, legalizing leasing of land, institutional support for marginal and small landowner and strengthening women farmers. The tenancy laws framed by central government were mostly amended by the state government from time to time.

The amended tenancy laws adopted by various states have main objectives of defining tenants, regulating rent, ensuring security of tenure, strengthen landlord's right to resume leased land for personal cultivation, conferment of ownership rights to tenants, giving up tenancy rights with mutual consent, prohibition of future tenancies, tenant's right of pre-emptive purchase, building up correct tenancy records, to abolish oral tenancies, etc. In the Eleventh FYP, central government had already declared to legalize leasing of land in 'limited' manner but still some states have restrictive nature of tenancy laws which hampers the supply of land in lease market. Table 1.1 shows the nature of restrictions in tenancy laws in different states of India.

Table 1.1 *Restrictive Nature of Tenancy Laws in Various States*

States	Nature of Restrictions in Tenancy Laws
Kerala and Jammu and Kashmir	Leasing-out of agricultural land is completely prohibited without any exception.
Telangana, Bihar, Jharkhand, Karnataka, MP, Chhattisgarh, UP, Uttarakhand and Orissa	Only certain categories of landowners such as disabled, minors, widows, defence personnel, etc., are allowed to lease out their land.
Punjab, Haryana, Gujarat, Maharashtra and Assam	Tenants can acquire ownership rights on tenanted land after a specific period of creating tenancy but leasing out of agricultural land is not banned.
AP, Rajasthan, TN and West Bengal	No restrictions in land leasing but in West Bengal only sharecropping leases are legally permitted.
In Scheduled Tribe areas of AP, Bihar, Orissa, MP and Maharashtra	Transfer of land from tribal to non-tribal community is prohibited without permission of a competent authority.

Source: Report of the Committee on 'State Agrarian Relations and the Unfinished Task in Land Reforms', Department of Land Resources, Ministry of Rural Development, Government of India (GOI).

After independence, the average share of leased-in area was high across the states but it started declining in 2002–2003 and again showed an increase during 2012–2013. Some states like AP (10%–36%), Bihar (12%–23%), Punjab (18%–24%), TN (6%–14%), Odisha (13%–17%) and West Bengal (9%–15%) showed a sharp increase in leased-in area by the tenants. So, it clearly indicates that lease restrictions in the states should be relaxed at the earliest possible (Mani, 2015). Table 1.2 shows statewise proportion (in %) of operated lease-in area.

Figure 1.1 shows some positive correlation between increase in area of lease-in land and agricultural GDP (nominal GDP) growth of various states of India. Hence, it indicates that there is some positive impact of leasing land, by allocation of land to able cultivator, and productivity of the land. Therefore, bans on leasing-in land existing in some states

Table 1.2 *Proportion (in %) of Operated Area Leased-in in Different States*

NSSO Reports	Rep36 (8th Round)	Rep215 (26th Round)	Rep330 (37th Round)	Rep388 (48th Round)	Rep492 (59th Round)	Rep National Sample Survey Key Indicators KI (70/18.1) (70th Round)
States	1953–1954	1972–1973	1981–1982	1992–1993	2002–2003	2012–2013
AP	21.2	9.0	6.2	9.6	9.97	35.70
Assam	43.0	16.7	6.4	8.9	5.06	4.20
Bihar	12.4	14.5	10.3	3.9	11.76	22.67
Gujarat	19.4	3.9	2.0	3.3	5.08	5.82
Haryana	39.8	23.3	18.2	33.7	14.38	14.82
Himachal Pradesh	N.A.	15.9	3.2	4.8	2.87	5.33
Jammu & Kashmir	22.1	8.1	2.5	3.7	0.32	0.20
Karnataka	21.5	15.9	6.0	7.4	3.68	6.90
Kerala	20.2	8.6	2.1	2.9	4.18	8.93
MP	19.8	7.5	6.6	6.3	2.83	5.14
Maharashtra	19.7	6.2	5.2	5.5	4.59	3.44

(Table 1.2 Continued)

(Table 1.2 Continued)

NSSO Reports	Rep36 (8th Round)	Rep215 (26th Round)	Rep330 (37th Round)	Rep388 (48th Round)	Rep492 (59th Round)	Rep National Sample Survey Key Indicators KI (70/18.1) (70th Round)
States	1953–1954	1972–1973	1981–1982	1992–1993	2002–2003	2012–2013
Odisha	12.6	13.5	9.9	9.5	13.15	16.96
Punjab	39.8	28.0	16.1	18.8	17.84	24.42
Rajasthan	21.0	5.3	4.3	5.2	2.81	7.11
TN	27.0	13.1	10.9	10.9	6.10	13.54
UP	11.4	13.0	10.2	10.5	3.49	7.89
West Bengal	25.4	18.8	13.4	10.4	9.42	14.73
All-India	20.6	10.6	7.2	8.3	6.60	10.41

Source: National Commission for Enterprises in the Unorganized Sector (2008), 'A Special Programme for Marginal Farmers' based on National Sample Survey (For data from 1953–1954 to 1992–1993); National Sample Survey Office (NSSO) Reports:Rep-492 (59th Rd) for 2002–2003 and Rep-NSS KI (70/18.1) (70th Rd) for 2012–2013 data.

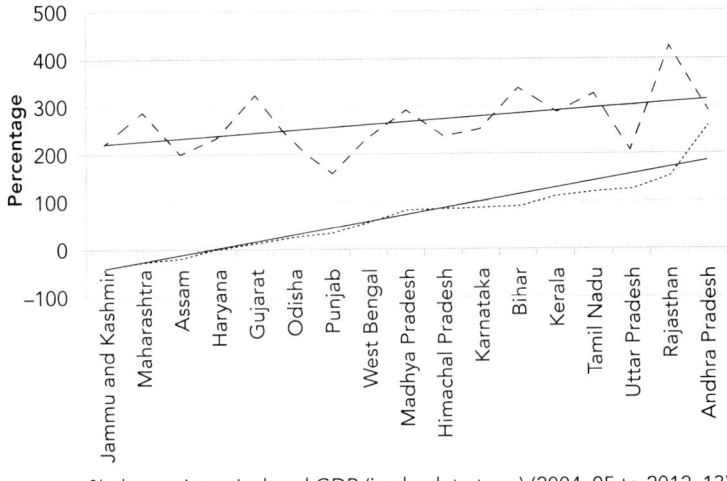

Figure 1.1 *Graph Showing Correlation between Lease-In Land and Agricultural GDP (Nominal)*

Source: NSSO reports (59th round for 2002–2003 data and 70th round for 2012–2013 data) and Ministry of Agriculture, GOI, for agricultural GDP data (2004–2005 to 2012–2013).

should be relaxed keeping in mind that the marginal and small farmers should not suffer. In previous studies, some cases of reverse tenancy have been found in some states, which is redundant for them.

SHARECROPPING IN INDIA

Sharecropping is a form of land tenancy in which the landowner permits the tenant to use his land in return for a stipulated share of the output. It is an institutional arrangement which has prevailed in both developing countries and less-developed countries. It may apparently seem that since under sharecropping, a certain portion of the output has to be surrendered to the landowner, there is a loss of incentives to invest. However, a close look reveals that it has certain advantages which are not offered by tenant farming. Sharecropping seeks to achieve a compromise between peasant proprietorship and tenant farming. It is an institutional arrangement designed both to share risks and to provide incentives to both the parties. Sharecropping represents a compromise, while rental contracts provide perfect incentives since the sharecropper is able to retain all of his value or marginal productivity of labour, however, it provides no risk-sharing. On the other hand, wage contracts shift all the risk on to landlords, who principally should be in their best position to bear such risks.

In actual reality, the sharecropping contract has certain optimality properties; the contract seeks to maximize the welfare of the worker, subject to the landlord obtaining a particular value of expected rents from his land. Even the inefficiency associated with the worker receiving less than the value of his marginal product may be mitigated with long-term contracts; workers who fail to produce a sufficiently high level of output over an extended period of time run the risk of termination of their contract. Mainly for this reason, we find the persistence of sharecropping mainly in developing countries.[11]

An important feature of sharecropping is cost sharing. The landowner has an incentive to encourage the tenant to use inputs such as fertilizer which raise the workers' marginal product and which, therefore, results in the workers putting extra effort (i.e., working hard). This explains why the landlord might bear a fraction of the cost of inputs that exceed the fraction of the output that he receives. This is the principal-agent view of sharecropping.

Sharecropping might invoke certain positive externalities. Important externalities might arise between land markets and credit markets (we will discuss this in detail in the forthcoming chapters). These externalities can explain the interlinkages between credit and land markets that are frequently observed in developing countries (i.e., the landowner is also a moneylender). An increase in the amount of outstanding debt affects both workers' efforts and their choice of technique (risk). These, in truth, affect the return to the landowner. Conversely, a change in

---

[11] There has been a large amount of literature which tries to explain the rationale behind sharecropping contracts. See Eswaran and Kotwal (1985), Newbery (1977) and Stiglitz (1974) among others. The explanations range from the risk sharing properties of sharecropping to the existence of moral hazard and/or adverse selection. The fact remains that sharecropping shows no sign of becoming extinct.

the terms of the sharecropping contract will, in general, affect the probability of default and the return to the lender.

DIMINISHING SHARECROPPING IN INDIA

Owing to the continued pressure of population on limited land resources, tenancy has persisted through informal contracts. Because of the ceiling on land holdings, sub-division and persisting pressure on land as a source of livelihood there has been an increase in the number of small and marginal operational holdings, owned as well as leased. In view of Hanumantha Rao, with the widespread adoption of technology and rise in input intensity, the incentives for investment and for capturing the returns on investment seem to be predominating over the need for sharing yield risks leading to natural replacement of sharecropping tenancy by the fixed crop and cash rents.

According to T. Schultz, farm lease contracts are essentially institutional devices for allocating risk among landowners and tenants. Cash rents guaranteed in advance of production means the risks of production are shared entirely by the tenants, while crop-sharing rentals indicate the distribution of such risks among the tenants and the landlords in proportion to their respective shares in output. In contrast, fixed-kind rents settled in advance of production imply the sharing of price and allocate the yield risks entirely to the tenants. Fixed-cost rents are preferred by landowners where there exists a significant scope for entrepreneurship. The reason is that such rents offer a foretold advantage—they permit the tenants also to capture the returns expected from their own decision-making. Such rent also protects those who lease out their land against the possible risks arising from the production decisions of the tenants. Under uncertain situations, there is limited scope for entrepreneurial functions. In such situations, there may be a requirement for the tenants to reduce fluctuations in their income by shifting part of their risk to the landowners through sharecropping arrangements.

Thus, it logically follows that in situations where the element of uncertainty is smaller and there is hardly any role of the entrepreneur, the landowners find it profitable to lease out a portion of land on a share-rent basis, rather than cultivate the entire holding by using hired labours. While referring to the inefficiency of sharecropping, Alfred Marshall brought into focus a very important point—the rent under this system would be lower than the fixed rent or net income from one's own cultivation even if the tenants were free to restrict their household income. In Marshall's view, sharecropping (tenancy) may be advantageous when the holdings are very small and is not suitable for holding large enough to give scope to the enterprise of an able and responsible tenant.

In 1969, Cheung presented an interesting theory of the choice of contracts on the basis of the 'gains from risk dispersion'. However, his theory suggests that share contracts can be expected to be more widespread in areas characterized by a high degree of uncertainty than in areas of relative certainty, if transaction costs are equal. But in the Indian context, Hanumantha Rao argues,

> Relative economic certainty in the sense of limited scope for decision-making seems to be necessary for the prevalence of sharecropping. Otherwise, individual anticipations regarding input-output rates and prices may differ, making it difficult for the parties concerned to arrive at an agreed choice as to the product mix and the amount of inputs to be committed (Hanumantha Rao, 1971).

In contrast, situations of high uncertainty call for fixed-cash rents.

Cheung notes 'the tenant's incentive to use an amount of input less than that stipulated in a share contract' suggests the role of transaction costs in determining the lease arrangements. In making this suggestion, Cheung implicitly assumes that the proposition between land and labour inputs can be varied over a significant range for share-rented crops. However, if production functions are characterized by relatively inflexible input combinations, then the costs of enforcing tenants' input would be lower and the incentives for share-contract would be in areas where share-cropping is widely practised and where landowners prefer to leave out land, owing to managerial discounts of crop cultivation with hired labours.

LAND-SHARING COMPANIES IN AGRICULTURE SECTOR

Singh et al. (2015) found some scope of intervention of land-sharing company in agricultural sector in India. However, in reality, land-share concept does not exist in India. They say that it could be a viable option for small and marginal farmers who account for more than 80 per cent of land holding to manage agricultural production professionally with their limited capacity and reach. They also believe that land-sharing company will not only provide economy of scale but will also facilitate forward and backward linkages to production system. This concept does not exist in India, but it could be possible for the farmers to float a land share agro-processing company in which the farmers will have the option to become a shareholder of that company in proportion to their size of holding. It is likely expected that the development of such companies will trigger agricultural and non-agricultural development in rural areas. To promote these companies, some concessional credit and other investment subsidies may be allowed by the local government or NGOs.

MAIN OBJECTIVES OF THE STUDY

Indian agriculture is gradually opening up on lines of the global pattern and has become internationalized through the system of CF. As the system is fast expanding, it becomes essential to evaluate CF in a wider framework to make an objective assessment. In a number of cases, it has been found that CF is relatively more viable for the large farmers and it exploits the smaller ones.

The present study systematically analyses CF in the broader framework of existing land and lease-market system. As land acquisition is becoming more and more complex, there is a new thinking on the lines of developing land-lease and land-sharing companies. Recently, Rajasthan state assembly passed an amendment bill (The Rajasthan Land Laws Amendment Bill, 2014) enabling farmers to lease their agricultural land to power generation companies namely, solar and wind energy, for 30 years. The states of Gujarat, MP, Karnataka and Maharashtra have recently allowed agribusiness firms to buy and operate large land holdings for R&D, and export-oriented production purposes. Punjab government is planning to raise the ceiling on holdings in order to encourage large-scale farming for making farming a viable proposition in the state. Karnataka state government has decided to amend the Karnataka Land Reforms Act (KLRA), 1974, to allow farmers to lease out their agricultural land to private agro-companies, who in turn will have to use technology to increase yield on the leased land. The other states also are likely to step in a similar way.

This study examines CF, vis-à-vis, land leasing and land sharing (farmer to farmer and if available, companies to farmers) to find out the pros and cons of the above system from the point of view of different farm categories. The specific objectives of this study are:

- To analyse the merits and de-merits of promotion of CF, land leasing and land sharing from the point of view of farmers.
- To assess the impact of CF, land leasing and land sharing on various stakeholders including agricultural cultivators and agricultural labourers.
- To document the legal framework and regulatory mechanism required to deal with disputes and issues arising from the proposed policy.
- To document best practices and models adopted in India and abroad.

DATABASE AND METHODOLOGY

The study is primarily based on a primary survey. We selected two states in the North and two states in the South for conducting this study. In the North, Punjab and Haryana and in the South, Karnataka and AP (including Telangana) were selected for carrying out this study. In the aggregate, 500 farm households—comprising 400 farmers belonging to the category of contract farmers, land leasing farmers and sharecropping farmers and 100 farmers from the control group not belonging to any of the above-mentioned categories—were selected in each state.

The selection of the sample broadly involved the following stages. At the first stage, firms involved in CF in each state were contacted and a list of farmers who were active participants in CF during the preceding year was obtained. The list included the names and addresses of the farmers and their contracted area, crop wise. Similarly, information was collected about land-leasing/land-sharing farmers in the selected villages in each state. Based on this list, farmers were chosen by the Stratified Random Sampling Method. For the selection of non-contract farmers, no such list was available. Therefore, keeping in mind the objective of the study to prepare a baseline to make comparison, non-contract farmers were selected in the peripheral areas with a similar cropping pattern as that of contract/lease farmers. It was tried to give a proportionate representation to different-size classes while selecting the sample farmers.

In order to study the institutional and governance mechanism, company's perspective was construed directly by the guided interviews and informal discussions with company management, officials and other field employees of the company indulging in contract, lease or land sharing. Further, international experiences of successful models of CF, land-leasing and land-sharing companies were documented through the literature review, whereas the best practices were captured during the field survey as well as through the literature review.

SCOPE OF THIS STUDY

In the recent past, CF has started becoming popular among many states; for example, wheat in MP by HLL, Rallis and ICICI. Rallis supplies agri-inputs and know-how and ICICI finances farm credit while HLL, the processing company, provides the buy-back arrangement for the farm output. Similarly, ACC, the ginning and trading house from Pollachi (TN), is providing a buy-back guarantee to the growers of cotton seeds in Coimbatore. The ACC formula of CF has been so successful that the TN Government is now keenly interested in replicating this model in various cotton growing districts of the state. Ugar Sugar Works Limited-led CF in barley in Belgaum (Karnataka) is another success story of CF. Encouraged by these examples, several state governments including AP, Gujarat, Karnataka, Punjab and TN are promoting CF, changing laws to enable and support it and providing companies interested in it with a variety of incentives including lifting of land ceilings, subsidies and tax rebates.

In the previous sections, we saw pros and cons of CF globally. A few observations made by studies on India (Rangi & Sidhu, 2000, 2003; Singh, 1997, 2002, 2004, 2005a) are that the results of contracting are very promising in the early years. Farmers benefit from the improved technology and higher productivity quality and production. However, once farmers deploy themselves into the new technology, problems start cropping up. If the market price is more advantageous than the contract price, farmers renege on the contract. Generally, the contracts are not written and the legal enforcement system is too tedious for both growers and firms. In the existing models, farmers are largely price takers, while the contracting firms make the price. Other criticisms levelled against CF in these cases is that it generally prefers labour-saving farm practices, low level of commitment of corporate over rural development, lack of transparency and lack of institutions and NGOs for proper dissemination of information for the success of CF. Therefore, this study systematically analyses CF in the broader framework of existing land and lease-market system.

The study is summed in 10 chapters. The next chapter presents comprehensive analysis of existing land market in India, explaining the system of land transactions and land-leasing system. Chapter 3 presents review of literature on CF, land tenancy and land reforms in India and elsewhere. Next three chapters are based on household survey data, whereas Chapter 4 presents household characteristics, cropping pattern followed by contract, lease and control farmers, resource use and productivity at the household level for the selected farmers. The chapter also presents the gross value of output, cost and net returns to the contract, lease and control farmers in the aggregate level and across various farm-size holdings. Chapter 5 concentrates on the nature of existing CF in India and among the selected farmers, the resource use, productivity and profitability among the contracted crops in comparison to leased crops and control crops. Chapter 6 looks into product disposal by the three categories of farmers, employment gen-eration by the contract, lease and control farmers, the various sources of non-farm income among selected households and farmer's opinion related to various aspects of CF, land leasing and lease companies. The chapter also provides farmers suggestions on how to improve CF and land tenancy. Chapter 7 presents existing contract companies in the selected states and various success stories of CF. This chapter provides detailed analysis of the present state of land leasing Act, the Model Act on Contract Farming formulated by (National Institution for Transforming India) NITI Aayog and various aspects of land-leasing and land-sharing companies. Chapter 8 presents labourers' perspective on CF. Chapter 9 presents the institutional/legal framework of CF and land leasing in India while the last chapter summarizes the study and offers conclusions and policy suggestions.

Chapter 2

Land Market Development in India

GLOBAL OPERATIONAL LAND MARKET

Land is regarded as a part of the culture of a nation and people are ready to fight for it whether at national or individual level. The Food and Agriculture Organization (FAO) defines land and land resources as,

> A delineable area of the earth's terrestrial surface, encompassing all attributes of the biosphere immediately above or below this surface, including those of the near-surface climate, the soil and terrain forms, the surface hydrology (including shallow lakes, rivers, marshes and swamps), the near-surface sedimentary layers and associated ground-water and geo-hydrological reserve, the plant and animal populations, the human settlement pattern and physical results of past and present human activity (terracing, water storage or drainage structures, roads, buildings, etc.) (FAO, 2011).

Throughout history, several issues happened for the entitlement of ownership of land. The probable reason is that land is not like other commodities which can be bought and sold as a movable commodity. Structures built upon it can be dismantled, soil can be dug up and taken away, but the space occupied by the land area cannot be moved. With regards to owning a land, some argue that government should determine allocation of land. Others say that a regulatory framework should be established by the governing bodies to achieve optimum use of land through the operation of free market forces (Mahoney et al., 2007).

Land Market

Land market is said to exist when and wherever it is possible to exchange rights on land in return of agreed amount of money. An efficient land market underpins the capacity of financial institutions to lend money to landowners to invest. A significant difference of efficiency of land market has been found in developed and developing societies. Developing societies failed to create an efficient land market for various political and cultural reasons and ultimately, they remain undercapitalized societies. The ultimate ownership of land remains with the state which retain the right to use private property for the benefits of public and regulate the land in the manner it is to be used by planning legislation. Many societies permit possession of land as a private property in which landowner has maximum degree of freedom on how and when the land may be used. Sometimes, the private rights in land are exchanged for a consideration, usually money, and this creates a kind of land market when the numbers of such exchange (transaction) cross a critical threshold. Figure 2.1 shows the transitions in life cycle of land markets.

Usually, land markets are governed through land tenure and land administration systems prevailing in the nation/state. The key elements in the land tenure system includes extent of selling and buying the land,

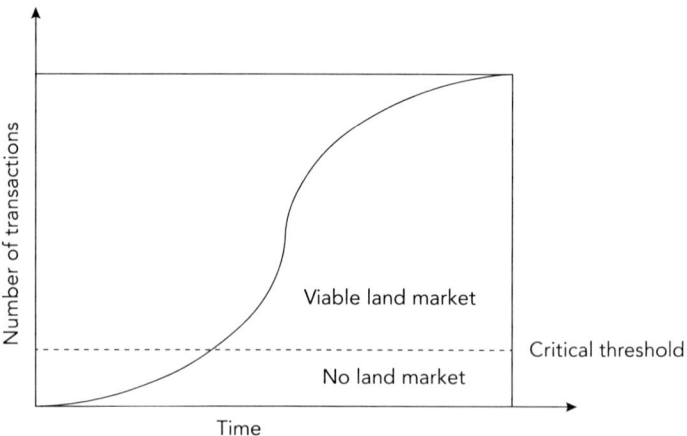

Figure 2.1 *Transitions in Life Cycle of Land Markets*

whether it can be used as collateral property against loan grants, who will take over the land property if someone fails to repay the loan, the rules governing inheritance of land and some additional use rights and obligations. These all elements collectively enable the security of tenure system and strong land administration system. If there is any weakness in the land administration system, then it will affect the level of trust and it ultimately leads to inefficient land market or no land market (Mahoney et al., 2007).

Theories Determining Land Prices/Rent

In traditional societies, land is a common good and cannot be alienated nor sold. But in a modern, free market, land is treated as a commodity that is desired and can be exchanged. Its value and price are controlled by offer (supply) and demand and the underlying benefits that can be generated from it. Price usually indicates the land values in functional market. The price of land is determined by its production potential and other services or externalities offered in present and future times. In modern times, land has also become a subject of speculation. Land is finite in extent and the demand for it is rising continuously due to the aspirations of growing population. Therefore, the value of land is expected to increase in the coming future.[1] Following are some theories established to explain the rent and price mechanism of land.

Ricardian Theory of Rent

David Ricardo (1772–1823) was one of the founders of the Classical School of economics. He gave the concept of economic rent which is defined as:

> Economic rent on land is the value of the difference in productivity between a given piece of land and the poorest (and/or most distant), most costly piece of land producing the same goods (e.g., bushels of wheat) under the same conditions (of labour, capital, technology, etc.) (Blaug, 1978; Ricardo, 1817, 1821).

---

[1] http://www.eolss.net/sample-chapters/c19/e1-05-03-03.pdf

This concept of economic rent is based on following six assumptions:

1. At the initial stage of development with a stable and low level of population, only the best lands (in terms of productivity, convenience, location, etc.) are brought under cultivation.
2. Due to population growth, eventual diminishing returns on current cultivated lands are forced into cultivation of new lands which are inferior in fertility, more difficult to work and involves high production and transportation costs.
3. The extra addition of inferior lands in production system give rise to high cost of producing extra bushels of grain to feed the growing population (assuming all people are fed).
4. In a given market zone, there is only one price of an agricultural produce.
5. The final or 'equilibrium' price of the produce is equal to the cost of producing that last bushel of grain from the last unit of land forced into the production to feed that larger population.
6. The total sales revenue generated from the last unit of land is equal to the total costs without any surplus or 'profit'.[2]

With an extra addition of cultivated land, the production cost would increase while the economic rent would decrease. This would continue till the production cost of last unit of land becomes equal to the price of the bushels of grain produced from that piece of land. However, Ricardian theory has limitations as it assumes rent as a reward for differential properties of land. The modern economists offered a better explanation of rent. Modern theory says that rent is the payment for the use of land and the payment is determined by the demand for and the supply of land. In this theory, demand for land is derived from the demand of products produced from land. If the demand of the products rises or falls, then it will also lead to increase or decrease of demand for land and, ultimately, the rent of the land. The supply of land is considered to be fixed for the community concerned, but it may vary individually if someone buys/sells or leases land from others. However, overall for the community, the land remains practically fixed. But in

---

[2] https://www.economics.utoronto.ca/munro5/ECONRENT.pdf

the case of an individual firm, supply of land is not fixed. The supply can be increased by offering more rent. Rent varies with the change in demand and supply of land in the case of inelastic and elastic supply of land.[3] In the case of inelastic supply, the total supply of land is fixed and any increase in demand will result in increase in rent without any increase in the supply. This is also true for the case of supply of land for the entire community or at an aggregate level. On the other hand, for individual firm or household level, the supply of land is elastic and supply can be increased by offering higher rent.

Modern Land Rent Theory

In highly developed countries, consumption models have shifted to more pro-ecological models, which make land to create utilities such as the environmental values of landscape, biodiversity, leisure, cultural inheritance, a guarantee of food security, a rural culture and tradition and local activities (Brouwer, 2004; Daly, 2007; Fałkowski, 2010; Sapa, 2009; Vatn, 2010). During the course of development of a market economy, different stages of land rent valorization can be seen. At a certain stage of economic development, the market or institutions valorize some intrinsic utilities of land such as the landscape, biodiversity, leisure facilities, a guarantee of food safety, rural culture, etc., and give them a financial character. These utilities are created without any additional input of capital in agricultural production. Therefore, in modern land theory, two important assumptions have been derived—the existence of intrinsic land utilities (which are converted into monetary terms) and assumption of the informational efficiency of the agricultural land market which allows the valuation of those utilities in the market-land price (Czyżewski, 2016).

DETERMINING PRICE OF LAND BY USING HEDONIC PRICING METHOD

If land price is determined through the auctions or negotiating with potential buyers, then hedonic pricing method is used to fix the price of land. In this method, price of a marketed good is estimated based

---

[3] http://www.economicsdiscussion.net/theory-of-rent/ricardian-theory-of-rent-with-diagram/1799

on the characteristics or the services provided by it.[4] The prices are determined at the point where willingness to pay of buyers equals willingness to accept by sellers. A hedonic price function is the equilibrium relationship between the characteristics of the good and its price. The price function of the same goods can emerge differently in competitive and non-competitive markets. Hüttel et al. (2016) used hedonic pricing method to analyse how institutional sellers within the privatization process shape price formation in agricultural land markets in Germany.

Factors Affecting Land Market

Deininger et al. (2001) say that the main factors affecting participation in land market are agricultural-production process, labour supervision cost, credit access, the risk characteristics of an individual asset portfolio and the transaction costs associated with market participation. The effect of these factors on land market varies from factor to factor. For example, if an owner-operated farm is more productive than hired-labour farm, then it is not necessary that the land will be shifted to owner-operated farm. Hence, it implies that if financial markets are imperfect, then land-market operation should be considered in broader context focussing on access to other markets and availability of other alternative assets. Broadly, the factors affecting land market are classified into following categories.

Institutional Arrangement

In a given setting, land use regulations can affect land market in positive, negative or neutral ways (Wu, 2006; Wu & Plantinga, 2003). However, the overall effect of land use regulations is very difficult to estimate for various reasons. The land use regulations are themselves very complex and to characterize them quantitatively is also difficult (Quigley, 2007). The effects of land use regulations have suffered from small samples for distinct regulations imposed in a locality or town or metropolitan area (Quigley, 2007). Some studies have tried to estimate the effect of land

---

[4] http://www.ecosystemvaluation.org/hedonic_pricing.htm

use regulations on property values which has positive 'amenity effects' that affects demand positively. So, as a result, the positive effect of land regulations on land prices are either due to supply shifts or demand shifts (or some combination of both; Phillips & Goodstein, 2000). Most of the existing literature has assumed that any relationship between land regulations and land prices are due to supply effects rather than demand effects (Malpezzi et al., 1998; Quigley, 2007). Jaeger (2013) attempted an empirical approach to estimate the overall demand for land in a given urban area as a function of population, income and other factors such as spatial dispersion of land development and price gradients or constraints on land use within a specified zone. In his study, he found that the elasticity of land development with respect to population is in between 0.79 and 0.82 based on open city model. Similarly, the elasticity of developed land area with respect to per capita income is 1.7–2.0. Chesire and Vermeulen (2009) also found that a wide range of land use regulations, in terms of institutional arrangements, form and restrictiveness, make it impossible to summarize the effects on housing market and social welfare in few facts and figures. However, the land use regulations which do not impose any binding restrictions, neither generate benefits to society nor impose costs; but the places which have a strong grip for planning on housing supply and urban form impose substantial adverse welfare effects, sometimes it accounts for large share of household income.

IMPACT OF COMMON AGRICULTURAL POLICY (CAP) ON EUROPEAN UNION

In European Union (EU), a CAP measures such as market price support, production subsidies, factor subsidies, both coupled and decoupled payments, etc., have been implemented to boost farmer's income. The result of these implemented policy measures influenced (increased) farmer's income with varying effects across policies. The farm subsidies not only had an impact on farmer's income, but it also induced second-order adjustment through altered farmer incentives on factor demand, inter-sectoral factor allocation and factor ownership. In addition to CAP, other policies might also have affected land market in EU. For example, in Finland, under rural development programme, start-up support grants for new farmers have increased intergenerational transfers between relatives. In Belgium, the 'manure action plans' forced the intensive animal-producing farmers to make arrangements with other landowners to internalize the environmental costs they caused. The implemented policy resulted in an increase in land demand and also exerted upward pressure on land prices not only in animal breeding region, but in whole Flanders. Similar effect of Nitrate Directive was seen in Netherlands too (Ciaian et al., 2012).

EFFECT OF OFF-FARM EMPLOYMENT ON LAND RENTAL MARKET IN TRANSITION COUNTRIES

In transition countries like Vietnam, provision of clear, enforceable and secure long-term land rights, even if they fall far short of full ownership rights, is an essential pre-condition for the sales and rent land market. Off-farm employment is also a major factor in developing land rental markets (Deininger & Jin, 2003). However, in Hungary, a well-functioning labour market does not lead to better functioning land market (Vranken & Mathijs, 2001). In rural China, land rental transactions became more active after being dormant for almost 15 years after the rural reforms. This development of land rental market is due to the development of off-farm labour market. Off-farm work pays several times more than the agricultural work, so the villagers who have access to off-farm activities tend to rent out their land (Kung, 2002).

TRANSNATIONAL LAND DEALS IN SUB-SAHARAN AFRICA (SSA)

In the last 10 years, SSA has witnessed an increasing interest in agriculture and land investments for the production of food and energy crops (Anseeuw et al., 2013; Cotula, 2012; Deininger et al., 2011). Giovannetti and Ticci (2016) estimated the determinants of large-scale transnational land deals for investment in biofuel crops in SSA. In their study, they found that foreign investors tend to select countries which have better institutional arrangement and higher endowment of land and water resources. Also, the investors prefer countries with weaker protection of land rights, which facilitates the investors to acquire land and water resources at favourable conditions.

IMPERFECTION IN FACTOR MARKETS

In early days, most of the land was cultivated with traditional technologies and existence of non-agricultural labourers was virtually absent, so the majority of land transactions were carried out between large landowners and small tenants with few alternate options. As the technologies advanced and other markets grew, it affected the nature and direction of rental contract (Deininger et al., 2008). Deininger et al. (2002) believe that land markets are driven by three factors—household's agricultural ability (unobserved), labour market imperfections in the form of supervision constraints and capital market imperfections.

Credit Market Imperfection

Poor access to credit not just affects land sales market, but also land rental market. Lack of farm profitability and imperfect credit market constrain farmers to get access to credit. Imperfection in credit market restricts the development of land sales market in different ways. First, under poor access to credit, buyers would have to finance the land purchasing by their own savings. Second, if the value of currency is low, then the owner of land will not tend to sale or rent his/her land. Third, land may be purchased or hedged against inflation or used as an asset for investment in the absence of alternative investment or hedge option. Fourth, due to constrained access to credit, farmers will tend to invest less on technology, equipment or quality inputs for land. These all factors will lead to lesser productive value of land than sale price of land (Ciaian, 2012).

Credit market imperfection can also eliminate the advantage of supervision cost of family farmers. For example, if credit markets do not function well and farmers need urgent working capital to invest in their land, then the access to capital will depend upon the farmer's initial wealth and operational size of land holding. In that way it will give rise to positive relationship between farm size and land holding. Also, in rental market, tenant would prefer for share contracts rather than fixed rent contract due to less access to credit. However, credit market imperfection will not undermine the tendency of rental market to transfer land to more productive farmers. Sometimes, farmers are forced to sell their land at low prices when the agricultural production is very risky and insurance is not available. Also, if non-agricultural land (tax and subsidy) policies and macroeconomic conditions increase the land value above the profit generated from agricultural production (for specific groups), then it makes it more difficult for the productive farmers to acquire land. Absence of long-term credits makes it more difficult for the small and productive farmers to acquire land through sales market. Therefore, it is expected that rental markets are more efficient than sales markets in imperfect credit market (Deininger & Jin, 2003).

Labour Market Imperfection

Imperfections in rural labour markets are mainly due to the supervision cost which arises from the unobservable nature of wage worker's true effort except in very limited circumstances. So, this implies that wage workers will have limited incentives to put efforts and either need to be supervised at a cost or offered contracts of high incentives. In case of family members, they have higher incentives to put efforts than hired labour, so it implies that renting-in land for abundant family labour will be advantageous to utilize their family labour with no supervision cost. Also, it will be advantageous for the landowner, who have abundant land, to rentout to the abundant family labour households rather than entering into the labour market transactions that incur supervision costs (Deininger & Jin, 2003).

In China, it has been observed that growth of off-farm labour market activities is the main catalyst of rising land rental activity. With the development of off-farm labour market, more people started leaving the farm and the scope of land renting activity increased. This process of land renting activity is also affected by the income gap between off-farm work and agricultural work. The wage employment pays more than twice and self-employment—three to five times as much as agricultural work. This income gap is a strong influential factor for farm households to send their members to seek employment and income opportunities in non-agricultural sector (Kung, 2002).

Hungarian land-rental market also has a similar kind of story as that of China. However, there is a huge variation in the share of households participating in rental market (from 1% to 38%) in different counties. This variation is due to the enormous differences in the percentage of leasing-out agricultural land by the households. Also, it is observed that renting-out land is more frequent than renting-in land. The reason behind renting-out land is lack of labour and machinery. Lack of labour and machinery also impedes households to rent (more) agricultural land. Therefore, it implies that there is a strong link between the functioning of land rental market and labour market (Vranken & Mathijs, 2001).

TRANSACTION COSTS

Transaction costs can also have an important impact on agricultural land markets. However, transaction costs are distinguished into two types.

Explicit transaction costs: These are the administrative costs associated with renting or buying a plot of agricultural land. These include registration costs, notary fees, etc. These costs are more prevalent in sales market.

Implicit transaction costs: These costs are also associated with renting and buying agricultural land. These include search and negotiation fees. Such costs are widespread in the countries where land markets are characterized by severe land market imperfections owing to the dominance of large-scale corporate farms. This phenomenon is mainly seen in the new member states (NMS) accessed in EU (Ciaian et al., 2012).

Explicit Transaction Costs

Taxes on the sale and purchase of land can affect the supply and demand of land and, also, affect the price of agricultural land. High-transaction cost (taxes or fees) hinders the structural change in the agricultural sector as they limit the reallocation of land from less-productive farms to more-productive farms. On the other hand, if there are low costs associated with land transaction, then there is possibility of more purchase by non-agricultural investors. In most countries, there is a provision for registration tax if land is purchased but it varies in magnitude from country to country. In EU, for member state this tax rate can amount to 18 per cent of the purchase value of land (e.g., Italy) while it is substantially low in non member states (NMS); for example, in Bulgaria and Slovakia it is 0 per cent. Explicit costs are more significant in the sales market of agricultural land. In some cases, this transaction cost can be seen in the rental market too. Usually, rental market is a mutual agreement between two parties, but in some cases, it needs to be registered (Ciaian et al., 2012).

Implicit Transaction Costs

The NMS who became member of EU have high implicit transaction costs which are closely related to the privatization and land-reform process which began in the early 1990s. Following are the three implicit costs associated with this process:

1. **Imperfect competition in land market:** During transition of the newly joined member states of EU, agricultural land was restituted to former owners. Majority of these owners are not active in agriculture and they opt to rent-out land to the historical users of the land, particularly to large-scale corporate farms. In the NMS, there has been seen a large share of rented land and strong correlation between farm structure and agricultural land use. For example, in Slovakia, corporate farms use more land which is generally rented land. As these corporate farms hold more share of rented land, it creates imperfections in the rental market. Also, the large corporate farms use their market power to influence land prices and rental contract condition in their favour (Ciaian et al., 2012).

2. **Imperfection in property rights:** Imperfection in property rights is also one of the factors affecting land market. In NMS, the two important causes of imperfections in property rights are— unresolved ownership and unknown ownership or co-ownership. A large share of agricultural land is still owned by the state and subject to future privatization and restitution. Due to uncertainty about future ownership, it had some effect on the (lack of) transactions associated with such land and its use. Similarly, unknown ownership and co-ownership also affect land transactions. In the NMS, landownership registration was poorly maintained. So, the loss of

information on registration and clear boundaries resulted in a large number of unknown owners in some transition countries (Dale & Baldwin, 2000). Apart from that, some unsettled land inheritance within families during socialist regime gave rise to widespread fragmentation in landownership and a high number of co-owners per plot of land. For example, in Slovakia, in 2003, approximately 9.6 million plots were registered with roughly a size of 0.45 ha per plot and each plot was owned by an average of 12–15 persons (OECD, 1997). Likewise, there are other NMS who have large number of owners in each plot which affected the land sales market as well as rental market in the respective countries (Ciaian et al., 2012).

DISTRESS SALE OF LAND

Distress sale of land is a phenomenon in which farmers are exposed to undiversifiable residual risks where they resort to liquidation of their assets during the period of severe crisis. This implies that during bad crop years (due to weather shocks), prices of land become low due to insignificant effective demand and high supply (Bidinger et al., 1991). Cain (1981) highlighted the link between unmitigated production risk and distress sales in which he examined the implication of different insurance mechanisms on distress sales and the landownership distribution between 1960 and 1980 for the adjacent villages of India and Bangladesh. The villages were facing high production risks but they had different risk insurance mechanisms. For example, in Maharashtra, India, it was observed that 97 per cent of all households participated in employment guarantee scheme to save their land from distress sales during disaster. But in Bangladesh, such schemes were absent after the major flood episodes, therefore 60 per cent of land sales in Bangladesh were undertaken to obtain food and medicine.

LAND MARKET IN INDIA

As such, there is nothing called an 'Indian land market', or in other words, formal land market does not exist in India. In the seventh schedule of Constitution of India, land is predominantly a State subject. Therefore, land market in India is not a homogeneous market but it consists of series of state land markets with varying levels of ownership, usage and revenue rights. Due to heterogeneous nature of land market in various states, it has an important implication for transacting land freely. Each state is independent to frame policies to manage its own land market. Therefore, the rules and regulations which govern agricultural and urban lands are different across different Indian states (Krishnan et al., 2016).

Post-Independence Drivers of Land Market in India

Since the 1980s, market liberalization reforms had been implemented which triggered growth in mining industries, steel companies, automobile factories, private ports, real estate developers, etc. Therefore, these companies/industries started acquiring land through Land Acquisition Act of 1894. For example, in Gujarat state, government-led land acquisition for industries soar up from 2,891 ha in 1947–1960 to 136,596 ha in 1981–2004 (Lobo & Kumar, 2009). This encroachment of lands by companies/industries made a massive 'land grab' which was highlighted in media such as 'Biggest Land Grab after Columbus' (Misra, 2009) and 'The Great Land Grab: India's War on Farmers' (Shiva, 2011).

Gandhi (2006) believes that the economic reforms are hostile to the poor. The reforms should not only facilitate overall economic growth, but it should also focus on development of labour-intensive employment and rural growth, which alleviates poverty in rural areas. Also, it is expected that liberalization of the economy should help agriculture to create the potential for raising rural output, wages and employment. During 1990–1991 and 1997–1998, he found that 92.5 per cent of the households in Gujarat did not show any change in the land owned. However, there were frequent changes in the operated land but there is evidence of both increases and decreases in particular land holding sizes. Also, it was found that leasingin was more common than leasingout, but transactions were of very small magnitude ranging between 0.1 to 5 acres. Table 2.1 shows that 84 per cent of the households did not participate at all in the lease market. Only 7.5 per cent of the households are involved in lease-in market and 9.2 per cent in lease-out market. But the participation of the households in lease-in market has increased considerably over the reform period from 2.5 per cent to 7.5 per cent and for lease-out market from 5.8 per cent to 9.2 per cent. The land transactions in terms

Table 2.1 *Leased-In and Leased-Out Land Holdings (%)*

	Leased-in		Leased-out	
	1990/1991	1997/1998	1990/1991	1997/1998
No	97.5	92.5	94.2	90.8
Yes	2.5	7.5	5.8	9.2

Leased-in/Leased-out

Leased-in	Leased-out		Total
	No	Yes	
No	84.2	8.3	
Yes	6.7	0.8	7.5
	Total	**9.2**	

Source: Gandhi (2006).

of leasein and leaseout only are commonly seen in the households owning land, irrigation as well as livestock. The leasing of land in most cases are seasonal either for kharif (monsoon) or rabi (winter) or summer seasons. However, 45 per cent of total leasing was reported for the whole year.

Sathe (2011) attempted to describe the causal link between political factors which create hostile land market conditions for non-agricultural sector to expand. The author says that India has huge amount of land but the land required by the non-agricultural sector for its development process is very specific and limited. According to him, land market is segmented into agricultural land, non-agricultural land (i.e., land where factories, IT offices, cities, towns, etc., exist) and appropriate land (i.e., land possessed by agricultural sector but it can be occupied by non-agricultural sector for their development). Due to increase in population and lack of employment opportunities, the stress on land has increased in India. This creates a situation in which non-agricultural sector wants this appropriate land and farmers do not want to leave their land for various reasons such as poor package offered for their land, emotional attachment, source of livelihood security, etc. As per NSSO report 2005, 40 per cent of the farmers in any case do not want to engage in farming and this percentage is expected to rise in the near future. Sathe (2016) says that a large number of farmers are willing to accept a viable alternative. On the other way around, wherever industrialization (manufacturing and services) and urbanization have taken place at high rates, some land acquisition has occurred peacefully. It is also observed that in southern and western states (including some pockets of Haryana and western Uttar Pradesh [UP]) of India, land acquisition by non-agricultural sector has occurred in a big way.

Akter et al. (2006) did an interesting study on the importance of land rental market in land use redistribution in 12 Indian villages from AP and MP states. They found that the rental market in these states had been transferred land to those tenants who had smaller holding, greater ability of cultivation, more investment assets, more adults available for labour and fewer off-farm employment opportunities. In their study, they found a few important factors responsible for creating land market in the selected villages. First was, unavailability of off-farm employment opportunities for young farmers who could be engaged in those activities. These young farmers generally leased-in land from other landlords who were not able to cultivate their land or engage in non-farming activities. They found statistical probability of one family member to get an off-farm job decreased with probability of renting-in land by more than 50 per cent and increased in the case of renting-out land by at least 50 per cent. Second was the location of the villages; villages which were farther from mainstream infrastructure and institutions had shown relatively higher number of renting-in activities in the same region or district. So, it indicates that possibilities to earn a livelihood from non-farming activities are strong for landless and near-landless households, whereas these alternatives are absent in more remote villages. Therefore, the poorer households in remote villages are bound to rent land to make a large contribution to their livelihood from farming.

DETERMINANTS OF FARMLAND PRICE IN INDIA

We have already seen that India does not have any kind of formal land market across the states. Each state has their own rules and regulations to control land market in their territory. However, some factors determining agricultural land prices are found to be common in most of the states. Kumar et al. (2005) did a district and state-level (across 18 states, 94 districts and 373 villages) survey to investigate the major determinants of farmland prices at micro as well as macro level. In their study, they found that the states (Punjab and Haryana) which have highest productivity do not have highest farmland prices. The probable reasons could be other factors which negate the positive effect of farm productivity on farmland prices. On the other hand, the states of West Bengal and Kerala were found to have highest farmland prices despite low agricultural productivity. In these two states, tenancy reforms were effectively enacted under which the ceiling-surplus land was redistributed to the landless and marginal farmers which greatly reduced the inequalities of ownership of farmlands. In Kerala, another factor was seen in playing role for increasing farmland prices. A huge influx of foreign currency from gulf countries which was remitted from the migrated Keralite labourers had increased the demand for real estate development in the state. Therefore, with rising demand of land the price of farmland surged in the state and this state has one of the highest population densities in the country which was also a reason for the highest farmland prices.

At micro level, Kumar et al. (2005) found that in majority of states' population density in rural areas, productivity (food grain yield) of farmland and distance from the nearest town were significantly affecting irrigated farmland prices. Population density in rural areas was significant for increasing farmland prices in AP, MP, TN, Maharashtra and UP whereas farm productivity was significant in AP, Himachal Pradesh, Orissa, TN and UP. In Haryana, Himachal Pradesh, Kerala, MP and TN the distance from the nearest town/city was playing a significant role in increasing farmland prices. Haryana has a similar kind of price trend of agricultural land as compared to some regions in the USA. Both regions have highly commercialized and developed agriculture sector; and distance from an urban area is a determining factor for agricultural land prices (Shi et al., 1997). In the case of unirrigated farmland, population density in rural area and food grain yield were the significant factors to determine farmland prices in majority of the states. AP, Himachal Pradesh, MP, Punjab, TN and UP had shown a significant positive correlation between rural population density and farmland prices, while food grain yield was significant for Orissa, TN, Himachal Pradesh and UP (Kumar et al., 2005).

At macro level, only rural population density among the significant variables at micro level was found to be significant. The other variables, namely, distance from urban centre, urban population density, food and non-food grain yield was found insignificant at all-India level. The rural population density was found significant in both irrigated as well as unirrigated farmland. Some other secondary variables such as road density, rural poverty, non-agricultural worker ratio with agricultural worker ratio and marginal holding were the major determinants of irrigated farmland prices. In the case of unirrigated farmlands, rural population density, rural poverty, agricultural productivity and State Gross Domestic Product from non-agricultural sector were the significant variables for determining farmland prices (Kumar et al., 2005).

INCREASE IN CULTIVABLE LAND USE IN INDIA

According to data published by the Ministry of Agriculture, GOI, since 1950 to 2014, contribution of agriculture to the country's GDP has drastically reduced from 50 per cent to less than 15 per cent, but the amount of agricultural land has remained the same with some seasonal fluctuations in net sown crop area based on weather conditions. Figure 2.2 shows the land use statistics of India from 1950–2014.

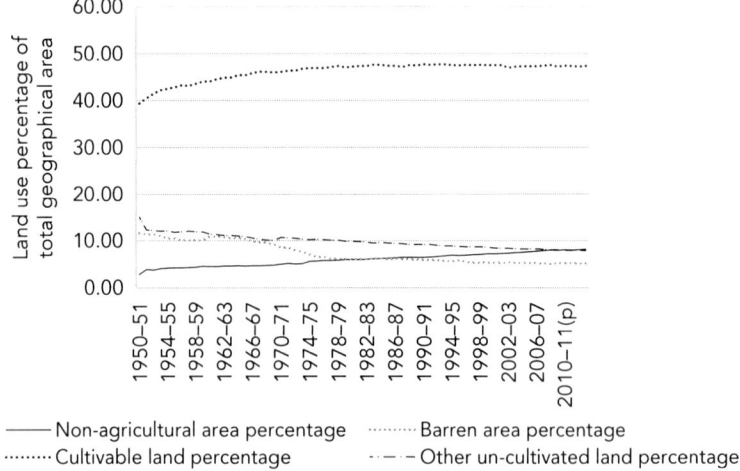

Figure 2.2 *Land Use Statistics of India from 1950 to 2014*

Source: Ministry of Agriculture, GOI.

In Figure 2.2, the amount of non-agricultural land use which includes industries, residential areas and infrastructure has increased from 2.85 per cent to 8.19 per cent during 1950–2014 but it still remains a minuscule proportion of total geographical land area of the country. On the other hand, cultivable land-use area increased from 39.37 per cent to 47.33 per cent which indicates a growing demand of food by the increasing population. The cultivable area has been increased by bringing the barren and other uncultivable land area under cultivation (which includes permanent pastures, grazing lands, miscellaneous tree crops and groves and culturable waste lands). The barren land reduced from 11.61 per cent to 5.16 per cent and uncultivable land reduced from 15.04 per cent to 7.86 per cent during 1950–2014. However, the data provides only aggregate estimates of change in land area in different sectors but the Ministry of Agriculture should investigate deeper in these to show how the land transactions are happening in states as well as country, as a whole.

DEVELOPMENT OF LAND RENTALS IN INDIA

As per the legal status of land leasing, various regions of India are broadly grouped into five categories from legally banned to no-legal ban on leasing out/in land. In some states, leasing-out land is permissible for certain categories of landowners like disabled, widows, minors, defence personnel, etc. In some other regions, tenant acquires the right to purchase the leased land from the owner within a specified period of tenancy. In tribal regions, transfer of tribal land to non-tribal land (even on lease basis) is only permitted by a competent authority (Haque, 2012). The study by Haque further argues that land leasing can be an important source of access to land and livelihood for rural poor if the land lease market is activated by the process of legalization and liberalization (Bansil, 2004). This study further adds to this literature by comparing productivity, cost and profitability on owned and rented land based on primary survey in two regions, namely, North and South India. The study also looks into the response of cultivating households on the question of development of land and rental market in India. This discussion is carried on based on primary survey in the forthcoming chapters.

Chapter 3

Contract Farming and Land Tenancy
A Review of Literature

The phenomenon of CF has remained a controversial subject in the literature. The agribusiness proponents advocate CF as a key strategy for rural transformation based on a dynamic partnership between smallholders and agro-industrial enterprises. It provides opportunities to both the parties to benefit from modern technology, marketing facilities and other services to boost their incomes. Because of its potential to promote private sector-oriented development and to increase and diversify agricultural exports it has found a prominent place in the International Monetary Funds–World Bank inspired Structural Adjustment Programmes (Glover & Kusterer, 1990; Grosh, 1994; Little & Watts, 1994). However, there is a counter argument regarding the benefits of CF to the smallholders. The opponents of CF reject the idea of equal partnership in these schemes. They argue that CF may subjugate the peasantry to increased control and exploitation by capital, leading to a peculiar form of proletarianization (Feder, 1977; Payer, 1980).[1] A brief review of the literature on CF is presented further.

At the macroeconomic level, contracting can help to remove market imperfection in case of credit, land, labour and agricultural produce. During the course of time, this contracting system may lead to better

---

[1] For a comprehensive list of the advantages and disadvantages of CF, see Roy (1972, pp. 9–11).

coordination between supply chain entities starting from input supply to retailing of the produce (Grosh, 1994; Key & Runsten, 1999). Key and Runsten (1999) further argue that contractual agreement will not only be restricted to increasing grower's income, but it will also positively impact on employment generation, infrastructure and market development in an economy. On similar lines, Christensen (1992) views CF as an institutional arrangement for agricultural development in the fields of inputs, product exchange and product upgradation.

For agribusiness firms, according to Buch-Hansen and Marcussen (1982), besides providing assured and stable-quality raw material supplies, the contracts are more flexible in the face of market uncertainty. Contracts make smaller demands on scarce capital resources and impose less of an additional burden of labour relations and ownership of land and farm production activities on management as compared with arrangements under captive farming. It even allows the firm access to unpaid family labour and state funds directed at farmers by development agencies indirectly through the agricultural production sector (Clapp, 1988; Kirk, 1987; White, 1997).

Contract farmers may learn the skill through CF to include record keeping, the efficient use of farm resources, improved methods of applying chemicals and fertilizers, understanding the importance of quality and desirable crop characteristics and the demands of export markets (Eaton & Shepherd, 2001). A guaranteed fixed price structure reduces price risks for the farmers. Whereas technology and extension services from the agribusiness firms leads to reduction in the yield risks (Simmons, 2003).

The opponents of CF, however, reject these benefits to consumers and farmers. They argue that contracting develops only when there is a diminished role of the state in agriculture and there is increased specialization of agricultural production in the absence of a proper and efficient set-up for marketing, credit and other infrastructure. In fact, a section of critics argue that contract production is one mode of capitalist penetration of agriculture for capital accumulation and exploitation of the farming sector. This even leads to processes of 'self-exploitation' of the farmers and the companies gain indirect control of land.

Michael Watts has been a particularly outspoken critic of CF. Drawing on studies from North America, Africa and Asia, he observes that the history of contracting is 'replete with company manipulation and abrogation of contracts' and the basis of peasant contracting is essentially self-exploitation, labouring more intensively (longer hours) and extensively (using children and other non-paid household labour; Watts, 1994, pp. 63–64). For Feder (1980), the relations between corporations and peasant out growers are similar to those between slave owners and slaves. Clapp (1988) in turn argues that peasant out growers are little more than the company's piece workers who must bring tools to the job. In the African context, Carney and Watts (1990) observe that CF has disrupted power relations and increased tension within farm households especially between male heads-of-household and their wives and children. Similarly, Bulow and Sorensen (1993) find in the context of tea production in Kenya that tea fields are neglected because of conflicts between spouses associated with contract tea production.

CF has also been criticized as being a tool for agro-industrial firms to exploit growers' weak power relationship with the firms. It is speculated that farmers may become overly dependent on firms by investing too much in fixed assets and altering their cropping pattern. If this will be the case, then farmers will have very limited options to exit and that will result into putting them at receiving end of the contract. At a macroeconomic level, big agro-industrial players can influence the policymakers by colluding with them and formulate the policies in best of their interests (Watts, 1994).

There are other ecological concerns of CF such as overexploitation of ground water, salination of soils, fertility decline, etc. (Siddiqui, 1998; Torres, 1997). The effect of contracting on non-contract farmers and the surrounding areas is also a matter of concern; in that, what is favourable for the contracting firms and farmers may harm other actors and sectors of the local economy (Little & Watts, 1994; Porter & Phillips-Howard, 1995). CF tends to shift agricultural production in favour of export-oriented and cash crops at the cost of basic food crops. This can lead to higher food prices and may harm non-contracting small farmers and other poor sections of the society. Another fear raised is that because of its tilt towards large farmers who are better able to meet contracting requirements, CF may encourage a socially undesirable, dual agricultural development (Dunham, 1995; Korovkin, 1992; Little & Watts, 1994; Sachikoyne, 1989).

There are evidences which suggest that a farmer's risk (production risk, market risk and external capital risk) increases after participating in the CF schemes (Eaton & Shepherd, 2001). Further, Simmons (2003) reported that agribusinesses corporations mostly prefer to deal the contracts with large farmer groups because they have lower-average costs and are more reliable suppliers in terms of quality and quantity.

Finally, Little (1994) offers a more balanced view of CF in its broader development context. While avoiding blanket condemnation, he points to the problems arising from the highly unequal power relationships that are usually involved and the fact that market instability and management problems often make contracting schemes unsustainable in the long term. Nonetheless, he suggests the importance of assessing contract schemes in the light of realistic alternative options for increased production and incomes. He concludes that the diversity of CF in scale, conditions of contract and so on is so great that it is better to focus on the motives and power relationships of the contracting parties than on the generic institution (Little, 1994, pp. 67–69).

DEFINITION OF CF

Manarungsa and Swanjindar (1992) defined CF as 'a way of co-coordinating the flows of goods through a vertical chain of production and marketing'. Charles and Shepherd (2001) defined CF as 'an agreement between a farmer and processing and/or marketing firm for the production and supply of agricultural products under forward agreements, frequently at predetermined prices'. Minot (2007) defined CF as 'agricultural production carried out according to a prior agreement in which the farmer commits to producing a given product in a given manner and the buyer commits to purchasing it'.

Chakraborty (2006) observed that CF, in India, leads to agricultural and rural development. Contract firms were located usually at agri-export zones. Kaur and Singla (2016) defined CF as 'an institutional arrangement where a farmer grows an agricultural product for a vertically integrated corporation under a forward contract'.

GLOBAL EVIDENCES OF CF

Macdonald et al. (2004) reported that CF in the USA depended mainly on the farm size. It reduced income risks and production risks, ensured market access and higher returns for the producers. For processors and other buyers of the produce, it ensured product flow and traced health issues. CF increased the productivity and improved the responsiveness to consumer demand. Patrick (2004) reported that CF in Indonesia reduced absolute poverty but increased relative poverty. Contract firms chose irrigated land and farmers who participated in agricultural groups. Smallholders participated in contract for availability of credit.

D'Silva (2005) envisioned the growing adoption of contracts in developing nations as an instrument for agribusiness development. High-valued crops and livestock, destined to processing or export markets, were better candidates for contracting. Sriboonchitta and Wiboonpoongse (2008) examined farmers in Thailand who sold 20 per cent of the tomato produce in the open market and 80 per cent to companies to overcome lower prices. Market certainty and price factors were the prime reasons for farmers to participate in CF followed by opportunistic mode of CF for farmers due to lack of alternatives. Contract firms provided assured price, timely income, extension services and input supply. There was no evidence that small farmers were excluded from contracting.

Sarkar et al. (2011) found that contract growers of Bangladesh, for tomato seed production, used more than the recommended quantity of fertilizer which decreased the yield below its potential level. This was due to lack of education of farmers and poor advice given by the firms. Majida and Hassan (2014) indicated that broiler production increased in Malaysia for about 70 per cent due to CF which provided technical support by the veterans and helped in adoption of latest technologies by farms.

Bellemare (2015) concluded that CF in developing countries eliminated price risk of the growers. Provision of inputs supply and contracted supply being used as collateral enabled small farmers to make required investments for adoption of new technology and technical assistance increased the yields of crops. In contrast, little or no local demand for the contracted crops created monopsony power, lacunae to meet quality and sanitary requirements created contract rigidity and presence of local market for the contracted crop otherwise led to leakage or side selling of the produce.

Ashok et al. (2016) examined small farmers in Nepal engaged in CF with input and output conditions, gained higher yield per ha, total revenue and total profits when compared to the other contract farmers. Farmers under contract had lower fixed costs and total costs with higher profits as compared to independent paddy seed growers.

INDIAN EVIDENCES OF CF

Birthal et al. (2005) examined milk, broiler and vegetable firms in Punjab, AP and Delhi. They observed that contracting firms provided technical support and assured market to producers. In contrast, input supply, control of the firm over production process, price risk averseness and influence on producer's decision varied. Nevertheless, institutional arrangements on producers reduced transaction costs of firms and increased net revenue of farmers, irrespective of farm size of land holders. In another study, Birthal et al. (2008) concluded that CF of milk in Rajasthan decreased transaction costs due to the presence of intermediaries between processor and producer. This also increased the competition in the local-milk markets.

Dev and Rao's (2005) study in AP revealed that large and medium farmers were engaged in oil palm contracts whereas small farmers in gherkin contracts. This was due to labour intensive nature of the crop and type of incentive provided by the state government for gherkin cultivation. The contracts were oral in both the cases but there was presence of facilitator in gherkin contract while there was no assured price in the case of oil palm.

Kumar's (2006) study in Punjab observed two types of firms in CF. The first type belonged to those agribusiness firms which had direct contract with farmers. Second type was those companies operating through Punjab government. First type was operating effectively over the second type contracts. The study indicated that medium and large farmers were skewed towards CF and three-fourth of the land was kept under non-contract to avoid risk of crop-rejection in contracting. The government supported contracts were not successful in diversification of cropping pattern from paddy and wheat to other crops. The productivity was higher in the case of direct contracts and there was positive relationship in productivity and farm size.

Gulati and Landes (2008) and Rao et al. (2007) examined CF in the context of traditional versus high-value commodities. They observed that fruits and vegetables, dairy and poultry sectors in India appeared more beneficial for CF with less transaction costs as most of the costs were borne by the contracting firms. Mutual trust and confidence in the farm-firm relationship was the driving factor for CF arrangements. CF enabled large farmers to get additional income whereas for small farmers, it was an opportunity to rise above subsistence farming.

Pandit et al. (2009) found that contract farmers in the study area were more experienced and had more years of schooling and social participation. The contract method of production was more efficient than non-contract production. CF was found as an economically viable enterprise for the farmers in Punjab. Singh (2012) found that generally, firms contracted medium and large famers; whereas in exceptional cases—in states like Karnataka, TN and AP—small and marginal farmers were contracted due to the nature of the crop under contract. Gherkin and baby corn, the high-value crops grown for export purpose and maize for feed industry needed the utmost care which could be provided only through personal care by the family labour, hence small farmers were contracted. Firms did not prefer small farmers due to high transaction costs, scattered nature, quality standards, business attitudes and ethics. Instead they preferred, generally, large farmers, who possessed irrigated land that is more suitable for contracted crop, land located near main roads and higher literacy level of the farmers.

Chitrambigai et al. (2013) concluded that technical assistance and forecast of disease outbreak were the main factors influencing farmers to contract Japanese quail in TN. Other factors that played a secondary role were aversion of price risk, removal of middlemen and provision of remunerative price. Mallika (2013) revealed that benefit–cost ratio of contracted crops grown in the study area (Hassan, Tumakuru, Kolar and

Koppal) were higher as compared to non-contracted crops. There was percentage increase in the economic status of the contracted farmers, over a period of time, after contract. Contracted farmers faced financial and labour constraints as compared to technological and extension constraints. Increase in economic status encouraged farmers to accept CF to a greater extent.

Kaur and Singla (2016) revealed that CF companies in India operated through written contracts with farmers. Companies procured produce mainly through bipartite and tripartite models with the collection of produce from the farm gate. Companies in Punjab preferred medium and large farmers because of lesser-transaction costs, whereas in West Bengal, Karnataka and Maharashtra, small famers were contracted due to their dominance in the state. Problems faced by the farmers included—undue quality cuts, delayed payments, low price for high-quality produce, poor technical assistance and not procuring entire quantity due to glut in the market.

FACTORS INFLUENCING CF

Singh (2007) concluded that increased competition for procurement instead of monopsony, guaranteed market price for produce, effective repayment mechanism, market information, reduced transaction costs and no alternative source of raw material for firms led to the successful binding between firms and producers in India towards CF. Failures of CF projects were due to poor design of the project by default or due to any of the contracting parties. Nagaraj et al. (2008) explained the differences between foreign and domestic contracting firms. Domestic firms offered compensation in the event of crop failure whereas, foreign firms never gave compensation. Foreign firms were entirely export oriented whereas, domestic firms were supplying to local and international markets. Farmers under CF borrowed less-crop loans as compared to large farmers who were under contract. Delay in payments, delay in delivery of inputs, lifting of produce, access to seeds were the problems faced by famers whereas, decreased initial investment, fair price and assured market, production information and transportation facilities were the advantages under CF.

Miyata et al. (2009) found that farmers were guaranteed fixed and high price, which were the main factors for the farmers to accept CF followed by access to the information on improving quality and inputs. The apple growers under CF had more agricultural assets, lived closer to village head, had older trees, higher family labour productivity and higher per capita income as compared to independent growers. Kaur (2014) examined that firm did not contract with small famers due to their lack of knowledge about modern inputs, lack of land to adopt modern technology and proper use of modern inputs. Small farmers earned more profit by leasing-out land on rent than doing agriculture. There were written contracts signed between firms and famers and only educated farmers had the written agreement with the firm.

ADVANTAGES AND DISADVANTAGES OF CF

Singh (2000) revealed that CF had ill effects on the livelihoods of producers, institutions and environment in Africa, Latin America and few Asian countries. In the short-run, they increased income and employment but in the long-run, worsened relationship between firm and farm resulted in degradation of economy and environment of local production systems. Contracts in less-developed countries were unfair and uncertain. State had to regulate the contract to alleviate exploitation of farmers by firms. Singh (2003) stated that CF promoted child labour participation in AP. This stopped the girls from having school education, pulsated health due to application of high pesticides for the cotton seed production and men habituated towards drinking habits. Whereas, in Punjab, women labourers were paid less for more intensive work. Women with infants were also encouraged to work which increased the employment of women but were paid less.

Singh (2006) revealed greater advantage of CF over corporate farming. It had positive impact like producer link up with profitable markets, better farm incomes, skill upgradation due to transfer of technology and sharing of market risk. He observed that CF does not make small farmer landless unlike corporate farming and does not contribute to environmental degradation. Bijman's (2008) study observed that CF reduced uncertainty and improved incentives for farmers to make specific investments. Small famers engaged in CF due to easy accessibility to credit, inputs and technical assistance along with assured incomes. Contractors preferred large farmers for lesser transaction costs and small famers for reliability in supply and their incompetence for alternative marketing opportunities and sources of inputs and credit.

Kumar and Kumar (2008) revealed that average gross farm income was higher in contract than non-contract farms, but off-farm income and income from livestock was higher on non-contract than contract farms. The rate of employment was more under contract than non-contract farms and women were highly employed because of less wage rate and loyalty. Non-contracted farmers were interested to join CF, provided the problem of irrigation was solved. Sharma (2008) concluded that operational holdings of contract farmers in Amritsar, Jalandhar and Ludhiana districts of Punjab were higher than non-contract farmers. Largely, medium and large farmers went for leasing land to increase operational holding, since companies preferred large holdings. Availability of institutional credit enabled farmers to participate in CF to escape from the clutches of moneylenders. Older farmers preferred less of CF and educated farmers accepted more of CF. Off-farm income holders and membership in cooperatives encouraged to participate in CF. There was increase in crop productivity and farm income under CF.

Ramaswami et al. (2009) examined that income from poultry production did not vary between contract and non-contract farmers but contract growers gained risk reduction. Farmers adopted improved technology and management practices which reduced feed conversion ratio and firms gained lower grower margins. Bellemare (2010) indicated that CF had positive impact on welfare of the households involved. They experienced shorter hunger seasons and income volatility when as compared to non-contract farmers. Farmers who were youngsters and had good family labour availability responded positively towards CF.

Clemente and Silva (2013) indicated that contract provided incentives and subsidies by the firm which stimulated farmers to put more efforts towards better productivity. Small-scale farmers with low level of formal education also followed fully the technical instructions given by the firms and adopted modern technologies in farming. Sharma and Singh (2013) observed that assured returns, less risks and stable markets for paddy and wheat crops due to the existence of MSP system prevented farmers to participate in CF for other crops in Punjab. Contract firms therefore entered into contract indirectly through Punjab Agro Foodgrains Corporation (PAFC). CF had failed to diversify crops in Punjab (till 2009) due to conventional growing of crops such as paddy and wheat by farmers and withdrawal of incentives to firms provided by PAFC.

Manzoor (2014) concluded that CF exposed farmers to mechanized agricultural technology. The contracting firms provided technology, healthy seedlings and technical advice and farmers obtained assured price and market for their produce. In return, the contracting companies enjoyed uninterrupted and regular flow of raw materials for their processing industry. Vath and Kirk (2014) concluded that famers under contract had lower profit than non-contract farmers. However, they showed 10 per cent higher profitability when they were offered with inputs and credit. Manas (2015) found CF as a better farming option over cooperative farming in view of easier access to credit, inputs, information and technology and product market for small famers. He observed that indiscriminate opening up of agricultural sector to corporate companieswill imbalance the social and economic equilibrium of the country, whereas contract faming does not do so.

Vicol (2015) revealed that economically sound farmers were beneficial for CF rather than resource-poor marginal farmers. When farmers experienced crop loss due to drought conditions they lost their contracts, land rights and assets. Lack of capital made marginal farmers employ family labour and casual labourers became seasonally unemployed. In summary, CF benefitted medium and large farmers rather than marginal and small farmers. Kadrolker (2016) observed that provision of input supply, access to credit, adoption of better technology, skill improvement, assured price and reliable market were the advantages experienced by farmers. On the other hand, sponsors gained quality products, escaped from land restriction barriers and political problems. The problems faced by farmers were greater risk in growing a new crop with no local market condition, over-capitalization and unemployment due to mechanization, rejection of produce by sponsors when quality specifications were not met and collapse of the contract.

The problems faced by sponsors were related to limited land availability, social attitudes of farmers and traditional farming affecting introduction of new crops, disloyalty of the farmers, low quantity produce and open market competitions.

LITERATURE REVIEW ON LAND TENANCY
Abroad

Grossman (1992) defined lease types in the USA as tenancy for years, year-to-year tenancy, tenancy at will and tenancy at sufferance. The termination notices vary from state to state. The farming in 1987 was carried out by 11.5 per cent of full tenants and 29.2 per cent of part owners. The landlords of Georgia in the USA were well protected with the doctrines of emblements and usufruct. In case of usufruct, the landlord did not pass on the ownership to the tenant if the lease term was less than five years. In the case of emblements, the tenant was able to grow in the land on an annual basis and if the term ended before the harvest, the doctrine enabled the tenant to enter the land till the harvest of the crop.

Lin (1992) observed that the shift in collective farming to individual responsibility farming in China, during the period 1978–1984, increased the productivity to 14 per cent. Subjected to poor land quality, earlier, he predicted that due to the reform the productivity would turn out larger in the long run, since investments would take time.

Besley (1995) reported that investment in land in Angola and Wassa of Ghana with the rights to sell, rent, mortgage, pledge, bequeath and gift was more as compared with land that was stringent in rights. The land that was registered and with lineage was more acceptable for transactions than the lands that were bought unregistered or as gifts.

Ashby and Ashby (2011) revealed that Royal Institute for Chartered Surveyors report on Agricultural Tenancy Act of 1995 in England had a positive impact on the landowners and tenants to enter into agreements subjected to freedom of contract. Lands with no structural changes were leased for four years, whereas lands that would be subject to structural changes were leased-in for nine years. The benefits of land leasing in UK turned the fixed-factor land into a liquidity factor and flexibleness in farm business to expand, contract or enter, irrespective of landownership. He also pointed out that share farming, share partnership and CF arrangements would meet the margin-level aspects of farming, whereas leasing would be the only sustainable solution for farming. The rural leasing agreements in the USA were subjected to market forces, whereas in UK, it was by the legislation.

Ciaian et al. (2012) noticed that short-term rental contracts allowed farmers to adjust their production with the external environmental changes, whereas the long-term contracts were not. At the same time, the short-term rentals were unable to get the full security rights which made them to invest less. The types of rental contracts followed in European member states and candidate countries include lease contracts for 9 years, 18 years and career contract, which is the difference between the age of the farmer and age of 65. The minimum duration limit to the career contract was 27 years. The other contracts include *recht van* postal and *erfpacht*. In the former one, the maximum duration was 50 years with the right to buildings in the plot confirmed by the notary; and in the latter one, the limit was 27–99 years.

Cianian et al. (2012) noticed that Agricultural Tenancies Act (ATA), 1995, in UK favoured England and Wales but not Scotland and Northern Ireland, which allowed flexibility for tenants and their landowners to make agreements that would suit their circumstances. The successor of ATA was Farm Business Tenancy, which was a contract for not more than two years, and this allowed farmers compulsorily to allocate land for farm business. The 2006 Regulatory Reform Order allowed the farmers to make lease period agreements according to their wishes. Hakizimana et al. (2017) indicated that in Kenya, one-ha land was rented on annual basis at $146. Women engaged in CF leased, on average, 0.25ha land from relatives to grow French beans to sell on contract. The commercial coffee growers rented the land for land consolidation and accumulation, which was fragmented by inheritance of land.

Haugerud (2017) revealed the effects of 1950, Kenya's tenure reform which till today is said to spread over the entire continent. Issuing of official land title to the farmers was not in par with the actual patterns of land use and access, instead informal ways to gain access to land increased. The land under sale was higher than the annual net return from the crop grown on that land and rents were nearly inexpensive. This reform failed to meet the actual purpose of the reform objective, which was meant to convert into perennial crop cultivation, increase agricultural productivity and consolidate the scattered plots or fragmented plots. Instead farmers preferred scattered plots to reduce risk of total crop loss, adopt crop diversity and manage labour availability to annual cycle. The reform turned out primarily for future subsistence security for sons and cash-borrowing power.

Klaiber (2017) explained that land rental agreement in Germany was liberal with no regulations on contract duration and rental prices. The tenant pays cash rent with contract-specific expenses and receives the Single Payment Scheme (SPS) plus market revenue. One-third of the contracts were open-ended and the rest were short-term for one year, medium-term contracts were for five years and long-term contracts for 9–12 years. With SPS entitlement, the capitalization into farm rental rates had increased in Bavarian farms of Germany. Yaro et al. (2017) revealed that agriculture commercialization in Ghana had encouraged the poorer families, who were unable to access land or survive from current holdings, to lease-out land for bigger farmers. Medium and large farmers leased-in land for fruit cultivation and plantation.

Literature in India

Appu (1975) revealed that the tenancy reforms in India, till date, had failed to reform the traditional agrarian structure. In addition to this, the unrecorded landownership rights and sharecropping fuelled to non-adoption of modern agriculture. He highlighted that restrictions on leasing-out had left tenancies dead and this encouraged small farmers to sell their land and add to the growing unemployment population in the urban areas.

Besley and Burgess (2000) proved that among various land reforms in India, tenancy reform's abolition of intermediaries and change in tenancy terms had a significant effect on reduction in rural poverty. The impact of land reform on poverty was highest in those states that had greatest land inequalities. Along with this, the reform had an indirect impact on welfare of landless agricultural labourers. The reform of land consolidation had a positive effect on increase in agricultural output, whereas reforms on land redistribution had limited impacts on poverty and agricultural output.

Haque (2001) concluded that states like Karnataka and West Bengal that were bestowed with ownership or occupancy rights due to abolition of intermediaries and tenancy reforms yielded good results. Farmers showed interest towards farming and invested in soil and land improvement activities. Thereby land productivity and economic status improved. Few states such as Punjab and Haryana adopted reverse tenancy that gave small farmers time to earn from non-farm activities with secured rent, but the actual objective of improving their economic status failed. The states with regulated leasing allowed sharecroppers and tenants to access institutional credit thereby decrease in landowner's contribution regarding input sharing was observed.

Banerjee et al. (2002) studied the impact of 1978 land reform in West Bengal, that is, operation Barga, by comparing with the non-reformed Bangladesh, which has similar agro-climatic condition as West Bengal with religion and political differences. This comparison was made to highlight the tenancy reform of West Bengal which was accompanied by green revolution, reduction in cost of fertilizers and initiatives to promote irrigation structures at the same time. They revealed two major positive impacts of operation Barga. The registration rate by the tenant farmers was higher as compared to the previous Land Reform Acts in India. The rice yield in West Bengal increased by 69 per cent whereas, in Bangladesh, it was 44 per cent irrespective of faster adoption of high-yielding variety rice by Bangladesh. The overall agricultural productivity grew by 28 per cent in West Bengal due to the tenancy reforms.

Murty (2004) examined the share of landless, marginal and small farmers in total tenanted holdings in 1981–1982 which was 75.58 per cent and their share in tenanted area was 35.12 per cent. The large farmer's per cent share in leasing was 1.44 per cent and the leased-in area was 13.46 per cent. From the period 1981–1991, leasing-in decreased from 15.20 per cent to 10.99 per cent except proportion of the large farmers. Their proportion increased from 11.6 to 16.7 per cent due to spread of leasing from 8 states to 15 states in the same period. The reason for leasing land was farm mechanization, commercialization and agricultural development which needed land and majority of them were large farmers, who possess these capital assets and who already had land and required small proportion of land; whereas, small farmers needed more land to lease-in. Large farmers edged-out marginal farmers by offering fixed money invariably in the beginning of the season in return for lease of land.

Deininger et al. (2007) revealed that land rental restrictions in India had reduced the production efficiency due to impeding access by efficient farmers. His simulation models predicted that with elimination of restrictions on land rental markets 40–70 per cent of efficient producers would get land. Awasthi (2009) revealed that in the Bundelkhand region of UP, the small and marginal farmers were more prevalent in leasing the land as compared to medium and large farmers. The small and marginal farmers rented the land based on crop yield sharing basis, whereas, medium and large farmers rented based on cash-rent lease contracts. The output under sharecropped lease system was 13 per cent lower than the owner-cultivated land, whereas the cash rented land yielded 8–10 per cent less productivity with uncoupled investment in variable inputs. The major factors that affected marginal and small farmers to sell the land were uneconomic land holdings and migration to urban centres. The medium and large farmers sold the land for loan-repayment purposes and social ceremonies.

Deininger and Nagarajan (2009) reported that landlords, due to fear of losing the land, cultivated it but less efficiently. The states that were outlawed on rent kept land fallow even in the main cropping season. The reform legislation allowed the tenants for inheritable security of land from eviction but not ownership, where the tenants had to pay the rent. This prevented both the tenant and the landlord in making land-related investments and sub-leasing that further led to decrease in allocative efficiency. This, in turn, affected the leasing market that de-promoted the productive farmers to access land and those who are unable to cultivate to migrate to non-agricultural economy.

Besley et al. (2013) discussed that the land reforms introduced before and after the states' reorganization in southern India favoured relatively wealthier tenants; while SC/ST saw decrease in landholdings and depended on agriculture-labour income. In turn, there was decrease in demand for tenants and increase in demand for agriculture-hired labour, which increased the agricultural wages.

Jayadev and Ha (2015) stated that land reforms in Kerala had neither increased the productivity of crops nor solved the problem of marginal and small farmers. Despite eradicating landlordism, the plantation owners turned out to be landlords. The reform failed to access the communities such as fishing. There was a decline in paddy cultivators since it was cultivated by small farmers. Lack of maintenance of records failed to fetch information of land holdings exceeding the ceiling limit.

Mani (2015) stated that amongst various terms of lease, the term of lease against share of produce had decreased over the last four decades but was important form of tenancy in Assam and Karnataka. Fixed money as a term of lease had gained importance, especially, in agriculturally advanced states like Punjab and Haryana. The leasing from relatives under non-specific terms was common in Himachal Pradesh and Kerala. States such as AP, Bihar, Punjab, TN, Odisha and West Bengal, which showed decline in leased-in area, had shown an increasing trend in 2012 that suggests relaxing the ban on leasing-in land.

Roy (2016) explained that post 1970, reforms in Kerala abolished landlordism, aroused land fragmentation and marginal farmers increased instantaneously. Coupled with land markets and increase in land value after the 1970's converted land to be an asset and was used for speculative purposes. Exceptional provision of ceiling restriction on plantation sector led to leasing-out by erstwhile monarchs to plantation-crop growers to a period of hundred to thousand years.

SUMMARY

In India, it has been realized that economic condition of Indian farmers (especially small and marginal) cannot be improved unless they diversify their cropping pattern as per the fast-changing tastes of global community.[2]

---

[2] See, for example, Johl Committee Report (1986, 2002) on Diversification of Punjab Agriculture.

The smallholders need to move away from cereals production towards more perishable commodities like fruits, vegetables and high-value crops to stabilize their income and employment.[3] Agricultural system can be made more dynamic by reducing the cost of cultivation, which can either be done by cutting costs directly or increasing returns to the producers by value addition. It is imperative to open more scope of processing and marketing of raw products to add more value to the agricultural produce (Kumar and Sharma 2005). It is in this context that CF brings in both the objectives of cost reduction and value addition by making available good quality seeds, fertilizers, technical know-how and efficient marketing channels to the producers.

In the recent past, CF has started becoming popular among many states, for example, wheat in MP by HLL, Rallis and ICICI. Rallis supplies agri-inputs and know-how and ICICI finances farm credit while HLL, the processing company, provides the buy-back arrangement for the farm output. Similarly, ACC, the ginning and trading house from Pollachi (TN), is providing a buy-back guarantee to the growers of cotton seeds in Coimbatore. The Appachi formula of CF has been so successful that the TN government is now keenly interested in replicating this model in various cotton-growing districts of the state. Ugar Sugar Works Limited-led CF in barley in Belgaum (Karnataka) is another success story of CF.[4] Encouraged by these examples, several

---

[3] It is now a forgone conclusion that the green revolution (wheat and rice) technology supported by the MSP system is no longer a viable option both for the state as well as the farming community. See, for example, Nadkarni (1988), Johl (1996) and Chand (1999).

[4] At present, many firms are practicing CF in different states. A few examples are: Pepsi—in potato, green chilli and citrus fruits in Punjab, Green Agro Pack—gherkins in Karnataka, Reliance Agrotech—cashew, mango, bamboo and teak in MP, A.V. Thomas Group Kochi—marigold in AP and TN, HLL—chicory in Gujarat, basmati rice in Punjab and dairy in UP, Coimbatore Cots and Coatings Ltd—cotton in TN, Ion Exchange Enviro Farm Ltd—organic mango, banana, pineapple, pulses and vegetables in Maharashtra, Mittal Farms—medicinal plants and herb in Gujarat, Semi Labs and Natural Remedies—medicinal plants in Karnataka, C&M Group—maize and soyabean in Maharashtra, Rallis India/Tata Chemicals—wheat in MP, basmati rice and hyola in Punjab, Soguna Broilers—broiler in TN, Global Ostrich (India) Pvt. Ltd and Chamundi Hatcheries—ostrich farming in Karnataka and Shri Bhumi Farms Pvt. Ltd—red bananas in Karnataka.

state governments—including AP, Gujarat, Karnataka, Punjab and TN—are promoting CF, changing laws to enable and support it and providing companies interested in it with a variety of incentives, including lifting of land ceilings, subsidies and tax rebates.

A few observations made by studies on India (Rangi & Sidhu, 2000, 2003; Singh, 1997, 2002, 2004, 2005) are that the results of contracting are very promising in the early years. Farmers benefit from improved technology and higher productivity, quality and production. However, once farmers deploy themselves into the new technology, problems start cropping up. If the market price is more advantageous than the contract price, farmers renege on the contract. Generally, the contracts are not written and the legal enforcement system is too tedious for both growers and firms. In the existing models, farmers are largely price takers while the contracting firms make the price. Other criticisms levelled against CF in these cases is that it generally prefers labour-saving farm practices, low level of commitment of corporate over rural development, lack of transparency and lack of institutions and NGOs for proper dissemination of information for the success of CF.

Chapter 4

Household Characteristics, Cropping Pattern and Land Productivity

This study is primarily based on a primary survey. Two states in the north and two states in the south were selected for conducting this study. In the North, Punjab and Haryana and in the South, Karnataka and unified AP (including Telangana) were selected. In the aggregate, 500 farm households—comprising 400 farmers belonging to the category of contract farmers, land leasing farmers and sharecropping farmers and 100 farmers from the control group not belonging to any of the above-mentioned categories—were selected in each state.

The selection of the sample broadly involves the following stages. At the first stage, firms involved in CF in each state were contacted and a list of farmers who were active participants in CF during the preceding year was obtained. The list included the names and addresses of the farmers and their contracted area, crop wise. Similarly, we collected information about land-leasing/land-sharing farmers in the selected villages in each state. Based on this list, farmers were chosen by the Stratified Random Sampling Method. For the selection of non-contract farmers, no such list was available. Therefore, keeping in mind the objective of the study to prepare a baseline to make comparison, non-contract farmers were selected in the peripheral areas with a similar cropping pattern as that of contract/lease farmers. It was tried to give a proportionate representation to different-size classes while selecting the sample farmers. The details of households selected are presented in Table 4A.1. This chapter outlines the household and demographic characteristics of the selected households, general cropping pattern followed by them and overall productivity of the selected households.

HOUSEHOLD CHARACTERISTICS AND DETAILS OF OPERATIONAL HOLDINGS

The number of households selected in each state by contract farming, leasing/sharecropping and control group and their area operated per household is provided in Table 4.1. In the aggregate, a total number of 2,014 households were selected in all the four states. It is to be pointed out here that the selected households in AP belong to erstwhile AP which is now divided into AP and Telangana since 2 June 2014. As in most of the cases, tenancy existed only in terms of cash payment on seasonal or yearly basis and tenancy in terms of sharecropping was almost non-existent or existed to a limited extent, the two categories are clubbed together for the sake of preserving numbers of observations (Table 4.1 provides details of tenancy in cash and sharecrop basis). Therefore, our analysis primarily consists of CF, leased-in and control groups, while the latter includes those households who operated purely on their own land without any support from the contracting firms and without any area leased-in or leased-out.

Out of 2,014 selected households, the distribution across four states was almost equal with 500 households in Punjab, 502 in AP, 503 in Haryana and 509 in Karnataka. Majority of the selected farmers belonged to CF as that was the design of the study proposed. The total number of contract farmers selected in the four states was 1,408 farmers, with 402 in AP, around 300 each in Punjab and Haryana and 408 in Karnataka. The numbers of leased-in farmers surveyed was 341 with highest numbers in Haryana and Punjab—136 and 138, respectively and 59 in AP, while only 8 farmers belonged to leased-in in Karnataka. Similarly, the control group farmers, who were neither having any CF nor any leased-in or sharecropped land, were 265 with 93 farmers from Karnataka, 68 from Haryana, 63 from Punjab and 41 from AP.

Table 4.1 *The Number of Households Selected and Their Area Operated in Acres/HH*

Farm Size	Contract		Leasing-in		Non-Contract		Sum Total	
	HH	Acres/HH	HH	Acres/HH	HH	Acres/HH	HH	Acres/HH
AP	402	4.20	59	4.80	41	3.60	502	4.20
Haryana	299	18.90	136	15.30	68	8.10	503	16.50
Punjab	299	23.50	138	16.70	63	8.20	500	19.70
Karnataka	408	3.24	8	3.31	93	3.00	509	3.20
Aggregate	1,408	11.14	341	13.77	265	5.64	2,014	10.87

It is evident from the table that on average, operated area was highest among the tenant farmers, who in addition to their own area also leased-in area to make their holdings more economical. The leased-in farmers operated 13.8 acres per household followed by contract farmers who operated 11 acres, whereas the control group farmers operated only 5.6 acres per household. In the aggregate, the average holding size was 10.9 acres per household with operational holding size highest in Punjab—19.7 acres, followed by Haryana—16.5 acres, AP—4.2 acres and Karnataka with lowest holding size of 3.2 acres per household. Comparing the regions of north and south, holding size was higher for contract farmers in both Punjab and Haryana as compared to leased-in farmers; while in the south, holding size was higher for leased-in farmers as compared to contract farmers in both AP and Karnataka; whereas in all the four states, control group had the lowest holding size. Table 4.1 shows that among the selected farmers, the number of marginal and small farmers was highest in AP and Karnataka, whereas, in Punjab and Haryana large farmers constituted the majority. This was true with regards to contract farmers, lease-in farmers as well as control groups.

Table 4.2 presents demographic profile of the selected farmers. The household size varied from less than five members to around eight members in different states. It was highest in Haryana, followed by Punjab, AP and Karnataka in the descending order. On average, the numbers of members in the house were highest among leased farmers followed by control group and contract farmers. However, contrarily, numbers of earners in the household were highest among contract farmers, followed by control group and leased-in farmers. Respondents were mostly males and they were generally the head of the households. Looking at the age composition of the respondents, more number of contract farmers were in less than 50 years of age, followed by leased-in farmers; while more number of household respondents with above 50 years were in the control group. Thus, contract farmers were younger in age as compared to other categories and this was same across all the four states without any single exception. In addition to being younger, they were also more educated as compared to the other two categories in all the four states. In the aggregate, around 9 per cent respondents in the category of contract farmers were educated up to graduation, as compared to around 6 per cent respondents in the case of leased-in and

Table 4.2 Demographic Profile of the Selected Farmers (% of Households)

Characteristics		AP			Haryana			Punjab			Karnataka			Aggregate		
		Contract	Leasing-in	Non-contract	Contract	Leasing-in	Non-contract	Contract	Leasing-in	Non-contract	Contract	Leasing-in	Non-contract	Contract	Leasing-in	Non-contract
No of HH		402	59	41	299	136	68	299	138	63	408	8	93	1,408	341	265
Household size (numbers)		5.36	5.38	5.12	7.3	6.5	7.8	6.5	6.3	6.3	5.56	4.75	5.35	6.07	6.18	6.17
Average numbers of earners		2.9	2.6	2.9	2.16	2.09	2.13	2.2	2.1	2.3	2.93	2.25	2.77	2.60	2.19	2.51
Gender (% of respondents)	Male	98.51	100	100	100	99.26	100	98.66	100	100	97.79	100	98.92	98.65	99.71	99.62
	Female	1.49	0	0	0	0.74	0	1.34	0	0	2.21	0	1.08	1.35	0.29	0.38
Age group of the respondents (%)	≤ 30	16.17	15.25	19.51	15.38	11.03	17.65	18.73	15.22	15.87	5.88	0	8.6	13.57	13.20	14.34
	>30 – ≤ 50	58.96	59.32	51.22	54.85	59.56	32.35	56.86	47.83	39.68	63.48	100	60.22	58.95	55.72	46.79
	>50	24.88	25.42	29.27	29.77	29.41	50	24.41	36.96	44.44	30.64	0	31.18	27.49	31.09	38.87

(Table 4.2 Continued)

(Table 4.2 Continued)

Characteristics		AP			Haryana			Punjab			Karnataka			Aggregate		
		Con-tract	Lea-sing-in	Non-contract	Con-tract	Lea-sing-in	Non-contract	Con-tract	Lea-sing-in	Non-contract	Con-tract	Lea-sing-in	Non-contract	Con-tract	Lea-sing-in	Non-contract
Identity of respon-dents (%)	Head	94.28	94.92	97.56	75.59	83.82	80.88	76.25	85.51	80.95	94.61	100	89.25	86.58	86.80	86.42
	Others	5.72	5.08	2.44	24.41	16.18	19.12	23.75	14.49	19.05	5.39	0	10.76	13.42	13.20	13.58
Education status of respon-dents (%)	Illiterate	43.28	67.8	51.22	9.36	14.71	19.12	0	0	0	26.23	0	35.48	21.95	17.60	25.28
	Up to primary	18.41	11.9	17.07	9.7	17.65	10.29	19.73	24.64	33.33	14.95	37.5	16.13	15.84	19.94	18.87
	Up to secondary	33.08	16.95	21.95	65.89	61.03	60.29	62.21	66.66	60.32	51.47	62.5	39.78	51.56	55.72	47.17
	Up to graduation	3.98	3.39	7.32	12.04	5.88	8.82	14.72	7.97	3.17	6.37	0	6.45	8.66	6.16	6.42
	Above graduation	1.24	0	2.44	3.01	0.74	1.47	3.34	0.72	3.17	0.98	0	2.15	1.99	0.59	2.26

Caste (% of respondents)	SC	12.19	35.59	19.51	6.69	21.32	11.76	5.69	5.8	4.76	5.39	0	3.23	7.67	17.01	8.30
	ST	4.23	1.69	0	0.67	0.74	0	0.33	2.9	0	2.7	0	4.3	2.20	1.76	1.51
	OBC	72.14	59.32	80.49	13.38	24.26	14.71	92.98	2.17	0	50.25	37.5	35.48	38.21	21.70	28.68
	General	11.44	3.39	0	79.26	53.68	73.53	1	89.13	95.24	41.67	62.5	56.99	51.92	59.53	61.51
Main occupation of respondents (%)	Farming	95.27	93.22	100	93.65	95.59	89.71	95.99	93.48	93.65	98.53	100	97.85	96.02	94.43	95.09
	Self-business	0.75	0	0	3.34	3.68	2.94	0	0	4.76	0.99	0	2.15	1.21	1.47	2.64
	Salaried/Pensioners	0.75	0	0	1	0	2.94	0.67	2.9	0	0.25	0	0	0.64	1.17	0.75
	Wage earners	3.23	6.78	0	1.67	0	4.41	1.67	2.9	1.59	0.25	0	0	1.70	2.35	1.51
	Others	0	0	0	0.33	0.74	0	1.67	0.72	0	0	0	0	0.43	0.59	0.00

control groups. Similarly, 52 per cent contract farmers were educated up to secondary level as compared to 47 per cent of control farmers.

Looking at the socio-economic characteristics, 38 per cent of contract farmers belonged to the category of Other Backward Class (OBC) as compared to 22 per cent leased and 29 per cent control group farmers. On the other hand, 52 per cent of contract farmers belonged to General category as compared to 60 per cent of leased farmers and 62 per cent of control farmers. Similarly, CF was observed existing among the SC and ST categories as well, albeit their percentage was slightly less among the SC farmers. Thus, contrary to the general thinking that CF exists only among upper-caste farmers, we observed that CF was widespread across various social class structures. Among the selected farmers, farming was the main occupation of the respondents as their involvement in self-business, salaried work or wage activities was almost negligible and the same was true for contract, leased and control farmers.

Table 4.3 presents operational holdings of selected farmers in the four states. The average operated area was much higher in Punjab and Haryana as compared to AP and Karnataka. Not only the size of owned land was higher, but the proportion of net leased land was also much higher in Punjab and Haryana as compared to the other two selected states. The size of owned land per household was 3.9 and 3.1 acres in AP and Karnataka, respectively, while it was 8.8 acres in Haryana and 9.7 acres in Punjab. Similarly, net leased-in land was less than 1 acre in AP and Karnataka; while in Haryana, net leased-in land was around 8 acres and in Punjab it was around 10 acres per household. Sharecropping existed in a small quantity only in Haryana. Most of the land leasing was in terms of short-term lease, not exceeding one year while miniscule cases were found of long-term lease of two years or more. Out of NOA of around 10.9 acres, around 10.4 acres were irrigated which consists of around 96 per cent operated area irrigated. While in Punjab and Haryana, almost the whole operated area was irrigated, in AP—78 per cent operated area was irrigated and in Karnataka around 82 per cent operated area was irrigated. Whereas in Punjab and Haryana, generally percentage of irrigated area is the reflection of the actual situation; in AP and Karnataka our sample area is much highly irrigated than the state averages because of our purposive sampling.

Table 4.3 Characteristics of Operational Holdings (Acres per Household)

Particulars	AP	Haryana	Punjab	Karnataka	Aggregate
Owned land	3.91	8.81	9.74	3.13	6.38
Net sharecropping	0	0.26	0	0	0.06
Net short-term lease	0.72	7.52	9.97	0.28	4.60
Net long-term lease	0.14	0.05	0	0.08	0.07
Fallow and current fallow	0.53	0.22	0.006	0.27	0.26
Pastureland	0.04	0.02	0	0.02	0.02
Net operated area (NOA; acres/HH)	4.2	16.48	19.72	3.2	10.87
Net irrigated area (NIA; acres/HH)	3.25	16.2	19.7	2.64	10.41
NIA as a % of NOA	77.45	98.3	99.9	82.44	95.83
Gross cropped area (GCA; acres/HH)	4.78	31.99	41.41	5.49	20.85
NIA as a % of GCA	68.05	50.64	47.58	48.07	49.95
Cropping intensity	113.82	194.12	209.96	171.5	191.85

The cropping intensity was almost two crops in a year per acre in Haryana and more than two crops in Punjab, as compared to much less than two crops in Karnataka and nearly one crop in AP. Whereas in Karnataka and AP, percentage irrigated area and cropping intensity was higher among marginal and small farmers as compared to the large farmers. In Punjab and Haryana, there was no significant difference between small and large farmers.

Looking at the sources of irrigation (Table 4.4), almost whole area in Haryana and Punjab was irrigated by borewell except a small area irrigated by canal and some area being irrigated by both borewell and canal. In contrast, around 10 per cent area in AP and around 3 per cent area in Karnataka was irrigated by open well, whereas 44 per cent area in AP and 76 per cent area in Karnataka was irrigated by the borewell. The declining importance of tanks in South India is clearly seen in our study as only two per cent area in AP and almost negligible area was irrigated by tanks in Karnataka. Among the selected farmers, around 23 per cent operated area in AP and around 18 per cent area in Karnataka was unirrigated while no area in Punjab and Haryana was found unirrigated. Among different size of holdings, marginal and small farmers had more area irrigated by borewell while large farmers had more area irrigated by canals in AP. On the other hand, in Punjab and Haryana, borewell area was less in the case of marginal and small farmers as compared to large farmers and their area irrigated by canal was more as compared to large farmers, a trend that was completely opposite to that of AP. In Karnataka, canal area was miniscule for both small and large farmers.

Looking at the tenure of leasing and leasing-out as displayed by Tables 4.5a and 4.5b, net leased-in area in the aggregate was around 4.6 acres and it was mostly irrigated area and the tenure of lease was mostly short term. State wise, lease-in area varied from less than half an acre in Karnataka, 1 acre in AP, around 8 acres in Haryana and 10 acres in Punjab. The rent paid for leasing per acre on average was ₹14 thousand in AP, ₹16 thousand in Karnataka, ₹34 thousand in Haryana and as high as ₹41 thousand per acre in Punjab for the cultivation of land for one year. Although long-term lease was only in miniscule cases but it did exist and has important implications for this study. Although

Table 4.4 *Source of Irrigation (% of NOA)*

Sources of Irrigation	AP	Haryana	Punjab	Karnataka	Aggregate
Open well	9.75	0	0.3	3.08	1.30
Bore/tube well	43.62	85.82	96.23	76.04	85.72
Canal	9.02	1.06	3.31	0.31	2.78
Tank and others	2.29	0	0	0.49	0.26
Open well and borewell	4.48	0	0	2.52	0.62
Open well and canal	1.67	0	0	0	0.16
Open and others	1.92	0.02	0	0	0.19
Borewell and canal	2.3	11.39	0.05	0	4.56
Borewell and others	0.83	0	0	0	0.08
Borewell, canal and others	0.57	0	0	0	0.05
Open well, borewell & others	1	0	0	0	0.10
No irrigation	22.55	0	0.1	17.56	3.52

Table 4.5a *Tenure of Leasing-in and Prevailing Rate of Leasing-in Land*

States	Short-term lease-in			Long-term lease-in			
	Irrigated (Acres per HH)	Unirrigated (Acres per HH)	Rent Paid (₹ per Acre)	Irrigated (Acres per HH)	Unirrigated (Acres per HH)	Rent Paid (₹ per Acre per Year)	Duration of Lease (Years)
AP	0.67	0.06	14,442	0.123	0.016	9,597	2.62
Haryana	7.61	0.008	33,766	0.046	0	16,413	7.67
Punjab	10.1	0.00	40,910	0	0	0	0
Karnataka	0.24	0.03	15,974	0.078	0.002	9,260	3.52
Aggregate	**4.63**	**0.021**	**36,604**	**0.062**	**0.004**	**10,732**	**3.37**

Table 4.5b Tenure of Leasing-Out and Prevailing Rate of Leasing-Out Land

| States | Short-term Lease-Out | | Rent Received (₹ per Acre) | Long-term Lease-Out | | Rent Received (₹ per Acre) | Duration of Lease (Years) |
	Irrigated (Acres per HH)	Unirrigated (Acres per HH)		Irrigated (Acres per HH)	Unirrigated (Acres per HH)		
AP	0.008	0.001	14,105	0	0	0	0
Haryana	0.099	0	31,960	0	0	0	0
Punjab	0.096		37,135	0	0	0	0
Karnataka	0	0	0	0.02	0	11,821	3.13
Aggregate	0.051	0.0005	33,505	0.0051	0	11,821	3.13

the area under long-term lease was very small, however, it indicates the existing tenure of long-term lease and presents a comparative picture of long-term rent in which the leasing had taken place.

It is observed from the data that tenure of long-term lease varied from around 2.6 years to 7.7 years and it averaged slightly above 3 years. The rent for long-term lease was significantly lower as compared to short-term lease. Long-term rent per acre on annual basis was around ₹9.5 thousand in AP, ₹9 thousand in Karnataka and ₹16 thousand in Haryana while in Punjab, no long-term lease was observed. The long-term rent was around 66 per cent that of short-term rent in AP, less than half in Haryana and around 58 per cent in Karnataka. In the aggregate, long-term rent was only 29 per cent that of the short-term lease rent. Similar was the case of leasing-out land as presented in Table 4.5b. Although instances of leasing-out land were very few in our sample, but few cases existed for short-term leasing-out in AP, Haryana and Punjab and long-term leasing-out in Karnataka. The rent for short and long-term leasing-out was mostly similar to that of short- and long-term leasing-in. On average, rent for short-term leasing-out was ₹33.5 thousand per acre and long-term leasing-out was only ₹11.8 thousand per acre and the latter was only 35 per cent of the former. This has long-term implication for the tenants as with the rise in the duration of tenancy there is a decline in rent, which gives opportunity to small-holders to make their holding size more economical by leasing-in land if provisions are made for long-term lease.

The possible reason for decline in land rent at longer interval of lease could be such long-term lease gives landlords more security for their holdings and they can plan alternate options for themselves. This issue is discussed in a greater detail in the forthcoming chapters. Tables 4.3 indicates existence of reverse tenancy among the selected households in all the four states. It is seen from leasing-in and leasing-out trends that medium and large farmers leased-in more land as compared to small and marginal farmers, possibly to economize their size of holdings and making appropriate use of existing machinery with them.

Tables 4.6a, 4.6b and 4.6c present land transactions by the selected households including land purchased and sold during the current and last three years and the reasons for sale and purchase. There were only

Table 4.6a Land Transactions by the Selected Households

Farm Size	Irrigated		Land Purchased during 2015–2016						Gift Obtained
			Dry Land		Pastures		Non-agricultural		
	Acres per HH	Payment—₹ Lakh/Acre	Acres per HH	Payment—₹/Acre	Acres per HH	Payment—₹/Acre	Acres per HH	Payment—₹/Acre	Acres per HH
	1	2	3	4	5	6	7	8	9
AP	–	–	–	–	–	–	–	–	–
Haryana	0.004	22.00	0.001	13.33	–	–	–	–	–
Punjab	0.014	8.07	–	–	–	–	0.0007	227,2727	–
Karnataka	–	–	–	–	–	–	–	–	–
Total	0.004	11.25	0.0001	13.33	–	–	0.0002	2,272,727	–
Land Purchased during Last Three Years (2012–2013, 2013–2014 and 2014–2015)									
AP	0.006	5.85	0.014	2.20	0	0	0	0	0
Haryana	0.016	24.24	0	0	0	0	0	0	0
Punjab	0.010	30.60	0.001	22.00	0	0	0	0	0
Karnataka	0	0	0.020	0.46	0	0	0	0	0
Total	0.008	22.79	0.009	1.77	0	0	0	0	0

Table 4.6b *Land Transactions by the Selected Households*

Farm Size	Irrigated		Land Sold During 2015–2016						Gift Obtained
			Dry Land		Pastures		Non-agricultural		
	Acres per HH	Payment—₹/Acre	Acres per HH	Payment—₹/Acre	Acres per HH	Payment ₹/Acre	Acres per HH	Payment—₹/Acre	Acres per HH
	1	2	3	4	5	6	7	8	9
AP	–	–	0.008	294,118	–	–	–	–	–
Haryana	0.004	3,900,000	0.002	1,500,000	–	–	0.002	1,500,000	–
Punjab	0.024	1,586,667	–	–	–	–	–	–	–
Karnataka	0.001	600,000	–	–	–	–	–	–	–
Total	0.007	1,872,612	0.002	535,679	–	–	0.0005	1,500,000	–
Land Purchased during Last Three Years (2012–2013, 2013–2014 and 2014–2015)									
AP	0.007	210,000	0.028	220,588	–	–	–	–	–
Haryana	0.008	2,720,000	–	–	–	–	–	–	–
Punjab	0.004	1,100,000	–	–	–	–	–	–	–
Karnataka	0.001	260,000	0.003	100,000	–	–	–	–	–
Total	0.005	1,357,851	0.008	208,771	–	–	–	–	–

Table 4.6c *Reasons for Land Sale (% of Households Who Sold Their Land)*

States	Drought	Health Issues	Difficulty to Manage	Family Needs, Marriages, etc.	Not Able to Make Livelihood	Others
AP	0	10.00	0	40	20	30
Haryana	0	0	0	80	20	0
Punjab	0	0	28.57	71.43	0	0
Karnataka	0	33.33	33.33	33.33	0	0
Aggregate	0	8.00	12.00	56.00	12.00	12.00

a very few instances of purchase of land by the selected households during the current year that also occurred only in Punjab and Haryana while no transaction was noted in Karnataka and AP. On the other hand, land sale incidences were recorded during the current year in all the four selected states, albeit sale of land was only miniscule. We even tried to record the land transaction occurred among the selected households during the last three years but we found only a few abysmal cases in all the four states. This indicates that land market in terms of sale and purchase is almost absent. The principal reason for sale of land in those few cases was family needs as well as unmanageable size and not being able to make a livelihood with the given piece of land was the predominant. Thus, the existing nature of land tenancy laws and complete absence of land markets makes it impossible for cultivators to move away for alternate employment especially the small and marginal farmers, who find it very difficult to endure in agriculture with their small holding size.

SOURCES AND PURPOSE OF CREDIT BY THE SELECTED HOUSEHOLDS

Easy availability of credit at reasonable rate plays an important role in meeting with farmers' requirement of building farm assets to enhance their productivity. There is not only the shortage of cash flow for the farmers, but it is also irregular in nature. The literature also suggests that the funds are usurped usually by the well-to-do households, majority of whom belong to large farmers (Kumar and Sarkar, 2012). Tables 4.7a and 4.7b present the details of sources of credit accessed by the selected farmers in the four states. In the aggregate, total loan accessed by the selected farmer amounts to ₹3.6 lakh per household. However, the wedge between contract farmers, leased farmers and control group was too wide. Whereas contract farmers borrowed above ₹4 lakh per household, the amount was slightly less in the case of lease farmers—₹3.9 lakh, while control group had less than half of this amount around ₹1.1 lakh only.

Among different sources, institutional sources constituted almost 80 per cent whereas moneylenders, commission agents and friends and relatives constituted rest of the 20 per cent, while contracting firms provided almost negligible amount (to contract farmers). For contract farmers, institutional credit share was the highest—82 per cent, followed by control group—72.5 per cent and leased farmers in the descending order with 70.5 per cent share. Thus, access of institutional credit was not much different across contract, lease and control groups. Credit access across different states varied quite widely and variations were also observed across the three categories. On average, credit availed by Punjab farmers was ₹8.6 lakh per household, followed by Haryana farmers with ₹4.3 lakh, whereas the southern states had far less availability of credit, ₹1.25 lakh in AP and only ₹69 thousand by the Karnataka farmers. Comparing the contract farmers, the wedge was even wider. In Punjab, contract farmers accessed ₹11 lakh per household as compared to ₹5.2 lakh in Haryana, ₹1.3 lakh in AP and only ₹72 thousand in Karnataka. The leased farmers availed ₹5.8 lakh per household in Punjab, ₹3.2 lakh in Haryana, ₹1.4 lakh in AP and ₹35 thousand in Karnataka. In contrast, control group farmers had access of total credit of only ₹42 thousand in Punjab as compared to ₹2.7 lakh in Haryana, ₹76 thousand in AP and ₹59 thousand in Karnataka.

A part of explanation of higher credit in the North Indian states as compared to South Indian states can be seen in terms of more institutional credit accessible to the former as compared to the latter. In the aggregate, Punjab had access to institutional credit that was as high as 87 per cent of the total credit and Haryana's share was 76 per cent. In comparison, the intuitional proportion of total availed credit in Karnataka was 61 per cent and in AP it was only 46 per cent. Thus,

Table 4.7a Details of Outstanding Credit Amount by the Selected Households (₹ per HH)

Farm Type	Institutional Loan by Banks	Moneylenders/ Commission Agents	Loan Given by Contracting Firms	Friends/ Relatives	Others	Total
AP						
Contract farmers	63,742 (49.44)	10,988 (8.52)	473 (0.37)	53,614 (41.58)	124 (0.1)	128,941 (100)
Land leased-in farmers	40,100 (28.01)	23,020 (16.08)	0 (0)	80,040 (55.91)	0 (0)	143,160 (100)
Non-contract farmers	33,360 (43.87)	1,840 (2.42)	0 (0)	40,840 (53.71)	0 (0)	76,040 (100)
Aggregate	58,361 (46.31)	11,275 (9.23)	378 (0.3)	54,974 (44.09)	100 (0.08)	125,088 (100)
Haryana						
Contract farmers	424,314 (81.08)	81,856 (15.64)	(0)	17,142 (3.28)	(0)	523,312 (100)
Land leased-in farmers	187,390 (57.7)	124,213 (38.25)	(0)	13,169 (4.05)	(0)	324,772 (100)
Non-contract farmers	210,750 (79.13)	49,412 (18.55)	(0)	4,706 (1.77)	1,471 (0.55)	266,339 (100)
Aggregate	331,383 (76.2)	88,922 (20.45)	(0)	14,387 (3.31)	199 (0.05)	434,891 (100)

(Table 4.7a Continued)

(Table 4.7a Continued)

Farm Type	Institutional Loan by Banks	Moneylenders/ Commission Agents	Loan Given by Contracting Firms	Friends/ Relatives	Others	Total
Punjab						
Contract farmers	978,540 (88.89)	121,338 (11.02)	669 (0.06)	334 (0.03)	0 (0)	110,0881 (100)
Land leased-in farmers	474,935 (82.21)	98,406 (17.03)	0 (0)	4,348 (0.75)	0 (0)	577,689 (100)
Non-contract farmers	29,760 (70.12)	12,620 (29.74)	0 (0)	60 (0.14)	0 (0)	42,440 (100)
Aggregate	746,009 (87.47)	112,340 (12.31)	400 (0.05)	1,460 (0.17)	0 (0)	860,209 (100)
Karnataka						
Contract farmers	43,449 (60.21)	1,691 (2.34)	625 (0.87)	25,495 (35.33)	900 (1.25)	72,160 (100)
Land leased-in farmers	21,875 (62.5)	0 (0)	0 (0)	13,125 (37.5)	0 (0)	35,000 (100)
Non-contract farmers	40,048 (68.17)	32 (0.05)	0 (0)	18,667 (31.78)	0 (0)	58,747 (100)

Aggregate	42,488 (61.47)	1,362 (1.97)	501 (0.72)	24,053 (34.8)	721 (1.04)	69,125 (100)
Aggregate						
Contract farmers	328,697 (81.64)	46,777 (11.62)	458 (0.11)	26,406 (6.56)	296 (0.07)	402,634 (100)
Land leased-in farmers	274,390 (70.55)	93,347 (24)	0 (0)	21,168 (5.44)	0 (0)	388,905 (100)
Non-contract farmers	80,370 (72.53)	15,975 (14.42)	0 (0)	14,092 (12.72)	377 (0.34)	110,815 (100)
Aggregate	286,827 (79.25)	50,609 (13.98)	320 (0.09)	23,899 (6.6)	257 (0.07)	361,912 (100)

Note: Percentage share of loan borrowed from different sources are indicated in parenthesis.

Table 4.7b *Details of Source of Credit (Based on Outstanding Loan) by the Selected Households (₹ per Acre)*

Farm Type	Institutional Loan by Banks	Moneylenders	Loan Given by Contracting Firms	Friends/ Relatives	Others	Total Loan
AP						
Contract farmers	15,248	2,628	113	12,825	30	30,845
Land leased-in farmers	7,128	4,092	0	14,227	0	25,446
Non-contract farmers	11,405	629	0	13,962	0	25,997
Aggregate	**13,898**	**2,685**	**90**	**13,091**	**24**	**29,788**
Haryana						
Contract farmers	51,730	6,414	35	18	0	58,197
Land leased-in farmers	31,435	6,513	0	288	0	38,235
Non-contract farmers	27,104	11,494	0	55	0	38,652
Aggregate	**44,995**	**6,776**	**24**	**88**	**0**	**51,882**
Punjab						
Contract farmers	41,566	5,154	28	14	0	46,763
Land leased-in farmers	28,450	5,895	0	260	0	34,606
Non-contract farmers	28,807	12,216	0	58	0	41,080
Aggregate	**37,833**	**5,697**	**20**	**74**	**0**	**43,624**

Karnataka

Contract farmers	13,414	522	193	7,871	278	22,278
Land leased-in farmers	6,604	0	0	3,962	0	10,566
Non-contract farmers	13,254	11	0	6,178	0	19,443
Aggregate	**13,275**	**425**	**157**	**7,515**	**225**	**21,598**
Aggregate						
Contract farmers	40,041	4,948	54	2,048	27	47,117
Land leased-in farmers	28,375	6,028	0	1,130	0	35,533
Non-contract farmers	23,548	8,518	0	2,571	0	34,637
Aggregate	**36,412**	**5,423**	**39**	**1,887**	**19**	**43,780**

Punjab and Haryana farmers could invest more into machinery and other implements due to better availability of institutional credit as compared to Karnataka and AP. The access of institutional credit to contract farmers was 89 per cent in Punjab and 81 per cent in Haryana, as compared to 60 per cent in Karnataka and 49 per cent in AP. Among the leased farmers, institutional credit share was 82 per cent in Punjab, 58 per cent in Haryana, 62.5 per cent in Karnataka and only 28 per cent in AP. The less institutional credit availability to leased farmers in Haryana and AP indicates lack of banking credit on the basis of leased-in land as there is no legal sanctity of leasing-in in the country as yet. Possibly after proposed land tenancy reforms, there would be higher access to credit based on leased-in land as well.

The above analysis shows that credit access was much higher in Punjab and Haryana as compared to AP and Karnataka. However, a part of the huge difference between per household credit was because of land operated in Punjab and Haryana was also much higher as compared to the two South Indian states. Credit per acre takes care of differences in operated area across the states and various categories. Details of out-standing loans per acre are provided in Table 4.7b. In the aggregate, credit accessed per acre by the selected households was ₹44 thousand that varied from ₹47 thousand for contract farmers, ₹35.5 thousand for leased farmers and ₹34.6 thousand for the control farmers. Thus, huge difference in access to credit per household between the three categories of farmers was on account of differences in operated area. Nevertheless, even after taking care of operated area, the credit access was slightly higher for contract and leased farmers as compared to control group, albeit difference was not too high. It is interesting to note that per acre access to credit was highest in Haryana—₹52 thousand—followed by Punjab—₹44 thousand, AP—₹30 thousand and Karnataka—₹21.5 thousand. Thus, although Punjab and Haryana still had more access to credit but Karnataka and AP were not as deprived as was apparent from the per household credit access. Per acre institutional credit was ₹45 thousand in Haryana, followed by Punjab—₹38 thousand, AP—₹14 thousand and Karnataka—₹13 thousand. Thus, the difference in access to institutional credit among North and South still prevailed even after correcting for differences in operational area. Table 4.7c reveals that out of the credit availed by the selected households, 95 per cent was used

Table 4.7c *Percentage of Loan Borrowed in Reference Year Used for Productive and Non-productive Purposes*

States	Contract Farmers		Land-leased Farmers		Non-contract Farmers		Aggregate	
	Productive Use (in %)	Non-productive Use (in %)	Productive Use (in %)	Non-productive Use (in %)	Productive Use (in %)	Non-productive Use (in %)	Productive Use (in %)	Non-productive Use (in %)
AP	86.42	13.58	88.71	11.29	99.26	0.74	87.51	12.49
Haryana	93.37	6.63	91.03	8.97	94	6	92.92	7.08
Punjab	97.54	2.46	94.84	5.16	98.77	1.23	97.02	2.98
Karnataka	92.83	7.17	100	0	97.25	2.75	93.64	6.36
Aggregate	**94.95**	**5.05**	**92.70**	**7.30**	**96.90**	**3.10**	**94.62**	**5.38**

for productive purposes—mainly for agriculture and livestock activities while only 5 per cent of that was used for daily consumption, social ceremonies and other such activities. The productive use of credit was the highest—97 per cent—in Punjab, 94 per cent in Karnataka, 93 per cent in Haryana and 87.5 per cent in AP.

Further looking at differential access to credit per household and per acre by farm-size holdings, in Punjab, credit per household varied from ₹1 lakh for marginal farmer to ₹10.9 lakh by large farmers while small and medium farmers lied in between with ₹3.4 and ₹5.4 lakh, respectively. The corresponding figures for Haryana were ₹34 thousand for marginal farmers, ₹1.6 lakh for small, ₹2.5 lakh for medium and ₹6.7 lakh for large farmers. In AP, the difference among these four categories was much less. Marginal and small farmers availed around ₹1.0 and ₹1.2 lakh, respectively while medium and large farmers accessed ₹1.6 lakh and ₹2.6 lakh, respectively. Similarly, in Karnataka, per household credit availed varied from ₹44 thousand by marginal farmers to ₹88 thousand by small farmers, ₹1.03 lakh by medium farmers and ₹1.85 lakh by large farmers. Thus, across all the four states, credit access per household had direct relationship with holding size, possibly because of operated holdings also increased with farm size.

However, neutralizing the scale of holdings, per acre credit access shows diametrically opposite trends. There was inverse relationship between credit accessed and holding size indicating much higher credit per acre for the small holding size as compared to the larger ones in AP and Karnataka. Per acre credit amount was ₹63 thousand for marginal farmers in AP and ₹40 thousand in Karnataka that declined to only ₹18 thousand for large farmers in AP and ₹21 thousand in Karnataka. On the other hand, in Punjab and Haryana, there was variation across farm size but the credit access had no particular relation with holding size. The average credit per acre was ₹54 thousand for marginal farmers, ₹56 thousand for small, ₹66 thousand for medium and ₹38 thousand for large farmers in Punjab. Similarly, per acre credit was ₹21 thousand, ₹48.5 thousand, ₹41 thousand and ₹31 thousand, respectively, for marginal, small, medium and large farmers in Haryana. Thus, the credit access was scale neutral in Punjab and Haryana whereas it had inverse relation with holding size in AP and Karnataka.

OWNERSHIP OF PRODUCTIVE ASSETS

As mentioned in the previous section, institutional credit plays an important role in capacitating households to own assets and machinery that help farmers in raising their productivity and enabling them to overcome several limitations in farm operations related to labour, capital and land resources. Table 4.8 provides details of assets owned and operated by the selected households. In the aggregate, productive assets owned by our selected farmers valued at ₹3.9 lakh per household that varied from ₹7.6 lakh in Punjab, ₹5.2 lakh in Haryana, ₹2.4 lakh in Karnataka and ₹69 thousand in AP. Thus, our assertion that higher credit leads to higher investment in assets and machinery stands true, given the fact that above 90 per cent of the credit was used for productive purposes by the selected households. The household assets included the mechanical assets like tractor, trolley, other tractor-driven implements including threshing machine, combine harvester, pumpsets, bullock cart, etc., and milch animals and poultry/dairy shed. The highest investment was made in buying tractor and tractor implements, which alone accounted for almost half of the value of assets, in the aggregate. The milch animals accounted for around one-fourth of the total value of assets and milch animals and poultry and dairy shed together accounted for around 30 per cent of the total value of assets in the aggregate. Pumpset was the other major investment by the selected households, which accounted for around 15 per cent of the total value of assets and threshing machine accounted for around 5 per cent of the total value of assets.

Looking at per acre investment in assets that is scale free of land size operated, the total value of assets in the aggregate valued at ₹36 thousand. Interestingly, per acre asset value was the highest—₹74 thousand in Karnataka, followed by ₹38 thousand in Punjab, ₹31 thousand in Haryana and ₹16.5 thousand in AP. The assets value was the highest per acre in Karnataka on account of big expenses incurred in drilling a successful borewell as the water table in parts of the state has gone down due to overexploitation of ground water. In Karnataka, 30 out of 176 taluks are categorized as overexploited. Per acre expenditure on pumpset in Karnataka was ₹22.5 thousand as compared to 5.9 thousand in AP, ₹3.5 thousand in Punjab and ₹2.3 thousand in Haryana. Investment in tractor was the highest in Punjab—₹16 thousand per acre, followed by

Table 4.8 Ownership of Productive Assets in the Selected States

Assets	₹ per Household					₹ per Acre				
	AP	Haryana	Punjab	Karnataka	Aggregate	AP	Haryana	Punjab	Karnataka	Aggregate
Tractor	6,743	216,471	316,572	37,024	143,695	1,606	13,134	16,048	11,568	13,220
Trolley	1,285	34,406	56,588	6,002	24,479	306	2,088	2,869	1,875	2,252
Harrow	585	15,273	22,804	560	9,763	139	927	1,156	175	898
Tiller	249	5,774	21,655	275	6,950	59	350	1,098	86	639
Plank	137	2,546	4,859	108	1,904	33	154	246	34	175
Threshing machine	0	8,584	7,560	88	4,043	0	521	383	28	372
Combine harvester	4	25,272	42,560	0	16,879	1	1,533	2,158	0	1,553
Other reaper	324	3,658	6,078	2,130	3,042	77	222	308	665	280
Pumpset	24,814	38,693	70,856	72,306	51,713	5,909	2,348	3,592	22,592	4,758
Bullock cart	2,289	4,887	4,074	3,695	3,736	545	297	207	1,154	344
Fodder chaffer	9	6,068	7,772	5.89	3,449	2	368	394	1.84	317
Spray pump	2,860	5,097	6,707	3,707	4,588	681	309	340	1,158	422
Storage bin	16	1,853	2,507	98.23	1,114	4	112	127	30.69	102

Poultry sheds	202	2,389	0	206	699	48	145	0	64.45	64
Dairy sheds	226	12,684	19,740	12,072	11,176	54	770	1,001	3,772	1,029
Animals — Cows	12,642	25,856	36,416	82,624	39,531	3,011	1,569	1,846	25,816	3,637
Buffaloes	9,994	93,885	119,680	5,986	57,164	2,380	5,697	6,067	1,870	5,259
Calves	2,744	10,754	9,465	4,706	6,909	653	653	480	1,470	636
Any other animal	2,269	788	1,824	3,553	2,113	540	48	92	1,110	194
Other assets	2,092	1,368	520	2,049	1,510	498	83	26	640	139
Total	69,483	516,306	758,239	237,193	394,455	16,546	31,327	38,438	74,112	36,291

Haryana—₹13 thousand, Karnataka—₹11.5 thousand, while AP invested least in tractor—₹1.6 thousand per acre. Value of milch animals per acre was also highest in Karnataka ₹29 thousand as compared to ₹8 thousand in Punjab and Haryana (each) and ₹6 thousand in AP. Thus, productive assets per household had a similar trend as that of credit per household, whereas assets per acre showed a different pattern as compared to credit per acre among the selected households.

CROPPING PATTERN AMONG CONTRACT, LEASE AND CONTROL FARMERS

Table 4.9 depicts cropping pattern among the selected households in the four states. By and large, contract farmers were sowing a greater number of crops as compared to the other two categories indicating that CF was helping farmers diversify their crops. This disproves the literature which indicates that CF leads to unification of cropping pattern. The crops grown under contract included cereals like paddy, wheat, maize, ragi, bajra, cotton, barley, etc., mainly for seed purpose; vegetables like red/green chilli, cauliflower, capsicum, etc., and some other high-value crops like baby corn, gherkin, chilli, jalapeño and so on. Among our selected farmers, the major contract crops grown in AP were groundnut, paddy, gherkins, green and red chilli/jalapeño, cotton and maize seed and baby corn. In Karnataka, the major crops grown under contract were baby corn, ragi, tomato, gherkins and chilli/jalapeño. In Punjab and Haryana, the contract crops were mainly the seed crops of most of the cereals like paddy, wheat, jowar, bajra, maize and vegetables like potato, peas, carrot, radish, French beans, etc., and last but not least, cotton.

Among the leased-in and control farmers, major crops grown were dry chilli, cotton, jowar and maize in AP; tomato, baby corn and red/green chilli in Karnataka; paddy, wheat and potato in Punjab and wheat, paddy, mustard and bajra in Haryana. It is however mentioned here that while selecting the sample, particularly for the control farmers, we preferred those farmers who grew the crops which were similar to that of contract and leased farmers. The selected contract and leased farmers were not necessarily growing only the contract and leased-in crops. Out of the total cropped area by the contract farmers, only around

Table 4.9 *Cropping Pattern of the Selected Farmers (% of GCA for the Whole Year)*

Crops	Contract Farmers	Lease-in Farmers	Non-Contract Farmers	Aggregate
AP				
Groundnut	19.61	–	–	16.11
Paddy	16.14	3.47	3.97	13.85
Gherkin	9.53	–	–	7.78
Dry chilli	1.74	33.99	45.95	8.39
Green/red chilli	5.66	–	–	4.63
Commercial cotton	7.5	24.9	10.41	9.77
Seed cotton	4.3	–	–	3.55
Seed maize	4.02	–	–	3.29
Jalapeño	3.33	–	–	2.72
Jowar	3.03	10.75	17.19	4.84
Maize	4.81	11.01	8.26	5.77
Babycorn	2.12	5	–	1.73
Onion	2.95	2.77	3.64	2.97
Other crops	18.21	13.11	10.58	14.85
Karnataka				
Babycorn	44.73	22.11	43.21	44.08
Ragi	9.83	–	8.43	9.47
Tomato	6.61	35.79	14.3	8.46
Gherkin	8.91	–	–	7.20
Green/red chilli	3.41	14.74	8.58	4.15
Groundnut	5.87	–	–	2.76
Jalapeño	3.82	–	–	2.11
Coconut	–	–	6.08	1.07
Other crops	16.82	27.37	19.41	20.72
Punjab				

(Table 4.9 Continued)

(Table 4.9 Continued)

Crops	Contract Farmers	Lease-in Farmers	Non-Contract Farmers	Aggregate
Paddy	34.40	37.35	34.03	35.09
Wheat	23.45	34.44	34.72	26.55
Potato	12.64	7.14	5.22	10.99
Fodder	4.10	5.63	8.57	4.69
Cotton	–	3.08	5.59	3.87
Narma	2.45	1.94	–	2.35
Oat	2.36	1.54	2.84	2.20
Moong	2.39	1.61	1.37	2.16
Flowers	1.89	–	–	1.39
Peas	0.75	1.92	–	1.04
Carrot	0.83	–	–	0.60
Radish	2.39	–	–	0.57
Maize	–	1.92	2.57	0.31
French bean	0.33	–	–	0.26
Capsicum	0.06	–	–	0.04
Other crops	11.93	3.42	5.08	7.88
Paddy	34.40	37.35	34.03	35.09
Haryana				
Wheat	32.73	37.25	34.08	33.96
Paddy	33.81	33.3	22.09	32.92
Potato	7.59	–	–	6.11
Mustard	5.36	5.27	–	5.45
Berseem/fodder	3.68	3.83	6.19	3.88
Bajra	–	4.4	8.02	3.32
Cotton	–	–	7.76	3.11
Barley	1.64	–	–	1.87
Other crops	15.21	15.96	21.85	9.38

one-fifth share was under contract crops and similarly, out of the total leased-in area, only one-third area was leased-in crops and rest of the area was under open crops in their owned land.

Looking at the cropping pattern across farm-size holdings, by and large, the crops grown were same across marginal, small, medium and large farmers, although the percentage area under different crops varied across holdings' size. In AP, the marginal and small farmers concentrated more on groundnut, paddy and gherkins while medium and large farmers had more area under commercial cotton along with groundnut and paddy. In comparison, in Karnataka, all categories of farmers had more concentration on baby corn, ragi and tomato. Similarly, in Punjab and Haryana, although a number of crops were grown by our selected farmers, yet the major concentration was on paddy and wheat in both the states.

OUTPUT, COST AND RETURNS ON THE NET AREA CULTIVATED

Table 4.10 presents value of output produced by the selected households, their cost of production, net returns or farm-business income, income from other allied and non-farm activities and aggregate household income. In the aggregate, output of all the crops grown by the selected farmers averaged at ₹8 lakh per household, per annum. The value of output per household was highest among the leased farmers—₹9.3 lakh—followed by contract farmers—₹8.5 lakh—and it was lowest—₹4.1 lakh—in the case of control farmers. It is however noted that the categorization of contract famers and leased farmers in this case is only indicative as the value of output that has been calculated for all the crops grown by contract and leased farmers during the reference year; which includes both contract and leased crops as well as non-contract crops grown by the contract farmers as well as crops grown on the owned land by the lease farmers. It was noted in the cropping pattern that both contract and lease farmers had only a small proportion (around one-third) of their area under contract or lease crop and more than two-third was for the open market and crops grown on the owned land. More detailed analysis of contract, leased and control crops separately for each category and with details of each item with cost is given in the next chapter.

Table 4.10 Value of Output, Cost and Net Returns for the Survey Year—Sum of All Crops (in ₹)

Farmer Category	Value of Output (Main + By-product)		Cost of Production (Including Labour Cost)		Net Returns (Farm-business Income)		Non-farm Income per Household	Total Income per Household
	Per Household	Per Acre	Per Household	Per Acre	Per Household	Per Acre		
AP								
Contract farmers	214,207	51,241	117,792	28,178	96,415	23,064	49,052 (33.7)	145,467
Leased in farmers	304,824	63,934	164,080	34,414	140,744	29,520	49,429 (26.0)	190,173
Non-contract farmers	280,562	78,653	133,847	37,523	146,716	41,131	51,146 (25.8)	197,862
Aggregate	230,277	54,837	124,544	29,658	105,733	25,179	49,268 (31.8)	155,001
Haryana								
Contract farmers	1,252,664	66,221	456,791	24,148	795,873	42,073	68,340 (7.9)	864,213
Leased in farmers	893,937	58,310	333,857	21,777	560,080	36,533	53,663 (8.7)	613,742
Non-contract farmers	431,159	53,404	162,688	20,151	268,471	33,253	59,103 (18.0)	327,574
Aggregate	1,044,614	63,382	383,793	23,287	660,821	40,096	63,123 (8.7)	723,944

Punjab

Contract farmers	2,044,858	86,861	751,514	31,923	1,293,344	54,938	51,290 (3.8)	1,344,634
Leased in farmers	12,66142	75,715	27,446	27,446	807,177	48,269	56,290 (6.5)	863,467
Non-contractfarmers	602,258	73,453	26,367	26,367	386,073	47,087	32,006 (7.7)	418,080
Aggregate	1,648,165	83,551	30,584	30,584	1,044,846	52,967	50,240 (4.6)	1,095,086

Karnataka

Contract farmers	304,128	97,278	157,786	48,713	149,599	46,185	69,042 (31.6)	218,641
Leased in farmers	327,779	92,023	249,125	75,208	211,175	63,751	75,175 (26.3)	286,350
Non-contract farmers	327,230	108,300	161,540	53,463	165,690	54,837	74,338 (31.0)	240,027
Aggregate	313,414	97,927	159,907	49,963	153,507	47,963	70,106 (31.4)	223,613

Aggregate

Contract farmers	849,542	76,488	335,946	30,134	514,539	46,153	59,416 (10.4)	573,955
Leased in farmers	929,354	67,382	178,492	25,618	579,339	42,029	54,498 (8.4)	633,837
Non-contract farmers	412,062	73,149	125,415	30,274	241,521	42,875	56,777 (19.0)	298,298
Aggregate	806,678	74,218	174,902	29,174	489,587	45,044	58,236 (10.6)	547,823

Note: Figures in parentheses are respective percentage of the total income.

Across the four states, the value of output per household, as expected, was highest in Punjab—₹16.5 lakh, followed by Haryana—₹10.4 lakh, Karnataka—₹3.1 lakh and AP with ₹2.3 lakh per annum. In Punjab and Haryana, the value of output was highest for the contract farmers, followed by leased-in and control farmers, whereas in AP and Karnataka, it was highest for the leased-in farmers, followed by contract farmers and control farmers. The value of output per household for contract farmers was ₹20.4 lakh in Punjab, ₹12.5 lakh in Haryana, ₹3.0 lakh in Karnataka and ₹2.1 lakh in AP. In comparison, the value of output per households for the control group was ₹6.0 lakh in Punjab, ₹4.3 lakh in Haryana, ₹3.3 lakh in Karnataka and ₹2.8 lakh in AP. However, value of output per household may represent farmers' gross earning at the household level, but it is not a good indicator of farm productivity. To compare the productivity of our three categories of farmers, we need to compare value of output per acre instead, as that takes care of differences in value of output arising out of scale of holdings.

The value of output per acre, also known as value of farm productivity, is given in column three of Table 4.10. In the aggregate, value of productivity was not significantly different across the above mentioned three categories. Productivity value (per acre) was highest among the contract farmers—₹76 thousand—followed by control farmers—₹73 thousand—and it was least among the leased farmers—₹67 thousand. The comparison across four states reveals interesting trends. The highest farm productivity was observed in Karnataka—₹98 thousand, followed by Punjab—₹83.5 thousand, Haryana—₹63 thousand and it was least once again in AP—₹55 thousand per acre. Looking within each category in the selected states, the highest productivity in Karnataka was observed among the control group—₹1.1 lakh, followed by contract farmers—₹97 thousand and leased farmers—₹92 thousand per acre. In Punjab, it was highest among the contract farmers—₹87 thousand, followed by leased farmers—₹76 thousand—and control farmers—₹73 thousand. Haryana also shows same trends as that of Punjab with contract farmers' productivity measuring at ₹66 thousand, followed by leased farmers—₹58 thousand—and control farmers—₹53 thousand. AP had similar trends in productivity as that of Karnataka with the control group having highest productivity of ₹79 thousand followed by leased farmers—₹64 thousand—and contract farmers at the lowest—₹51 thousand.

To find the reasons for this contrast of highest productivity in Karnataka and its value being higher in control groups as compared to contract farmers both in Karnataka and AP, one needs to go through the cropping pattern followed by the selected farmers in the four states. Whereas in Punjab and Haryana, paddy and wheat were the predominant crops among both control and contract-farmer groups; it was baby corn, gherkins and tomato in Karnataka, and dry chilli and cotton in AP, specifically among leased and control-group farmers. The productivity and gross returns for the cereal crops are much less as compared to high-value commodities, especially in the case of gherkins, baby corn and chilli/jalapeño. It is further reiterated that in Karnataka, control farmers devoted around 43 per cent area to baby corn (which they sold in the open market) and 14 per cent area to tomato, while leased farmers devoted 22 per cent area to baby corn and 36 per cent area to tomato. Thus, in these two states, value of productivity for control and leased farmers competed well with the contract farmers.

The cost of production including both material cost and labour cost was also not significantly different among the three categories of contract, lease and control farmers. It was almost the same—₹30 thousand per acre among contract and control farmers and slightly less—₹26 thousand for leased farmers. Across the four selected states, the cost was highest in Karnataka like that of the value of output, ₹50 thousand per acre, followed by Punjab—₹30.5 thousand, AP—₹30 thousand and Haryana—₹23 thousand per acre. Thus, cost figures were consistent with the value of output as high-value crops not only have higher value of output, but also higher cost of production. Across various categories, cost of production per acre was the highest for leased farmers, followed by control and contract farmers in Karnataka, contract, lease and control farmers in Punjab and Haryana and control, leased and contract farmers in AP. It would be much more interesting to see the trends of net returns (after subtracting the cost) and how they are different from the gross returns, the analysis of which is provided in the next paragraph.

On average, net returns (value of output – cost of production) per household had similar trends as that of value of output per household (gross returns). Net returns per household (also called as farm-business income) averaged at ₹4.9 lakh per annum and it varied from ₹5.8 lakh for leased farmers to ₹5.1 lakh for contract farmers and ₹2.4 lakh for control farmers. The value was the highest—₹10.4 lakh—in Punjab, ₹6.6 lakh in Haryana, ₹1.5 lakh in Karnataka and ₹1.05 lakh in AP. However, it would be more interesting to compare net returns per acre that takes care of differences in holdings operated by different categories. Net returns per acre averaged at ₹45 thousand and its value was highest for the contract farmers—₹46 thousand, while it was almost the same—₹42–₹43thousand—for the other two categories of leased and control farmers. Thus, whereas gross returns were higher for the control group as compared to the leased farmers, net returns were almost equal for these two groups.

Across the four states, unlike gross returns that were highest in Karnataka, net returns per acre were highest in Punjab—₹53 thousand, followed by Karnataka—₹48 thousand, Haryana—₹40 thousand—and lowest in AP—₹25 thousand per acre. In Punjab, contract farmers earned ₹55 thousand per acre, while earning was ₹48 thousand for leased farmers and ₹47 thousand for the control farmers. In comparison, in Karnataka, net returns per acre were ₹64 thousand for leased farmers, ₹55 thousand for control group and ₹46 thousand for contract farmers. In Haryana, the value of net earnings per acre varied from ₹42 thousand to ₹36.5 thousand and ₹33 thousand for contract, leased and control farmers, respectively. In AP, control farmers earned ₹41 thousand per acre as compared to ₹29 thousand by leased farmers and ₹23 thousand per acre by the contract farmers. Thus, net returns per acre varied widely across the states and different categories of farmers. It was highest—₹64 thousand—among the leased farmers in Karnataka and lowest—₹23 thousand—among the contract farmers in AP. However, the categorization of contract and leased group is not in the true sense as two-thirds of the share of area constitutes non-contract or owned area. The contract and crop-leased productivity is discussed in the next chapter.

Details of income from allied and non-farm activities and total income of the selected households is given in the last two columns in Table 4.10 (figures in parentheses are percentage of total income). Non-farm income averaged at ₹58 thousand per household and it was the highest in Karnataka—₹70 thousand, followed by Haryana—₹63 thousand, Punjab—₹50 thousand, while AP was slightly less than Punjab—₹49 thousand per household. The aggregate household income including farm-business income and non-farm income aggregated at ₹5.5 lakh and it was highest—₹6.3 lakh for leased farmers and lowest, around ₹3 lakh, for control group, while contract farmers lied in between with an amount of ₹5.7 lakh. The share of non-farm income in total income on average was only 10.6 per cent which was highest—19 per cent—in the case of control group and lowest—8.4 per cent—for leased farmers. Among the four states, aggregate income was highest, around ₹11 lakh, in Punjab for which the contribution of non-farm income was less than 5 per cent only. Punjab was followed by Haryana with ₹7.2 lakh average household income in which non-farm income share was around 9 per cent. Karnataka followed Haryana with average household income of ₹2.2 lakh with contribution of non-farm income—almost one-third. AP lies at the bottom with per household income of ₹1.6 lakh whereby non-farm income contributed one-third, like in the case of Karnataka. Thus, non-farm income provided support to farm income and its share was inversely related to farm income. With decreasing farm income, share of non-farm income increased, although absolute amount of non-farm income does not support this hypothesis.

Some interesting trends were discernible about farm size–productivity relationship through value of output per acre across various farm-size holdings. There was inverse relationship between farm size and productivity in the two southern states, namely AP and Karnataka, while there was direct relationship between farm size and productivity in the two northern states, namely Punjab and Haryana. While value of output per acre was higher for small and marginal farmers as compared to medium and large farmers in AP and Karnataka, it was the reverse case in Punjab and Haryana. However, similar trends were also seen in the case of cost of production. In other words, total cost of production per acre was also higher for marginal and small farmers as compared to medium and large farmers in AP and Karnataka, while cost was higher for medium and large farmers as compared to marginal and small in Punjab and Haryana. The reason for such opposite trends in the two regions is more use of machinery and economies of scale because of dominance of medium and large farmers in Punjab and Haryana. Because of these reasons, productivity was higher for large farmers as compared to resources-poor marginal and small farmers in these two states. On the other hand, in AP and Karnataka, holding size was small and there was comparatively less use of machinery as compared to Punjab and Haryana. Consequently, per acre resource intensity including use of labour, fertilizers, pesticides, etc., went in favour of small and marginal farmers and thereby their productivity as well as cost of production was higher as compared to medium and large farmers. It is interesting to note that although there was clear-cut association between farm-size productivity and cost of production, net returns from farming as well as non-farm income did not reflect any such clear-cut associations. The returns per acre, although varied across farm sizes, did not reflect any particular direction or relationship. The particular components of non-farm income and cost of production are discussed in more details in the forthcoming chapters.

SUMMARY

A total number of 2,014 households were selected in all the four states. Majority of the selected farmers belonged to CF as that was the design of the study proposed. In most of the cases, tenancy existed only in terms of cash payment on seasonal or yearly basis and tenancy in terms of sharecropping, which was almost non-existent. The leased farmers operated 13.8 acres per household followed by contract farmers who operated 11 acres, whereas the control group farmers operated only 5.6 acres per household. The household size varied from less than five members to around eight members in different states. Generally, contract farmers were younger in age as compared to other categories and they were also more educated as compared to other two category in all the four states. The cropping intensity was almost two crops in a year per acre in Haryana and more than two crops in Punjab as compared to much less than two crops in Karnataka and near one crop in AP.

The proportion of net-leased land was much higher in Punjab and Haryana as compared to the other two selected states. The sharecropping existed in small quantity only in Haryana. Most of the leasing land was in terms of short-term lease, not exceeding one year, while miniscule cases were found of long-term lease of two years or more. There existed reverse tenancy in all the four states. Regarding access to credit, the wedge among contract farmers, leased farmers and control group was too wide. However, huge difference in access to credit per household between the three categories of farmers was partly on account of differences in the operated area. Among different sources, institutional sources constituted almost 80 per cent. Punjab and Haryana farmers could invest more into machinery and other implements due to better availability of institutional credit as compared to Karnataka and AP. By and large, contract farmers were sowing more number of crops as compared to the other two categories indicating that CF was helping farmers diversify their crops.

In the aggregate, output of all the crops grown by the selected farmers averaged at ₹8 lakh per household, per annum. The value of output per household was highest among the leased farmers—₹9.3 lakh, followed by contract farmers—₹8.5 lakh—and it was lowest—₹4.1 lakh—in the case of control farmers. Across the four states, the value of output per household, as expected, was highest in Punjab—₹16.5 lakh, followed by Haryana—₹10.4 lakh, Karnataka—₹3.1 lakh—and AP—₹2.3 lakh per annum. It was observed that the productivity and gross returns for the cereal crops were much less as compared to high-value commodities, especially in the case of gherkins, baby corn and chilli/jalapeño. On aver-age, net returns (value of output – cost of production) per household had similar trends as that of value of output per household (gross returns). Net return per household averaged at ₹4.9 lakh per annum and it varied from ₹5.8 lakh for leased farmers to ₹5.1 lakh for contract farmers and ₹2.4 lakh for control farmers. The value was highest—₹10.4 lakh—in Punjab, ₹6.6 lakh in Haryana, ₹1.5 lakh in Karnataka and ₹1.05 lakh in AP. Net returns per acre averaged at ₹45 thousand and its value was highest for contract farmers—₹46 thousand, while it was almost same—₹42–₹43 thousand—for the other two categories of leased and control farmers. Across the four states, unlike gross returns that were highest in Karnataka, net returns per acre were the highest in Punjab—₹53 thousand, followed by Karnataka—₹48 thousand, Haryana—₹40 thousand and lowest in AP—₹25 thousand per acre.

Some interesting trends were seen about farm size–productivity relationship. There was inverse relationship between farm size and productivity in the two southern states, namely AP and Karnataka, while there was direct relationship between farm size and productivity in the two northern states, namely Punjab and Haryana. The reason for such opposite trends in the two regions is more use of machinery and economies of scale because of dominance of medium and large farmers in Punjab and Haryana. The returns per acre, although varied across farm size, did not reflect any particular direction or relationship.

Chapter 5

Resource Use and Profitability
Contract, Lease and Control Farmers

It was discussed in Chapter 1 that mainly three types of CF exists in the literature, that is, market-specification contracts, resource-providing contracts and production-management contracts. In the market-specification contracts, private players facilitate the flow of market information which otherwise farmers do not have in the spot market. On the one hand, companies provide demand information to the producer concerning the crop, variety, quality, timing, location and acceptable price. On the other hand, buyers gather information of supply conditions of particular commodities through the process of finding and negotiating with growers. This system of contracting allows one buyer to coordinate numerous growers without any management problems of vertical integration at different efficient scales between stages (Minot, 1986). Defining the second type, there are certain factors which motivate private firms to do resource-providing contracts. Those factors include unavailability of productive inputs in the market. If the inputs are available in the market, private firms can provide them at lower cost (economies of scale) to encourage the use of certain inputs by subsidizing price or incentivizing their use. However, the 'subsidy' offered by the firms is implicitly covered in the commodity price (Minot, 1986).

In market-specification contracts, firms tell the grower what to produce but production-management contracts provide some instruction as to how to produce. It is obvious that unless growers know the value of production information, they would not pay for that.

Similarly, buy-back companies will not be providing extension services unless they can perceive a benefit. Under a contract, the cost of providing extension services can be captured by implicitly deducting the cost from the commodity price. To make it a successful contract, the contract must be enforceable or the buyer will be the only outlet for the commodity. Otherwise, the grower can breach the contract and sell the commodity to others by taking advantage of extension services (Minot, 1986).

It would be interesting to know the nature of CF prevailing in India, especially among the selected contracting households in the four states. In our field questionnaire, we tried to get some of these answers directly from the farmers as well as collected information regarding buy-back arrangements by the contracting firms, provision of extension services, price paid for the contracted product as well as their prevailing market price and so on. This chapter summarizes findings on these issues. The first section of the chapter covers issues related to the nature of existing contracts, information and service provision, major advantages and households' satisfaction from CF. The next section is devoted to resource use, productivity, price realized and net profitability of contracting farmers, vis-à-vis leased and control farmers. The third section provides various aspects of employment provision under CF while last section summarizes the chapter.

NATURE OF CF AMONG THE SELECTED HOUSEHOLDS

Table 5.1a presents selected contract farmers' response about the nature of contract they have with the firms and how they obtained information about CF and contracting firms. Out of our total 2,014 households selected, a sum of 1,408 farmers were engaged in CF, thus, making our sample of almost 70 per cent doing CF. Among various states, 80 per cent selected farmers were engaged in CF in AP and Karnataka and around 60 per cent were engaged in Haryana and Punjab. We enquired from the farmers how many numbers of years were they engaged in this practice. On average, all farmers had more than four years of experience with CF. Punjab farmers had more than six years while all other had more than four years of experience of CF. It is interesting to note

Table 5.1a *Details about the Nature and Source of Information of CF*

Details about CF	AP	Haryana	Punjab	Karnataka	Aggregate
Nature of Contract					
Percentage of household doing CF	80.08	59.44	59.8	80.16	69.91
How long following this practice (years)	4.94	4.04	6.09	4	4.72
Fixed-price contract (percentage of HH)	12.44	71.57	67.56	0	33.10
Input-supply contract (percentage of HH)	0.25	13.71	24.08	9.31	10.79
Input-supply and fixed-price contract (percentage of HH)	87.31	13.71	8.36	90.69	55.89
Oral contract (percentage of HH)	100	93.31	47.83	100	87.50
Written contract in English (percentage of HH)	0	7.69	52.17	0	12.71
Written contract in vernacular (percentage of HH)	0	0	0		0.00
Average registration amount paid (₹ per acre)	0	0	0	0	0.00
Source of Information about CF (Percentage of HH)					
Through mass media	0	10.04	8.03	11.41	5.90

Through contract extension agency	28.61	5.69	8.36	6.3	12.29
Through private firm	39.8	28.77	45.15	30.71	32.60
Through neighbouring farmers	14.93	25.41	50.17	29.92	25.71
Information from relative and friends	0.25	18.57	17.73	9.45	9.48
Through input supplier	8.21	0	0	0	2.34
Through neighbouring farmers, relatives and friends	7.96	0	0	0	2.27
Others	0.25	11.17	0	11.81	4.67

that while more than two-thirds of farmers in Punjab and Haryana were engaged in fixed-price contract without provision of extension and other services, almost 90 per cent farmers in AP and Karnataka were engaged in contract with provision of inputs and buy-back facility. In Punjab and Haryana, many farmers were engaged in contract with seed firms for crops like paddy, wheat, potato, mustard, etc., who were mainly providing buy-back facility, while in AP and Karnataka, CF consisted of commodities meant for export purpose like gherkins, jalapeño and baby corn—in which case, contracting firms closely monitored the quality of crops to meet the requirements of exports. The contract was mostly oral except in Punjab, where majority of the farmers had written contract in English (and not in the local language). However, the written contract in Punjab also was mostly on a plane paper without any legal sanctity and thereby cost of registration was nil in Punjab as well.

To our question, how farmers obtained information about CF and the firms which were carrying out CF, the answers of contracting farmers are summarized here. Around 6 per cent farmers indicated that they obtained information through mass media, while majority of them (around 45%) indicated that contracting firms or extension agencies themselves approached the concerned farmers. Around one-third of the farmers pointed out that they came to know about CF thought relatives and friends or through neighbouring farmers while a few of them indicated some other sources of information about CF. Across the four states, the source of information about CF was not very diverse.

Table 5.1b presents details of service provision by the contracting firms. On average, contract farmers were having only one crop under CF in a year except in the case of Haryana, where farmers indicated growing more than one crop under CF in a year. In Haryana, farmers were growing seed crops under CF whereby they covered both kharif (paddy) crop and rabi (wheat) crop under contract, but the nature of contract was only provision of buy-back arrangements. Thus, although farmers in the selected states were mostly producing two crops or more than one crop in a year as cropping intensity of the sample was 1.9, but only one crop was covered under CF. The average size of area under CF was only 4 acres, whereas the average operated area of the sample

Table 5.1b *Details about the Services Provided under CF*

Details about CF		AP	Haryana	Punjab	Karnataka	Aggregate
Service Provision under Contract						
No. of crops cultivated in a year under contract (No.)		1.03	2	1.05	1.01	1.23
Average area under contract in a year (acres/HH)		1.37	5.81	8.84	1.9	4.05
Seeds (percentage of HH)		65.34	92.31	81.59	99.75	84.49
Fertilizers (percentage of HH)		41.24	3.68	51.24	40.44	35.16
Crop protection chemicals (percentage of HH)		31.67	7.69	33.33	20.59	23.72
Farm advisory (percentage of HH)		45.62	30.43	56.97	20.59	37.55
Crop insurance (percentage of HH)		16.33	0	5.22	0.74	5.99
Crop loan (percentage of HH)		4.18	2.34	20.4	0	6.02
Farm machinery and implements (percentage of HH)		15.14	1.34	69.9	98.28	47.93
Soil testing facility (percentage of HH)		0	7.36	18.91	0	5.58
Others (percentage of HH)		0	5.02	0	38.48	12.22
Do you get advice from company?	Yes	93.28	54.51	55.85	38.48	61.22
(percentage of HH)	No	6.72	45.49	44.15	61.52	38.78

was around 11 acres and GCA was 21 acres. It indicates that only less than 20 per cent of the GCA of a particular household was under CF. In AP, out of 4.8 acres of cropped area, only 1.4 acres were under contract; in Haryana, out of 32 acres of cropped area, only 5.8 acres were under CF; in Punjab, out of 41 acres of cropped area, 8.8 acres were under contract and in Karnataka, out of 5.5 acres of cropped area, only 1.9 acres were under CF.

Looking at the services provision under CF, around 85 percent of the contracting farmers pointed out that contracting companies or firms provided seed for the contracted crop. Seed provision was 100 per cent in Karnataka, 92 per cent in Haryana, above 80 per cent in Punjab and 65 per cent in AP. Thus, in Punjab and Haryana, seed companies also provided seed to the contracting farmers for ensuring the procurement of high-quality output. In addition to seed, around 35 per cent selected contract farmers also pointed out that they were provided with fertilizer facility (of course on-spot payment or payment at the time of sale delivery) with the exception of Haryana, where very few farmers pointed out that they were provided fertilizer. Similarly, around one-fourth of the selected farmers also indicated provision of pesticides and other plant-protection chemicals, once again with exception of Haryana state. Farm advisory services were indicated by around 57 per cent farmers in Punjab, 46 per cent in AP, 30 per cent in Haryana and only 21 per cent contracting farmers in Karnataka. Crop loan, crop insurance and soil testing facility were almost negligible among the selected contract farmers. A large number of farmers in Punjab and Karnataka indicated that they were provided farm machinery and implements by the contracting firms. To our question of whether farmers received some advice on cultivation practices of contracted crops, a clear majority of farmers replied, 'Yes', including almost 93 per cent farmers in AP, around 55 per cent in Punjab and Haryana and 38 per cent in Karnataka.

As per farmers' opinion, the necessary requirements for farmers entering into CF include assured irrigation, labour availability and having reasonable size of holdings (Table 5.1c). Around two-thirds of the majority of selected farmers indicated that for implementation of any successful contract with the companies require assured

Table 5.1c *Necessary Requirements for Entering into CF for the Households*

Details about CF	AP	Haryana	Punjab	Karnataka	Aggregate
Necessary Requirements for CF					
Assured irrigation (percentage of HH)	71.39	55.85	59.2	72.3	65.77
Labour availability (percentage of HH)	22.39	20.74	26.09	16.18	21.03
Reasonable land acreage size (percentage of HH)	4.23	20.4	9.36	8.33	9.94
Tractor ownership (percentage of HH)	1.74	3.01	1.67	0.49	1.63
Social contacts (percentage of HH)	0.25	0	3.68	2.7	1.64

irrigation and farmers without having assured irrigation might not have successful participation in CF. Similarly, a thin majority of farmers also indicated that easy access of labour is required as CF involves more labour-intensive crops like the case of gherkins, baby corn and other vegetable cultivation. Reasonable size of holding might help CF but does not seem to be a necessary condition. Similarly, tractor ownership and having social contacts was not found as a necessary requirement for CF.

To our question of whether companies provided buy-back facility, there was no exception and selected farmers indicated that the contracted produce was being procured. We tried to ascertain whether companies procured the contracted produce from the farm gate or it was the responsibility of farmers to deliver it at the company gate. All farmers doing contract in AP and Karnataka indicated that the produce was procured by the companies from the farm gate while two-thirds of the majority of farmers in Punjab and Haryana pointed out that the companies asked the farmers to deliver the produce at the company gate (Table 5.1d). To the question even if the produce was procured from the farm gate or farmers were asked to deliver it at company gate but who really bore the transportation cost, most farmers in AP and Karnataka indicated that the cost was borne by the companies while in Punjab and Haryana, farmers' opinion was divided between farmers and companies. To our question whether some produce was rejected by the companies on quality or other grounds, we observed only a handful of farmers indicated very small quantity of produce being rejected in all the four states (Table 5.1d).

To a further question of whether farmers under contract ever breached the contract and in what circumstances, we observed almost negligible cases where farmers indicated that they did breach the contract. To another question of whether companies buy extra produce not covered in the contract, most of the households in AP and Karnataka indicated yes to this question, while mostly, households indicated no in Punjab and Haryana. Almost all farmers in all the four states pointed out, 'No', to the question whether companies frequently change terms of reference for contract or arbitrarily changed terms and conditions of contract (Table 5.1d).

Table 5.1d *Details about Product Delivery, Crop Rejection and Contract Breach*

Details about CF	AP	Haryana	Punjab	Karnataka	Aggregate
Mode of Delivery and Cost of Delivery					
At farm gate (percentage of HH)	100	18.06	12.71	99.51	61.17
At market yard (percentage of HH)	0	11.37	9.03	0	4.67
At company gate (percentage of HH)	15.79	66.56	78.26	0	37.99
Farm gate and market yard	0	2.01	0	0	0.46
Farm gate and company gate	0	2.01	0	0	0.46
Others (percentage of HH)	0	0	0	0	0.00
Cost borne by farmer (percentage of HH)	15.79	53.85	63.88	0	31.79
Cost borne by company (percentage of HH)	84.21	45.48	36.12	99.51	67.94
Cost borne by himself and company	0	0.33	0	0	0.08
Cost borne by other (percentage of HH)	0	0.33	0	0	0.08
Contract Produce Rejected by the Company Due to					
Excess supply (percentage of HH)	0.25	0.67	1	0	0.46
Not as per quality and specification (percentage of HH)	0	2.68	0.67	0	0.77

(Table 5.1d Continued)

(Table 5.1d Continued)

Details about CF		AP	Haryana	Punjab	Karnataka	Aggregate
Late delivery (percentage of HH)		0	0	0	0	0.00
Grading not done (percentage of HH)		0	0	0	1.23	0.29
Others (percentage of HH)		0	0.67	0.33	0	0.23
Did Farmer Breach Contract Any Time? If Yes, When?						
Market price above contract price (percentage of HH)	Yes	0	4.01	0.67	0	1.07
	No	100	95.99	99.33	100	98.93
Company not purchased entire produce (percentage of HH)	Yes	0	0.67	1.34	0	0.46
	No	100	99.33	98.66	100	99.54
Company not willing to buy due to lower price in the market (percentage of HH)	Yes	0	0	0	0.2	0.05
	No	100	100	100	99.8	99.95
Company closed in the middle (percentage of HH)	Yes	12.69	0.33	0	0	3.98
	No	87.31	99.67	100	100	96.02
Did company buy extra produce not covered in the contract (percentage of HH)	Yes	93.03	5.69	2.68	100	54.02
	No	6.97	94.31	97.32	0	45.98
Does company frequently change TOR (percentage of HH)	Yes	0	3.34	0.67	0	0.92
	No	100	96.66	99.33	100	99.08

Assured income, superior price based on quality product supplied and hassle-free marketing were the main advantages of CF as per majority of the farmers engaged in CF (Table 5.1e). However, good farm practices advised by the experts of the companies as a benefit to the farmers was expressed only by 5 per cent of the selected contract farmers. Similarly, provision of crop loan, crop insurance and coping mechanism of farm risk through CF was not preferred as a benefit by the contracting farmers. To our question of what were the major advantages of CF, around 56 per cent of selected farmers opined that yield increase was the major advantage, followed by 24 per cent as price increase as a major advantage of CF. Only 14 per cent of the selected farmers indicated getting the technical know-how from the company experts, whereas only 6 per cent expressed increase in employment as a major advantage of CF (Table 5.1e). We tried to seek whether contract farmers were satisfied with their association with the firms for last so many years. A clear majority of the contract farmers (58%) expressed that they were satisfied and another 24 per cent expressed as somewhat satisfied, while only 7 per cent of the farmers expressed very much satisfied. Only 10 per cent were not satisfied and less than half a per cent expressed totally dissatisfied. The households who were not satisfied, highest—21 per cent—were from AP and around 5 per cent each from the other three states.

RESOURCE USE PRODUCTIVITY AND PROFITABILITY: CONTRACT, LEASE VERSUS CONTROL CROPS

In the previous chapter, we discussed farm productivity, cost of cultivation and net returns among contract farmers, leased-in farmers and control farmers. However, cropping pattern indicated that out of total area cropped, only a proportion of that was under CF or under tenancy. Thus, the gross and net returns presented in the previous chapter were calculated in the aggregate by summing up all the crops sown by the households in each category. Therefore, difference in productivity, cost and returns were not strictly due to contract or lease farming at the crop level but in the aggregate which included both contract crops and non-contract crops by the contract farmers as well as crops from leased and owned area by leased farmers. Moreover, net and gross returns

Table 5.1e *Main Advantages, Benefits and Household Satisfaction from CF*

Details about CF	AP	Haryana	Punjab	Karnataka	Aggregate
Benefits from CF					
Assured income (percentage of HH)	54.98	52.84	62.54	53.68	55.75
Superior price on the basis of quality (percentage of HH)	14.43	39.8	27.42	10.54	21.45
Farm advisory and technical support (percentage of HH)	7.71	5.69	5.35	4.41	5.82
Crop loan (percentage of HH)	0	0.33	4.01	0	0.92
Insurance (percentage of HH)	0.25	0	0.67	0.25	0.29
Hassle-free marketing (percentage of HH)	22.64	0	0	29.17	14.99
Ability to cope with farm risks (percentage of HH)	0	1	0	1.96	0.78
Others (percentage of HH)	0	0	0	0	0.00
Major Advantages from CF					
Yield increase (percentage of HH)	48.76	66.22	71.91	40.93	56.21
Price increase (percentage of HH)	16.67	28.09	24.08	28.68	23.80
Employment increase (percentage of HH)	8.46	3.01	4.01	8.33	6.16

Increase in know-how for growing crops (percentage of HH)	26.12	5.35	0	22.06	14.44
Households Satisfaction from CF					
Very much satisfied (percentage of HH)	4.48	13.04	13.38	1.47	7.32
Satisfied (percentage of HH)	38.06	64.88	67.56	64.71	57.74
Somewhat satisfied (percentage of HH)	35.57	17.06	12.04	25.74	23.79
Not satisfied (percentage of HH)	20.65	5.02	7.02	7.84	10.72
Totally dissatisfied (percentage of HH)	1.24	0	0	0.25	0.43

were measured at the household level and not at the crop level. In this section, we present resource use productivity, cost of cultivation and net returns at the crop level purely for the crop area under contract, lease and control groups. As farmers were growing multiple crops under contract, lease and control, we have summed the value of all contract crops together and similarly, all leased crops and all control crops have been summed together to have broader comparison between these categories of farmers. The analysis is provided in the following paragraphs.

Before presenting the net returns, cost and profitability, Table 5.2 presents details about the crops grown under contract and lease among the selected contract and lease farmers in the four states. On average, only 28 per cent of cropped area by the contract farmers was under CF in AP. In Punjab, around 16 per cent of the cropped area by the contract farmers was grown under CF, while in Karnataka, it was 33 per cent and it was 23 per cent in Haryana. Thus, in the aggregate, only

Table 5.2 *Details of Crops Grown under CF and on Leased-in Area*

Name of the Crops Grown under CF	% Share	Name of the Crops Grown under Leased-in Rea	% Share
AP			
Gherkin	31.27	Dry chilli	58.33
Red chilli	20.25	Cotton	41.67
Seed cotton	15.02	Leased-in	100
Seed maize	14.38	Cropping intensity	102
Jalapeño	11.56		
Baby corn	7.15		
Beans	0.36		
Total contract area	100		
Cropping intensity	117		
Haryana			
Wheat	54.29	Wheat	69.12
Potato	24.40	Paddy	9.03

Barley	6.78	Mustard	7.96
Mustard	5.89	Barley	5.88
Paddy	4.20	Potato	5.47
Moong	3.57	Moong	1.72
Red gram	0.70	Red gram	0.74
Cauliflower	0.12	Tomato	0.08
Tomato	0.04	Total lease GCA	100
Total contract area	100	Cropping intensity	196
Cropping intensity	194		

Punjab

Potato	34.38	Potato	45.54
Wheat	31.82	Paddy	23.08
Barley	14.42	Wheat	18.89
Flower	9.42	Peas	5.80
Peas	4.14	Barley	4.58
Radish	3.29	Cotton	1.22
Carrot	1.39	Narma	0.61
French bean	0.81	Fodder	0.15
Capsicum	0.29	Maize	0.13
Cauliflower	0.04	Total lease GCA	100
Total contract area	100	Cropping intensity	205
Cropping intensity	212		

Karnataka

Babycorn	54.06	Tomato	45.71
Gherkin	22.20	Green chilli	28.57
Jalapeño	8.87	Baby corn	25.71
Green chilli	7.99	Total lease GCA	100
Tomato	6.61	Cropping intensity	179
Seed cotton	0.26		
Total contract area	100		
Cropping intensity	171		

20 per cent area of the contract farmers was under contract while 80 per cent area was under non-contract crops. Similarly, the share of leased area in the total GCA by leased farmers was 51 per cent in AP, 31 per cent in Haryana, 33 per cent in Punjab and 37 per cent in Karnataka. In the aggregate, only one-third area by leased farmers was actually leased for which they paid rent and cultivated it as tenant-farmer and rest of two-thirds of the area was their owned area. It would be interesting to see the nature of crops grown under CF and leased crops.

In AP, the major crops grown under CF were gherkin, red chillies, baby corn, maize-seed, cotton-seed and jalapeño with gherkins and red chillies constituting more than 50 per cent share and baby corn and jalapeño constituting less than 20 per cent share. In Karnataka, baby corn, gherkin, tomato, jalapeño and green chilli were grown under CF. Baby corn and gherkins together constituted above 76 per cent of CF area among the selected farmers, while jalapeño and green chillies together occupied above 16 per cent share of the contract area in Karnataka.

In Haryana, contract crops included paddy, wheat, potato, barley and mustard whereas wheat and potato constituted around 80 per cent share. In Punjab, contract crops were wheat, potato, barley, flower, carrot, radish, peas, Frenchbeans, cauliflower and capsicum. The wheat, potato and barley together constituted more than 80 per cent area under CF among the selected contract farmers in Punjab. Thus, in AP and Karnataka, mainly the export-oriented crops were being grown under contract, whereas in Punjab and Haryana, contract was either for seed companies that were mainly in cereals and oilseeds crops or for vegetable production, mainly for the domestic markets.

Comparing contract crops with the crops grown on leased land, and as mentioned above, in Punjab and Haryana contract crops were mostly for seed purpose except in the case of potato, in these two states leased crops were similar to that of contract crops. In AP, only two crops were grown on the leased land, that is, cotton and dry chillies, while in Karnataka, there were only few cases of leasing-in available who grew more number of crops as compared to crops under CF, except jalapeño and gherkin as there was no open market available for these products. It is to be mentioned here that while selecting the leased-in and control group households our guiding principle was the crops grown under CF. We tried to select only those households who had similar cropping pattern as that of contract farmers for the sake of comparison. Therefore, crops grown by leased and control farmers are fairly similar to that of contract farmers.

Tables 5.3a, 5.3b and 5.3c present resource usage and net returns per acre for contract crops, leased crops and control crops, respectively. As discussed in the last paragraphs, farmers were growing a select number of crops under CF in the selected states. Therefore, for the sake of comparison, value of output and costs of production for all crops under CF have been aggregated together. Similarly, all crops under leased and control groups have been aggregated in their respective categories. The analysis indicates that on average, value of crop output per acre was highest in the case of CF crops—₹52 thousand, followed by leased-in crops—₹43 thousand—and the least was control crops—₹38 thousand per acre. The value of output per cropped area under CF was highest—₹91 thousand—in AP, followed by Karnataka—₹68 thousand, Punjab—₹51.5 thousand—and it was least in Haryana—₹41 thousand per acre.

Thus, our results are completely opposite from what we presented in the case of total value of output of all the crops per acre of net sown area in the previous chapter. The reason for high value in AP and Karnataka as compared to Punjab and Haryana under CF and against the general trends of high productivity in the latter green revolution states lies in the nature of crops grown under CF. The two southern states were growing high-value commodities under CF like gherkins, baby corn, jalapeño and green chillies. In comparison, cereal crops like paddy and wheat were grown in Haryana and wheat and potato were grown in Punjab, albeit cereal crops were grown for seed under buy-back arrangements with seed companies. Except potato, most of the other crops grown in these two states had only low returns as compared to high-value crops which occupied major share in the southern states. It is especially mentioned here that in AP and Karnataka, new crops like gherkins, jalapeño and baby corn were grown by the farmers because of the initiatives of contracting firms like Global Green, Namdhari and Indo-Spanish companies. These firms not only provide seed to the farmers and ensure the buy-back facility, but they also provide training to the farmers, give technical know-how, mechanical implements and provide package of practices for the successful implementation of contract with the farmers. Therefore, these trends indicate the importance

Table 5.3a Net Returns per Acre of Cropped Area under CF (₹ per Acre)

Particulars	AP	Haryana	Punjab	Karnataka	Aggregate
Average area planted under contract (acres per HH)[a]	1.36	8.33	8.03	1.87	4.40
	(27.95)	(22.71)	(16.10)	(33.83)	(20.62)
Cost of seed and transplanting	4,406	5,284	7,560	4,284	5,964
	(9.61)	(15.53)	(20.55)	(10.08)	(16.41)
Manure & fertilizer	11,131	2,976	4,098	12,655	5,321
	(24.29)	(8.75)	(11.14)	(29.78)	(14.64)
Irrigation, canal, hired tube well and electricity charges	841	598	401	1,325	633
	(1.84)	(1.76)	(1.09)	(3.12)	(1.74)
Plant protection, pesticides, etc.	6,656	1,306	1,803	3,974	2,299
	(14.52)	(3.84)	(4.9)	(9.35)	(6.33)
Expenses for tractor/bullock in ploughing	3,982	2,062	2,138	3,673	2,459
	(8.69)	(6.06)	(5.81)	(8.64)	(6.77)
Harvesting material cost	62	60	24	0	39
	(0.14)	(0.18)	(0.07)	(0)	(0.11)
Repair, maintenance and depreciation[b]	1,571	3,074	1,691	4,289	2,918
	(3.43)	(9.04)	(4.6)	(10.09)	(8.03)

Rent paid for leasing land (per acre)	1,476	1,4309	9,948	1,040	8,851
	(3.22)	(42.06)	(27.05)	(2.45)	(24.36)
Hired-labour charges	11,769	4,243	7,139	8,976	6,610
	(25.68)	(12.47)	(19.41)	(21.12)	(18.19)
Marketing cost including grading, storage, transport, packing	688	34	11	27	82
	(1.5)	(0.1)	(0.03)	(0.06)	(0.23)
Market/mandi fee, etc.	517	1	0.17	27	49
	(1.13)	(0)	(0)	(0.06)	(0.14)
Miscellaneous	582	42	104	473	167
	(1.27)	(0.12)	(0.28)	(1.11)	(0.46)
Interest on working capital[c]	2,152	31	1,864	1,754	947
	(4.69)	(0.09)	(5.07)	(4.13)	(2.61)
Total cost	45,835	34,020	36,781	42,497	36,340
	(100)	(100)	(100)	(100)	(100)
Total cost without rent	44,359	19,711	26,833	41,457	27,489
Total revenue	90,665	41,449	51,538	67,647	51,760
Total revenue −total cost	44,830	7,429	14,758	25,150	15,420
Total revenue −total cost (without rent)	46,306	21,738	24,706	26,190	24,271

Note: [a]Figures in parentheses are respective percentage of GCA under CF; [b]Figures in parentheses are percentage of total cost and there is no statistical significance test involved here; [c]Interest on working capital is interest paid on the loans/borrowing divided in proportion to each crop sown during the year.

Table 5.3b *Net Returns per Acre of Cropped Area under Tenancy—All Crops (₹ per Acre)*

Particulars	AP	Haryana	Punjab	Karnataka	Aggregate
Average area planted under lease-in/ sharecropping (acres per HH)[a]	2.51	8.98	9.47	2.05	7.22
	(51.37)	(30.95)	(32.83)	(36.84)	(32.59)
Cost of seed and transplanting	2,537	1,552	4,450	4,646	3,127
	(4.73)	(4.28)	(12.57)	(8.16)	(8.82)
Manure & fertilizer	8,293	2,393	3,833	12,957	3,497
	(15.47)	(6.59)	(10.82)	(22.75)	(9.86)
Irrigation, canal, hired tube well and electricity charges	350	576	362	1,303	458
	(0.65)	(1.59)	(1.02)	(2.29)	(1.29)
Plant protection, pesticides, etc.	7,384	1,324	1,930	6,286	1,969
	(13.78)	(3.65)	(5.45)	(11.04)	(5.55)
Expenses for tractor/bullock in ploughing	3,881	1,746	2,400	3,543	2,203
	(7.24)	(4.81)	(6.78)	(6.22)	(6.21)
Repair, maintenance and depreciation[b]	986	2,030	2,030	4,309	2,010
	(1.84)	(5.59)	(5.73)	(7.57)	(5.67)
Rent paid for leasing land (per acre per HH)	10,108	23,455	12,067	4,105	15,292
	(18.86)	(64.63)	(34.08)	(7.21)	(43.12)

Hired-labour charges	12,829	3,032	6,323	15,146	5,302
	(23.93)	(8.35)	(17.86)	(26.59)	(14.95)
Marketing cost including grading, storage, transport, packing	1,902	43	25	3,257	145
	(3.55)	(0.12)	(0.07)	(5.72)	(0.41)
Market/mandi fee, etc.	1,431	2	28	583	90
	(2.67)	(0.01)	(0.08)	(1.02)	(0.25)
Miscellaneous	24	89	70	0	75
	(0.04)	(0.25)	(0.20)	(0)	(0.21)
Interest on working capital[c]	3,879	48	1,892	821	1,410
	(7.24)	(0.13)	(5.34)	(1.44)	(3.98)
Total cost	53,603	36,291	35,411	56,956	35,460
	(100)	(100)	(100)	(100)	(100)
Total cost without rent	43,495	12,836	23,344	52,851	20,168
Total revenue	69,631	30,124	49,816	90,971	42,689
Total revenue – total cost	16,028	–6,167	14,405	34,016	7,229
Total revenue – total cost (without rent)	26,136	17,288	26,472	38,122	22,521

Note: [a]Figures in parentheses are respective percentage of GCA under leased crops; [b]Figures in parentheses are percentage of total cost and there is no statistical significance test involved here; [c]Interest on working capital is interest paid on the loans/borrowing divided in proportion to each crop sown during the year.

Table 5.3c *Net Returns per Acre from Non-contract Crop—All Crops (₹ per Acre)*

Particulars	AP	Haryana	Punjab	Karnataka	Aggregate
Average area planted under non-contract (acres per HH)	2.05	11.82	16.3	2.98	8.27
Cost of seed and transplanting	2,127	1,387	1,089	1,509	1,297
	(8.24)	(9.87)	(6.35)	(6.84)	(7.66)
Manure and fertilizer	6,660	2,105	2,797	4,794	2,961
	(25.79)	(14.98)	(16.3)	(21.72)	(17.48)
Irrigation, canal, hired tube well and electricity charges	508	503	288	625	412
	(1.97)	(3.58)	(1.68)	(2.83)	(2.43)
Plant protection, pesticides, etc.	3,129	781	1,255	2,009	1,263
	(12.12)	(5.56)	(7.31)	(9.1)	(7.46)
Expenses for tractor/bullock in ploughing	3,668	1,506	1,965	1,361	1,833
	(14.21)	(10.72)	(11.45)	(6.17)	(10.82)
Material cost of harvesting	0	13	0	10	6
	(0)	(0.09)	(0)	(0.05)	(0.03)
Repair, maintenance and depreciation[a]	870	4,387	2,878	4,431	3,386
	(3.37)	(31.22)	(16.77)	(20.07)	(20)

Hired-labour charges	5,637	3,205	3,985	3,885	3,784
	(21.83)	(22.81)	(23.23)	(17.6)	(22.34)
Marketing cost including grading, storage, transport, packing	821	9	3	1,040	146
	(3.18)	(0.06)	(0.02)	(4.71)	(0.86)
Market/*mandi* fee, etc.	437	5	0.16	691	95
	(1.69)	(0.04)	(0)	(3.13)	(0.56)
Miscellaneous	7	5	19	7	12
	(0.03)	(0.04)	(0.11)	(0.03)	(0.07)
Interest on working capital[b]	1,956	146	2,877	1,712	1,740
	(7.58)	(1.04)	(16.77)	(7.76)	(10.27)
Total cost	25,820	14,051	17,157	22,074	16,934
	(100)	(100)	(100)	(100)	(100)
Total revenue	40,803	32,721	39,976	31,107	38,005
Total revenue – total cost	14,982	18,670	22,819	9,033	21,071
Total revenue – total cost (without lease rent)	14,982	18,670	22,819	9,033	21,071

Note: [a]Figures in parentheses are percentage of total cost and there is no statistical significance test involved here; [b]Interest on working capital is interest paid on the loans/borrowing divided in proportion to each crop sown during the year.

of CF in bringing diversification of cropping pattern towards high-value crops for which demand is rising at a faster pace with the rising living standard especially among the urban masses.

The value of crop productivity in the case of leased-in crops was not much different from that of contract crops. The value of output per cropped area was ₹91 thousand in Karnataka, ₹70 thousand in AP, ₹50 thousand in Punjab and only ₹30 thousand in Haryana. The reason for the difference across two regions was same as that of contract crops. In Karnataka, tomato, baby corn, green chillies and carrot were grown while in AP, dry chillies and cotton were grown on the leased area. Although these crops were not covered by the assured buy-back under CF and they had high price and market risk but at the same time, these crops entail much better profitability. In comparison, in both Punjab and Haryana, farmers were growing paddy and wheat for assured MSP but with average returns. Thus, assured MSP only yielded average returns to Punjab and Haryana farmers whereas market based risky crops entail high returns to the AP and Karnataka farmers.

In the case of control crops, the difference in productivity was much less across these four states probably because of coverage of low-value cereals and oilseed crops in all the four states. For these reasons, average value of output per cropped area of control crops was also low—₹41 thousand in AP, ₹40 thousand in Punjab, ₹33 thousand in Haryana and ₹31 thousand in Karnataka. Nevertheless, the net returns to the farmers are determined by not only the productivity and price obtained, or in other words, value of their productivity, but also their cost of production. It is also well known that high-value crops are not only risky, but also have higher cost of production on account of higher material cost as well as labour cost. Therefore, it would be interesting to compare the net profitability across selected states and across these three categories of crops.

Cost of production has been calculated by adding material cost and labour cost. The material cost includes cost of land preparation including cost for bullock or tractor for ploughing, etc., seed and trans-planting, farmyard manure (FYM), bio and chemical fertilizer, plant protection chemicals, irrigation charges that include canal, hired tube well and electricity charges, harvesting including threshing charges, repair and maintenance of implements including depreciation cost and cost for marketing the produce. Material cost also includes rent for land leased-in but imputed value of owned land has not been included in the total cost of production. Among the labour cost, only the paid-out labour cost has been included in the total cost of production and imputed value of family labour has not been accounted in the total cost.

Cost of production is presented in Table 5.3a for contract crops, Table 5.3b for leased-in crops and Table 5.3c for control crops for the selected four states. It is mentioned here that some items of cost are available in the aggregate and not at the crop level, for example, electricity and canal charges, diesel value of own tractor, repair, maintenance and depreciation, interest on working capital and so on. For calculating per crop cost of the above items, these costs have been divided by the GCA of the household to calculate their per acre cropped area value. The cost of per acre cropped area is still not comparable across contract, lease and control group farmers as rent for leasing-in land is included in the cost which is fully borne by the leased farmers and partly by the contract farmers in few cases, while control farmers do not have any leased land and thereby their total cost is free of rent charges. Therefore, while calculating net revenue we have presented both the cases by including and by excluding the rental charges for leased-in land in the case of contract crops and leased-in crops.

Comparing cost of cultivation per acre of cropped area, as expected, cost was highest for the contract farmers—₹36 thousand—but it was not very different for leased-in farmers whose average cost was ₹35 thousand. Both these categories bore some rent cost for the leased-in land, thereby their cost per acre was almost double than that of the control group, whose cost averaged at ₹17 thousand per acre as they did not lease-in any land and so there was no rent cost in their case. Comparing the cost of cultivation excluding rent charges, it shows that still the cost was highest for the contract crops, followed by leased-in and control-group farmers, however, the wedge between the three was much less—₹27 thousand, ₹20 thousand and ₹17 thousand per acre of cropped area, respectively for contract-, leased- and control-group farmers.

Among four states, cost including rent was the highest—₹46 thousand per acre—for contract crop in AP, followed by ₹42 thousand in

Karnataka, ₹37 thousand in Punjab and ₹34 thousand in Haryana. Thus, cost was in the same order as that of value of output in the four states. Among leased farmers, the cost per acre of cropped area was highest in Karnataka—₹57 thousand, followed by AP—₹54 thousand, Haryana—₹36 thousand and Punjab was slightly less—₹35 thousand per acre. The order of cost comparison was same even without including the rent charges, although rent was observed much higher in Punjab and Haryana as compared to AP and Karnataka. Among the control farmers also, the order of cost per acre was same—₹26 thousand in AP, ₹22 thousand in Karnataka,₹17 thousand in Punjab and ₹14 thousand in Haryana. Thus, value of output as well as cost per acre was higher for high-value crops in the two southern states as compared to traditional cereal and oilseed crops sown in Punjab and Haryana.

Looking at various components of cost of production, in the case of contract crops, there were four major items in the cost of production, namely seed, fertilizer and plant protection, rent paid for leasing-in land and the labour cost. On average, seed and transplanting constituted around 16 per cent cost of production. Although under CF, companies provided seed to the farmers but either they charged the cost at the time of delivery or they subtracted cost from the output delivered by the farmers and in no case, the seed was provided free of cost. Fertilizer and plant protection together constituted more than 20 per cent cost of production. Some farmers even reported having received some major and micronutrients from the contracting firms, but like seed, the cost was charged either at the time of delivery or during the product deliverance to the company. Leasing was more prevalent in Punjab and Haryana as compared to AP and Karnataka, therefore rent formed the major cost item in the former two states (27% and 42% respectively, in Punjab and Haryana) while in the latter two states it was less than 5 per cent. Labour charges, which also included most of the harvesting cost in all the four states, constituted almost 20 per cent of total cost. It is to be noted here that in the labour cost we have included only paid-out cost whereas family labour cost has not been included in the total cost of production. Comparing the four selected states, cost for seed, rent for leased-in land and repair and maintenance cost was higher in Punjab and Haryana whereas fertilizer and plant protection and labour cost was much higher in Karnataka and AP.

In the case of leased-in crops, the major cost components were—seed and transplanting, manure fertilizer and plant protection, rent for leased-in land, hired-labour charges, expenses for tractor or bullock for ploughing and repair and maintenance charges. Slightly less than half of the cost, on average, was rent paid for leased-in land that varied from 64 per cent in the case of Haryana to only 7 per cent in Karnataka, while share of rent in Punjab and AP was 34 and 19 per cent, respectively. Cost of fertilizer and pesticides constituted around 15 per cent of total cost that varied from around 33 per cent in Karnataka, 29 per cent in AP, around 16 per cent in Punjab and only 10 per cent in Haryana. Seed and transplantation cost were, on average, 9 per cent of the total cost that varied from 13 per cent in Punjab to 4 per cent in Haryana and AP and 8 per cent in Karnataka. The labour charges were highest—27 per cent—in Karnataka, 24 per cent in AP, 18 per cent in Punjab and 8 per cent in Haryana, while in the aggregate, labour cost averaged at around 15 per cent of the total cost.

Control farmers did not lease any land and therefore their cost for rent was nil. This was also one reason that their cost was least among the three categories, although control-farmers' cost was least when we don't consider land-lease cost but the difference was much less in the latter case. This points out very high cost of hiring land and among the selected states, the rent was much higher in Punjab and Haryana as compared to the other two selected states. Among various components of total cost of production for the control crops, the highest was fertilizer and pesticides (25%), followed by labour charges (22%), repair and maintenance (20%), interest on working capital (10%) and seed and transplanting (8%). While cost of fertilizer and pesticides was higher in Karnataka and AP, like in the case of contract and leased crops. However, it made an opposite trend in the case of labour cost whereby we found Punjab and Haryana having higher cost as compared to Karnataka and AP as against the trends found in the case of contract and leased crops. In the case of other components of cost, there were mixed trends among the selected four states.

Thus, given the fact that both value of output as well as cost of production were highest for contract crops followed by leased-in and control crops and both were higher for AP and Karnataka as compared to Punjab and Haryana, it would be interesting to see the net returns to farmers as that makes the farmers' income and that is what matters most for the farmers. As was mentioned earlier, rent for leasing-in land was almost half of the cost in Punjab and more than 60 per cent in Haryana whereas it was not more than 5 per cent in Karnataka and AP. Similarly, rent share in total cost was much higher among leased farmers as compared to contract farmers while it was nil in the case of control farmers. Therefore, in order to have comparison across the four states and three categories of farmers, we calculated net returns by excluding rent amount form the total cost.

On average, value of net returns, that is, total revenue – total cost excluding cost of rent for leased land, was not as diverse as were total revenue and total cost as discussed previously. Net returns although followed the same order, that is, contract crops followed by leased-in and control crops but their values varied from ₹24 thousand per acre for contract crops to ₹22.5 thousand per acre for leased crops and ₹21 thousand per acre for control crops. Its value for contract crops once again was highest in AP—₹46 thousand, followed by Karnataka—₹26 thousand, Punjab—₹25 thousand and Haryana—₹22 thousand. In the case of leased crops, net returns were highest—₹38 thousand—in Karnataka, followed by Punjab and AP both at ₹26 thousand and Haryana at ₹17 thousand. In control crops, Punjab and Haryana led the other two states with value of ₹23 thousand per acre in Punjab, ₹19 thousand in Haryana, ₹15 thousand in AP and least was Karnataka with per acre value of ₹9 thousand only. Thus, whereas in contract and leased crops, AP and Karnataka realized higher returns on account of growing high-value crops, but Punjab and Haryana gained more returns in the control group as in this category, cropping pattern was more similar across the four states and Punjab and Haryana had better economies of scale in growing these crops.

The above analysis highlights the fact that diversifying cropping pattern towards high-value crops like fruits, vegetables and animal products and paying more attention towards changing consumer pattern can help achieving the target of doubling farmers' income in a set time period. The role of CF in helping farmers adopting such a cropping pattern and disseminating information and technical know-how is highlighted by the above results. The results presented above were in the aggregate level for the four selected states. The results related to intra-size of holdings revealed that the marginal and small farmers had higher percentage of their GCA under contract as compared to medium and large farmers in Karnataka and AP. In comparison, medium and large farmers had higher percentage of area under contract in Punjab and Haryana thus these two regions presenting opposite trends in CF. Similarly, in the case of leasing also, marginal and small farmers leased-in more land in Karnataka and AP whereas medium and large farmers leased-in more land in Punjab and Haryana. Thus, there was reverse tenancy in Punjab and Haryana where medium and large farmers tried to increase their size of holding by leasing-in more area to optimize their economies of scale. In AP and Karnataka, on the other hand, there was direct tenancy whereby small and marginal farmers tried to make their holdings economical by leasing-in more land. The possible explanation of these two different trends could be that in Punjab and Haryana agriculture is more mechanized, thereby medium size farmers having most of agriculture implements try to optimize their use by leasing more holdings. On the other hand, in Karnataka and AP, where agriculture is still not as mechanized, small and marginal farmers having more access to family labour try to lease-in land to fully utilize the labour component, whereas medium and large farmers have less incentive to lease because of rising labour cost. In the previous section, it was seen that labour cost was much higher in southern states as compared to north.

Among the crops grown under CF, marginal and small farmers had comparatively higher area under gherkins and cotton, while medium and large farmers had more area under red chillies, maize and jalapeño in AP. In Karnataka, marginal, small and medium farmers had more contract area under baby corn and gherkin, while large farmers had comparatively higher area under tomato and jalapeño. In Punjab, all farmers had almost same percentage of area under contract in the case of wheat, while large farmers devoted more area under potato while marginal, small and medium farmers devoted higher area under barley. In Haryana, all farmers, small as well as large, had major proportion devoted to wheat and rice under CF mainly with the seed companies. In the case of leased crops, there did not appear any particular trend towards any particular crop across small versus large farmers.

Comparing productivity, costs and net returns across various farm-size holdings, there seems to be a particular trend in favour of medium and large farmers, especially in the case of contract crops. There was discernible a clear inverse relationship between value of output per acre and farm-size holdings indicating higher value of output per acre for large farmers as compared to small and marginal farmers. This was true in all the four states without any exception. In the case of leased crops also, there was a clear inverse relationship although leasing-in cases were not there for medium and large farmers in Karnataka. In all other states, value of output per acre was higher for medium and large farmers as compared to marginal and small farmers. In the case of control crops, however, the same was not found true. In AP, clearly marginal and small farmers had much higher value of output per acre as compared to medium and large farmers. Similarly, in Karnataka for control crops, value of output per acre was higher for marginal and small farmers as compared to large farmers. Against these trends, there was a direct relationship between value of output per acre and farm size, like in the case of contract crops and leased crops in the case of control farmers also in Punjab and Haryana.

Thus, these results indicate that whereas in Punjab and Haryana large farmers enjoy economies of scale in their productivity because of more mechanized agriculture, the same was true for contract and leased crops in Karnataka and AP against the general trends observed in control crops. This also indicates the natural inclination of CF towards large and medium farmers as compared to small and marginal farmers.

However, against the favourable trends in value of output realized by contract and leased farmers across all the four states, no such disadvantage was seen in the case of cost of production. Cost per acre for contract and leased crops in AP in the case of marginal farmers was higher as compared to medium farmers. Similarly, cost was higher for marginal farmers as compared to medium and large farmers for contract crops in Haryana and Karnataka and leased crops in Punjab. Therefore, it would be interesting to compare net profitability across various farm-size categories and across various groups of farmers.

Like in the case of total revenue, net returns per acre also showed clearly a direct relationship with farm size in the case of contract crops.

Whereas, marginal farmers earned ₹51 thousand per acre, large farmers earned ₹77 thousand per acre. In Haryana, marginal farmers were in net loss while small farmers earned only ₹7 thousand per acre, whereas large farmers' net profit per acre was ₹22 thousand. In Punjab, marginal farmers earned ₹15 thousand per acre while large farmers earned ₹25 thousand per acre. In Karnataka, the difference was highest. Whereas net returns per acre were ₹21 thousand for marginal farmers, it was ₹33 thousand for medium farmers and ₹1.09 lakh for the large farmers. Thus, clearly, large farmers had better profitability from contract crops as compared to small and marginal farmers.

In the case of leased-in crops, large farmers were having better profitability as compared to small and marginal farmers only in Punjab and to some extent in Haryana while in AP, medium farmers had highest profitability and in Karnataka, only marginal and small farmers had leased land whereby small farmers had better profitability as compared to marginal farmers. Among the farmers growing control crops, profitability was clearly more for medium and large farmers as compared to marginal and small farmers in Haryana, Punjab and Karnataka while only in the case of AP, marginal farmers enjoyed highest profitability followed by large farmers and medium farmers in that order and small farmers had the least profitability. Thus, by and large, the bigger-size holding enjoyed not only higher profitability on account of ploughing more area, but also had better per acre net returns on account of better economies of scale in Punjab and Haryana while in Karnataka and AP, they had more advantageous position with respect to contracting farming.

COMPARATIVE PRODUCTIVITY AND PROFITABILITY OF INDIVIDUAL CROPS

In this section, we compare net returns for the sample crops for which we have sufficient observations for all the three types of farming, that is, CF, leased and control groups. We have the case of chillies in AP, baby corn in Karnataka and paddy, wheat and potato in both Punjab and Haryana. Chillies were grown under contract in AP by around 50 contract farmers, around 34 leased farmers and 34 control farmers.

CF in chillies was done through Global Green Company. Table 5.4a presents details about area cultivated, inputs used, total revenue earned, physical productivity, net returns and the price at which final output was sold by the farmers. The total area devoted to chillies by the selected farmers was 34 per cent of GCA by the contract farmers, 48 per cent by the leased farmers and 38 per cent by the control group farmers. On average, area devoted to chillies varied from 2.2 acres for contract farmers, to 2.5 acres by leased farmers and 1.6 acres by the control-group farmers.

Table 5.4a *Net Return from Chillies Crop—AP*

Particulars	Contract Farmers	Lease-in Farmers	Non-Contract Farmers
Number of households	50	34	34
Average area planted under contract (acres per HH)	2.2	2.5	1.6
% share of baby corn area to GCA	34.44	47.59	38.20
Cost of seed and transplanting	4,387	4,276	3,866
	(6.04)	(5.48)	(5.9)
Manure & fertilizer	14,346	12,828	14,473
	(19.75)	(16.44)	(22.1)
Irrigation, canal, hired tube well and electricity charges	697	474	587
	(0.96)	(0.61)	(0.9)
Plant protection, pesticides, etc.	13,222	13,549	14,021
	(18.2)	(17.36)	(21.41)
Expenses for tractor/bullock in ploughing	4,934	5,105	4,643
	(6.79)	(6.54)	(7.09)
Repair, maintenance and depreciation[a]	1,031	1,032	1,213
	(1.42)	(1.32)	(1.85)
Rent paid for leasing-in land (per acre)	4,805	9,150	0
	(6.61)	(11.72)	(0)
Hired-labour charges	21,369	21,944	19,099
	(29.41)	(28.11)	(29.17)

Marketing cost including grading, storage, transport, packing	2,733 (3.76)	3,865 (4.95)	2,721 (4.16)
Market/*mandi* fee, etc.	2,754 (3.79)	3,418 (4.38)	2,270 (3.47)
Miscellaneous	9 (0.01)	42 (0.05)	12 (0.02)
Interest on working capital[b] 10% per annum	2,369 (3.26)	2,370 (3.04)	2,581 (3.94)
Total cost	72,655 (100)	78,054 (100)	65,486 (100)
Total revenue	133,386	98,026	101,463
Total revenue – total cost	60,731	19,972	35,978
Total revenue – total cost (excluding lease rent)	65,536	29,122	35,978
Output (red chilli) produced per acre (quintals)	15.45	–	–
Price per quintal of red chilli	2,200	–	–
Output (dry chilli) produced per acre (quintals)	14.12	17.82	16.24
Price per quintal of dry chilli	7,038	6,952	7,228

Note: [a]Repairs maintenance and depreciation are collected from the field for the existing machinery; [b]Interest on working capital is interest paid on the loans/borrowing divided in proportionate to each crop sown during the year.

The contract growers were selling both red chillies and dry chillies while leased and control farmers sold only dry chillies. Total revenue earned per acre was much higher—₹1.3 lakh—by the contract farmers as compared to 1.0 lakh by the control farmers and ₹98 thousand by leased farmers. Net profitability was also much higher for contract farmers—₹61 thousand per acre as compared to ₹36 thousand for control group and ₹20 thousand for leased farmers. The profitability was least in the case of leased-in farmers even when we adjust for rent paid for leasing-in land. The physical productivity among the three groups was not comparable as contract farmers had both red and dry chillies, while other two groups had only dry chillies. The price obtained by contract farmers for dry chillies was slightly less than that of control group but slightly more than the leased farmers. The highest net price was obtained by control group—₹72 per kg as compared to ₹70 per kg by contract farmers and ₹69.5 per kg by the leased farmers. Thus, despite receiving less price as compared to control farmers, contract farmers had much higher earnings as compared to theother two categories.

In the case of baby corn crop in Karnataka (Table 5.4b), a total number of 206 contract farmers cultivated this crop while 47 control farmers and only 3 lease-in farmers cultivated baby corn. There were two companies namely, Global Green and Namdhari which carried out CF in baby corn in Karnataka. Average area under baby corn per household was 2 acres by the contract farmers and 1.8 acres by control group that constituted around 30 per cent of the GCA by the respective farmers. The productivity per acre by contract farmers was slightly above both control group as well as leased farmers whereas price realized was almost equal in all the three cases. The gross revenue obtained by contract farmers was around ₹35 thousand per acre for contract farmers as compared to ₹36 thousand by leased farmers and ₹33 thousand by the control group farmers. Similarly, cost per acre was highest for leased-in farmers, followed by contract and control farmers.

Table 5.4b *Net Returns from Baby Corn Crop—Karnataka*

Farm Type	Contract Farm	Lease Farm	Non-Contract Farm
No. of HH	206	3	47
Average area under baby corn (acres per HH)	2.0	1.5	1.8
% share of baby corn area to GCA	33.17	31.03	29.71
Cost of seed and transplanting	2,306	2,511	2,554
	(10)	(8)	(12.4)
Manure & fertilizer	6,333	8,422	5,657
	(27.47)	(26.83)	(27.47)
Irrigation, canal, hired tube well and electricity charges	902	444	616
	(3.92)	(1.42)	(2.99)

Plant protection, pesticides, etc.	182.0	–	175
	(0.79)	–	(0.85)
Expenses for tractor/bullock for ploughing	2,830	3,000	2,865
	(12.28)	(9.56)	(13.92)
Repair, maintenance and depreciation[a]	4,061	6,034	3,262
	(17.62)	(19.23)	(15.84)
Rent paid for leasing land	509	3,793	0
	(2.21)	(12.08)	(0)
Hired-labour charges	4,963	5,458	4,002
	(21.53)	(17.39)	(19.44)
Marketing cost including grading, storage, transport, packing	1	–	8
	(0)	–	(0.04)
Market/*mandi* fee, etc.	2	–	–
	(0.01)	–	–
Interest on working capital[b]	964	1,724	1,451
	(4.18)	(5.49)	(7.05)
Total cost	23,056	31,387	20,591
	(100)	(100)	(100)
Total revenue	34,970	36,000	33,284
Total revenue – total cost	11,915	4,613	12,693
Total Revenue – total cost (excluding lease rent)	12,424	8,406	12,693
Output produced per acre (quintals)	39.35	35.60	36.30
Price of produce per quintal	601	600	608

Note: [a]Repairs maintenance and depreciation are collected from the field for the existing machinery; [b]Interest on working capital is interest paid on the loans/borrowing divided in proportionate to each crop sown during the year.

Comparing profitability by excluding cost for leasing-inleasing, it was almost same for the contract and control farmers and it was lowest for leased farmers. Thus, both in chillies as well as in baby corn, the contract farmers had edge over other categories both in productivity as well as cost of production resulting into better profitability while leased land realized least returns. These findings support our proposition that leased land generally have less priority of the farmers' both management as well as resources devoted as long-term investment falls short on such land as there is no security of tenure for the tenant. CF was found beneficial in both these crops as farmers obtained seeds and some other inputs from the contracting firms and the product was procured by the companies. We will discuss more details about the services provided by the companies in the next chapter.

There are three crops in Punjab and Haryana, for which we have sufficient numbers of observations to compare productivity and profitability between contract, lease and control farmers (Tables 5.4c–5.4h). In Haryana, out of these three crops, wheat and paddy contract was for seed companies namely, Prabhat seeds and Dhariwal seeds for wheat, Jai Bharat seeds, Haryana seeds and Super seeds for paddy and Goodrich and ITC Agri Technico for potato. In Punjab, contract for wheat was done with Modern Seed company, Braghu seeds, Rashtriya Beej Nigam and Pioneer Seeds and in potato contract was done with mainly McCains, Biocarb, Pagro and ITC Agri Technico, while some prominent companies like PepsiCo and FieldFresh did not provide the farmers' list for conducting survey. Whereas wheat and paddy contracts were mainly with seed companies, potato contract was for agri-business firms mainly Goodrich and ITC, who used potato as raw material for processing different products. In our sample in Haryana, 60 households were growing wheat crop under contract, 13 farmers grew paddy under

Table 5.4c *Net Returns of Wheat Crop—Haryana*

Farm Size	Contract	Lease-in	Non-contract
No. of HH	60	61	228
Average area under wheat crop (acres per HH)	23	12	8
% share of wheat crop area to GCA	35.65	35.27	27.02
Cost of seed and transplanting	1,339 (6.34)	1,186 (4.58)	1,327 (12.64)
Manure & fertilizer	2,226 (10.54)	2,419 (9.34)	1,875 (17.85)

Irrigation, canal, hired tube well and electricity charges	349	459	640
	(1.65)	(1.77)	(6.1)
Plant protection, pesticides, etc.	1,170	1,440	728
	(5.54)	(5.56)	(6.94)
Expenses for tractor/bullock in ploughing	1,694	1,669	1,351
	(8.02)	(6.44)	(12.87)
Harvesting material cost	5	6	32
	(0.03)	(0.02)	(0.3)
Repair, maintenance and depreciation[a] 10% per annum	3,662	1,396	1,622
	(17.34)	(5.39)	(15.45)
Rent paid for leasing-in land (per acre)	7,739	14,184	0
	(36.64)	(54.74)	(0)
Hired-labour charges	2,630	2,679	2,622
	(12.45)	(10.34)	(24.97)
Marketing cost including grading, storage, transport, packing	7	56	18
	(0.03)	(0.21)	(0.18)
Market/*mandi* fee, etc.	0	0	6
	0	0	0
Miscellaneous	49	88	41
	(0.23)	(0.34)	(0.39)
Interest on working capital[b] 10% per annum	252	329	239
	(1.19)	(1.27)	(2.28)
Total cost	21,122	25,912	10,501
	(100)	(100)	(100)
Total revenue	33,194	29,851	29,616
Total revenue – total cost	12,072	3,940	19,115
Total revenue – total cost (without lease rent)	19,810	18,123	19,115
Output produced per acre (quintals)	20	18	18
Price of output per quintal	1,553	1,502	1,504

Note: [a]Repairs maintenance and depreciation are collected from the field for the existing machinery; [b]Interest on working capital is interest paid on the loans/borrowing divided in proportionate to each crop sown during the year.

Table 5.4d *Net Returns from Paddy Crop—Haryana*

Particulars	Contract	Lease-in	Non-Contract
No. of HH	13	12	168
Average area planted under paddy (acres per HH)	8	9	19
% share of paddy planted area to GCA	36.12	40.77	43.97
Cost of seed and transplanting	922	923	1,116
	(4.7)	(3.37)	(9.93)
Manure & fertilizer	2,084	2,355	2,150
	(10.62)	(8.6)	(19.12)
Irrigation, canal, hired tube well and electricity charges	1,208	505	423
	(6.16)	(1.84)	(3.76)
Plant protection, pesticides, etc.	1,190	1,589	788
	(6.07)	(5.8)	(7.01)
Expenses for tractor/bullock in ploughing	2,154	2,281	1,564
	(10.98)	(8.32)	(13.91)
Repair, maintenance and depreciation[a] 10% per annum	1,621	1,393	1,617
	(8.27)	(5.09)	(14.38)
Rent paid for leasing-in land (per acre)	7,086	12,037	0
	(36.13)	(43.93)	(0)
Hired-labour charges	3,168	5,209	3,458
	(16.15)	(19.01)	(30.74)
Marketing cost including grading, storage, transport, packing	0	0	0
	(0)	(0)	(0)
Market/*mandi* fee, etc.	95	0	0
	0	0	0
Miscellaneous	86	0	0
	(0.44)	(0)	(0)
Interest on working capital[b] 10% per annum	0	1,107	130
	(0)	(4.04)	(1.16)
Total cost	19,615	27,398	11,247
	(100)	(100)	(100)

Total revenue	34,772	39,352	35,320
Total revenue – total cost	15,157	11,954	24,073
Total revenue – total cost (without leaserent)	10,695	23,990	24,073
Output produced per acre (quintals)	18	28	25
Price of output per quintal	1,095	1,397	1,397

Note: [a]Repairs maintenance and depreciation are collected from the field for the existing machinery; [b]Interest on working capital is interest paid on the loans/borrowing divided in proportionate to each crop sown during the year.

Table 5.4e *Net Returns from Potato Crop—Haryana*

Particulars	Contract	Lease-in	Non-Contract
No. of HH	97	13	21
Average area planted under potato (acres per HH)	6	5	8
% share of potato planted area to GCA	14.67	11.35	18.13
Cost of seed and transplanting	17,956	10,073	9,205
	(36.14)	(23.43)	(31.75)
Manure & fertilizer	5,526	4,065	4,992
	(11.12)	(9.46)	(17.22)
Irrigation, canal, hired tube well and electricity charges	638	615	394
	(1.28)	(1.43)	(1.36)
Plant protection, pesticides, etc.	2,158	2,451	2,127
	(4.34)	(5.7)	(7.34)
Expenses for tractor/bullock in ploughing	3,169	2,731	1,834
	(6.38)	(6.35)	(6.32)
Harvesting material cost	153	7	72
	(0.31)	(0.02)	(0.25)
Repair, maintenance and depreciation[a]	1,806	1,903	2,057
	(3.63)	(4.43)	(7.09)

(Table 5.4e Continued)

(Table 5.4e Continued)

Particulars	Contract	Lease-in	Non-Contract
Rent paid for leasing-in land (per acre)	8,766	13,970	0
	(17.64)	(32.5)	(0)
Hired-labour charges	9,214	7,040	8,154
	(18.54)	(16.38)	(28.12)
Marketing cost including grading, storage, transport, packing	107	0	63
	(0.22)	(0)	(0.22)
Market/*mandi* fee, etc.	0	30	72
	0	0	0
Miscellaneous	12	104	3
	(0.02)	(0.24)	(0.01)
Interest on working capital[b]	186	0	22
	(0.37)	(0)	(0.08)
Total cost	49,690	42,989	28,993
	(100)	(100)	(100)
Total revenue	74,699	55,396	47,160
Total revenue – total cost	25,009	12,406	18,167
Total revenue – total cost (without leaserent)	33,775	26,376	18,167
Output produced per acre (quintals)	107	89	77
Price of output per quintal	695	624	615

Note: [a]Repairs maintenance and depreciation are collected from the field for the existing machinery; [b]Interest on working capital is interest paid on the loans/borrowing divided in proportionate to each crop sown during the year.

Table 5.4f *Net Returns from Wheat Crop—Punjab*

Particulars	Contract	Lease-in	Non-Contract
No. of HH	49	35	116
Average area under wheat crop (acres per HH)	16	8	10

% share of wheat planted area to GCA	42	33	37
Cost of seed and transplanting	1,100	1,628	874
	(5.05)	(5.35)	(6.19)
Manure & fertilizer	2,596	2,393	2,465
	(11.92)	(7.87)	(17.46)
Irrigation, canal, hired tube well and electricity charges	533	550	482
	(2.45)	(1.81)	(3.41)
Plant protection, pesticides, etc.	1,163	1,462	1,116
	(5.34)	(4.81)	(7.9)
Expenses for tractor/bullock in ploughing	1,760	1,992	1,866
	(8.08)	(6.55)	(13.22)
Harvesting material cost	0	10	3
	(0)	(0.03)	(0.02)
Repair, maintenance and depreciation[a]	2,231	2,229	1,965
	(10.24)	(7.33)	(13.92)
Rent paid for leasing-in land (per acre)	6,376	13,550	0
	(29.28)	(44.56)	(0)
Hired-labour charges	2,834	3,628	3,203
	(13.02)	(11.93)	(22.69)
Marketing cost including grading, storage, transport, packing	1	2	4
	(0)	(0.01)	(0.03)
Market/mandi fee, etc.	0	0	0
	(0)	(0)	(0)
Miscellaneous	238	331	98
	(1.09)	(1.09)	(0.7)
Interest on working capital[b]	2,944	2,631	2,043
	(13.52)	(8.65)	(14.47)
Total cost	21,777	30,406	14,117
	(100)	(100)	(100)
Total revenue	33,476	32,209	29,456
Total revenue – total cost	11,699	1,803	15,339

(Table 5.4f Continued)

(Table 5.4f Continued)

Particulars	Contract	Lease-in	Non-Contract
Total revenue – total cost (without leaserent)	18,075	15,353	15,339
Output produced per acre (quintals)	19	20	19
Price of output per quintal	1,570	1,490	1,512

Note: [a]Repairs maintenance and depreciation are collected from the field for the existing machinery; [b]Interest on working capital is interest paid on the loans/borrowing divided in proportionate to each crop sown during the year.

Table 5.4g *Net Returns from Paddy Crop—Punjab*

Particulars	Contract	Lease-in	Non-Contract
No. of HH	–	22	294
Average area under paddy crop (acres per HH)	–	16	18
% share of wheat planted area to GCA	–	40	43
Cost of seed and transplanting	–	988	791
	–	(6.08)	(5.35)
Manure & fertilizer	–	2,279	2,670
	–	(14.04)	(18.06)
Irrigation, canal, hired tube well and electricity charges	–	229	233
	–	(1.41)	(1.58)
Plant protection, pesticides, etc.	–	1,810	1,155
	–	(11.15)	(7.82)
Expenses for tractor/bullock in ploughing	–	2,385	1,986
	–	(14.69)	(13.44)
Harvesting material cost	–	1	0
	–	(0.01)	(0)
Repair, maintenance and depreciation[a]	–	1,887	1,916
	–	(11.62)	(12.97)

Rent paid for leasing land (per acre)	–	0	0
	–	(0)	(0)
Family labour charges	–	0	0
	–	0	0
Hired-labour charges	–	4,516	3,986
	–	(27.81)	(26.97)
Marketing cost including grading, storage, transport, packing	–	3	2
	–	(0.02)	(0.01)
Market/*mandi* fee, etc.	–	0	0
	–	(0)	(0)
Miscellaneous	–	17	0
	–	(0.1)	(0)
Interest on working capital[b]	–	2,123	2,039
	–	(13.07)	(13.8)
Total cost	–	16,238	14,778
	–	(100)	(100)
Total revenue	–	41,599	42,082
Total revenue – total cost	–	25,361	27,304
Total revenue – total cost (without leaserent)	–	25,361	27,304
Output produced per acre (quintals)	–	28	29
Price of output per quintal	–	1,471	1,458

Note: [a]Repairs maintenance and depreciation are collected from the field for the existing machinery; [b]Interest on working capital is interest paid on the loans/borrowing divided in proportionate to each crop sown during the year.

Table 5.4h *Net Returns of Potato Crop—Punjab*

Particulars	Contract	Lease-in	Non-Contract
No. of HH	68	51	27
Average area planted under potato (acres per HH)	12	14	12

(Table 5.4h Continued)

(Table 5.4h Continued)

Particulars	Contract	Lease-in	Non-Contract
% share of potato planted area to GCA	15	20	8
Cost of seed and transplanting	17,804	8,104	7,024
	(32.46)	(19.13)	(19.1)
Manure & fertilizer	6,689	5,630	6,261
	(12.19)	(13.29)	(17.03)
Irrigation, canal, hired tube well and electricity charges	207	296	224
	(0.38)	(0.7)	(0.61)
Plant protection, pesticides, etc.	2,510	2,331	3,126
	(4.58)	(5.5)	(8.5)
Expenses for tractor/bullock in ploughing	2,705	2,659	2,312
	(4.93)	(6.28)	(6.29)
Harvesting material cost	0	0	279
	(0)	(0)	(0.76)
Repair, maintenance and depreciation[a]	1,548	1,589	1,806
	(2.82)	(3.75)	(4.91)
Rent paid for leasing-in land (per acre)	12,005	12,881	8,774
	(21.88)	(30.4)	(23.86)
Hired-labour charges	10,042	7,695	6,957
	(18.31)	(18.16)	(18.92)
Marketing cost including grading, storage, transport, packing	2	0	3
	(0)	(0)	(0.01)
Market/*mandi* fee, etc.	0	0	2
	(0)	(0)	(0)
Miscellaneous	0	0	0
	(0)	(0)	(0)
Interest on working capital[b]	1,345	1,188	0
	(2.45)	(2.8)	(0)
Total cost	54,855	42,373	36,769
	(100)	(100)	(100)
Total revenue	75,483	67,519	58,693

Total revenue – total cost	20,628	25,146	21,924
Total revenue – total cost (without leaserent)	32,632	38,026	30,698
Output produced per acre (quintals)	100	111	95
Price of output per quintal	753	609	618

Note: [a]Repairs maintenance and depreciation are collected from the field for the existing machinery; [b]Interest on working capital is interest paid on the loans/borrowing divided in proportionate to each crop sown during the year.

contract while 97 farmers grew potato under CF. In comparison, in Punjab, 49 farmers were growing wheat and 68 farmers were growing potato under CF while paddy contract was not found in Punjab. Per household wheat area under CF in Haryana was 23 acres while area under lease farming was 12 acres and control farmers' area under wheat was 8 acres. In comparison, area under paddy in Haryana for contract farmers was 8 acres, leased farmers was 9 acres and control farmers was 19 acres. In the case of potato, average per household area was six, five and eight acres, respectively for contract, leased and control farmers.

In Punjab, area under wheat was 16 acres under CF, 8 acres in leased farming and 10 acres for the control group. In the case of potato, average per household area was 12, 14 and 12 acres for contract, lease and control groups, respectively. Per household area under paddy in lease and control group in Punjab was 16 and 18 acres, respectively. Thus, area under CF as well as under lease and control farming in Haryana and Punjab was much higher as compared with AP and Karnataka. Comparing productivity among the three categories of farmers, in the case of wheat and paddy, productivity was not different significantly in Haryana as well as Punjab. In Haryana, productivity for wheat was 20 quintals per acre for contract farmers and 18 acres each for leased and control farmers.

Similarly, in Punjab, it was more or less 20 quintals per acre for all the three groups. In the case of paddy, productivity was least for contract farmers—18 quintals per acre as compared to 28 quintals for leased and 25 quintals for control group farmers. There was no case of CF in paddy in Punjab while for leased and control group productivity was 28 and 29 quintals, respectively. Similarly, there was not much advantage for contract farmers in terms of better price as in wheat as it was slightly above the other two categories in both the states but in paddy, it was the least among the three categories of farmers. Consequently, the net returns (excluding rent for leasing) was either same in all the three categories or it differed only marginally while in the case of paddy in Haryana, it was almost half for the contract farmers as compared to the other two categories. Thus, given the fact that wheat and paddy CF was only a buy-back arrangement by the seed companies and there was not much value addition, it was not very beneficial for the farmers in terms of better returns. The contracting companies only provided seed and provided buy-back arrangement mostly at the price marginally above the market rate. The extension services were almost absent and except seed, no other service provision was made. This was also the case of CF for seed purpose for other crops like moong, mustard and *arhar* in Haryana. In Punjab, although our majority of sample farmers were growing these two crops under contract, but we had other cases where farmers were growing flowers and vegetable crops, in which case net returns were better than these examples of seed crops.

Taking the example of potato in Haryana and Punjab, the productivity was much higher for contract farmers as compared to lease and control farmers in Haryana and better than control farmers in Punjab. Price paid for potato was also significantly more than that of leased and control farmers. The net returns per acre in Haryana were ₹34 thousand for contract farmers, ₹26 thousand for leased and ₹18 thousand for control farmers. In Punjab, net returns were ₹33 thousand for contract farmers as compared to ₹38 thousand for leased farmers and ₹31 thousand for control farmers. Thus, not only returns were higher for the contract farmers, but returns were much higher in general for potato (and other vegetable crops) as compared to wheat and paddy. It is mentioned here that in potato, companies provided seed as well as extension services and they arranged for advisory and some machinery to the needy farmers as compared to seed companies which only provided seed and no other services to the contract farmers.

Similar to the case of vegetables in Punjab and Haryana, in Karnataka and AP, CF was in gherkin, baby corn, chillies and jalapeños. In most of these crops, companies engaged in value addition through processing and very clearly, farmers gained through CF as their net returns were not only better than other traditional crops like cereal, pulses and oilseeds but also contract farmers earned better than their counterpart leased and control farmers who grew these crops without any support of CF. In our sample, farmers were growing many other crops under CF as well as on the leased land and control group. However, we do not have sufficient numbers of existing farmers in all the three categories. Therefore, we have presented here comparative profitability of only those crops for which sufficient comparable number were available. Nevertheless, in our previous analysis, we compared all crops grown under CF, leasing-in and control group of farmers which reinforce the point that contract farmers in the aggregate had better profitability although the advantage of CF was more in those products which had more value addition rather than only buy-back arrangement without having any processing activities attached to the product.

SUMMARY

Our enquiry with the farmers revealed that in Punjab and Haryana, farmers were engaged in contract with seed firms for cereal and pulse crops where companies were mainly providing buy-back facility alone, whereas in AP and Karnataka, CF consisted of commodities meant for export purpose like gherkins and jalapeño, in which case contracting firms closely monitored the quality of crops to meet the requirements of exports. The contract was mostly oral except in Punjab where majority of the farmers had written contract. Only less than 20 per cent of the GCA of a particular household was under CF. As per farmers' opinion, the necessary requirements for farmers entering into CF include assured irrigation, labour availability and having reasonable size of holdings. All the selected farmers indicated that the contracted produce was being procured. Only a handful of farmers indicated very small quantity of produce being rejected in all the four states. Similarly, breach of contract by the farmers was also almost negligible. Assured income, superior price based on quality product supplied and hassle free marketing were the main advantages of CF as per majority of the farmers engaged in CF. A clear majority of the contract farmers expressed their satisfaction with CF.

Comparing all contract crops, leased crops and control crops, on average, value of crop output per acre was highest in the case of CF crops—₹52 thousand, followed by leased crops—₹43 thousand and the least was by control crops—₹38 thousand. The value of output per cropped area under CF was the highest—₹91 thousand—in AP, followed by Karnataka—₹68 thousand, Punjab—₹51.5 thousand and it was least in Haryana—₹41 thousand per acre. The two southern states were growing high-value commodities under CF like gherkins, baby corn, jalapeño and green chillies. In comparison, cereal crops like paddy and wheat were grown in Haryana and wheat and potato were grown in Punjab. Except potato, most of the other crops grown in these two states had only low returns as compared to high-value crops, which occupied major share in the southern states.

The value of crop productivity in the case of leased-in crops was not much different from that of contract crops. In the case of control crops, the difference in productivity was much less across these four states probably because of coverage of low-value cereals and oilseed crops in all the four states. Both value of output as well as cost of production were highest for contract crops followed by leased-in and control crops and both were higher for AP and Karnataka as compared to Punjab and Haryana. On average value of net returns followed the same order, that is, contract crops followed by leased-in and control crops but their diversion was much less. Whereas in contract and leased crops, AP and Karnataka realized higher returns on account of growing high-value crops, but Punjab and Haryana gained more returns in the control group, as in this category cropping pattern was more similar across the four states and Punjab and Haryana had better economies of scale in growing these crops. The above analyses highlights the fact that diversifying cropping pattern towards high-value crops like fruits, vegetables and animal products and paying more attention towards changing consumer pattern can help achieving the target of doubling farmers' income in a set time period. The role of CF in helping farmers adopting such a cropping pattern and disseminating information and technical know-how is highlighted by the above results.

Chapter 6

Marketing, Employment and Farmers' Opinion about Contract Farming and Land Leasing

The previous two chapters presented household characteristics, their cropping pattern, nature of CF, resource usage, farm productivity and profitability with reference to contract, lease and control crops. This chapter starts with the disposal pattern of the final product by the selected farmers with comparison across farm categories and farm-size holdings. This is followed by a section on employment generated by contract, lease and non-contract crops. The third section presents earning sources from allied and non-farming activities. The last section of this chapter presents farmers' opinion about CF, tenancy and leasing companies and their suggestions for the better implementation of CF.

MARKETING PATTERN FOLLOWED BY CONTRACT, LEASE AND CONTROL FARMERS

By and large, contract farmers sold their product through contracting firms. However, as discussed in the last chapter, almost half to two-thirds of the GCA of contract farmers was for non-contract crops. Therefore, we have bifurcated total output sold by the contract farmers into contract and non-contract crops. The results are presented in Table 6.1. The crops grown on CF were, by and large, sold through the contracting companies without any exception. The results reveal that the entire output produced under CF was disposed of through

Table 6.1 *Marketing Channels through which Crops Were Sold by the Selected Households (% of Output)*

Particulars	Pre-arranged Company Contract	Wholesale Market/ Regulated Mandis	Local Market	Villagers (Directly)	Coo-perative	Government Agencies (Including FCI, CCI, etc.)	Sold to Merchant	Selling at Farm Gate	Others
AP									
Contract crops	99.67	0.20	0.03	0.04	0.00	0.05	0.00	0.00	0.00
Non-contract crops under contract group	7.63	42.03	28.98	0.49	0.18	0.49	11.40	7.76	1.04
Lease crops	0.00	71.50	14.20	0.83	0.00	0.00	3.66	9.81	0.00
Non-lease crops under lease-in group	2.58	68.41	11.89	0.00	0.00	4.52	4.46	7.49	0.65
Non-contract crops	0.00	62.67	12.54	0.00	0.00	3.01	0.99	20.79	0.00
Haryana									
Contract crops	93.69	1.11	0.57	0.05	0.00	2.86	1.72	0.00	0.00
Non-contract crops under contract group	28.01	18.29	5.14	0.29	0.00	34.98	13.15	0.00	0.14
Lease crops	5.02	28.98	27.89	0.16	0.03	25.86	11.39	0.00	0.67
Non-lease crops under lease-in group	0.69	21.88	11.97	0.04	0.49	54.77	10.14	0.00	0.03
Non-contract crops	7.38	31.57	5.82	0.11	0.00	37.82	16.93	0.00	0.38

Punjab

Contract crops	99.45	0.00	0.55	0.00	0.00	0.00	0.00	0.00	0.00
Non-contract crops under contract group	14.13	33.98	10.88	1.10	0.00	21.16	18.10	0.61	0.04
Lease crops	18.97	27.83	8.87	0.34	0.23	21.49	15.85	5.03	1.38
Non-lease crops under lease-in group	6.05	25.42	30.36	0.46	0.00	17.32	17.19	3.20	0.00
Non-contract crops	0.00	34.44	21.72	1.85	0.81	9.78	31.19	0.00	0.22

Karnataka

Contract crops	99.42	0.00	0.06	0.00	0.00	0.00	0.00	0.00	0.52
Non-contract crops under contract group	0.00	11.51	80.87	3.82	0.00	0.32	3.03	0.15	0.30
Lease crops	0.00	83.57	11.43	0.00	0.00	0.00	5.00	0.00	0.00
Non-lease crops under lease-in group	0.00	1.18	95.05	0.17	0.00	0.05	3.55	0.00	0.00
Non-contract crops	0.33	6.26	78.05	10.40	0.00	0.92	3.93	0.00	0.09

contracting companies in AP, Punjab and Karnataka and with a few exceptions in Haryana as well. Crops grown without CF by the category of contract farmers were sold either through wholesale markets, which are known as regulated *mandis*, or through local markets, which are operating in the peripheral area of production centres, or they were sold through traders or merchants either at the farm gate or a place specified by the buyer.

In AP, around half of the output produced under non-contract crops by contract farmers was disposed of thorough regulated *mandis* while rest of the half was disposed though local markets, through merchants and intermediaries who lifted the produce at the farm gate. In Haryana and Punjab, a part of the non-contract produce was also sold through pre-arranged contract with the same companies or other companies as in both these states, CF was mainly for seed purpose in traditional crops. The other channels were mainly regulated *mandis* and government agency though minimum support-price system as government procurement was high in these two states. In Karnataka, non-contract produce by contract farmers was sold through local markets and a small proportion was sold through wholesale or regulated markets.

Even in the case of lease-in farmers (for lease crops and non-lease crops) as well as control farmers, majority of the produce in Punjab and Haryana was either sold through regulated *mandis* or though government agencies, that is, through MSP to Food Corporation of India (FCI) in the case of wheat and rice and Cotton Corporation of India (CCI) in the case of cotton. In Punjab, around 30 per cent output in the case of lease farmers and 22 per cent in the case of control farmers was sold in the local market and around 31 per cent output in the case of control farmers was sold to merchants. There were cases in Punjab and Haryana where local wheat flour mills procured wheat directly from farmers for processing wheat into wheat flour.

In AP, around 70 per cent produce belonging to leased farmers and around 63 per cent by control farmers was sold through regulated *mandis*. The other channels followed in AP were local market and selling at the farm gate through local traders. In Karnataka, only eight farmers were engaged in small quantity of leasing-in and almost whole of their produce under non-lease crops as well as all control farmers sold their produce through local markets, while the leased crops by a few farmers were sold thorough wholesale markets.

Among various farm-size holdings, all small as well as large farmers growing crops under contract disposed their product through contract companies in all the four states. The only exception was Haryana where marginal farmers, growing mostly wheat and rice under contract, disposed of their 33 per cent produce through MSP system to the government agency rather than through the contracting firm. In the case of lease and control farmers, in AP, both small as well as large farmers sold mostly through wholesale regulated markets. A part of the product was sold through the local market and at the farm gate through intermediaries but there was no particular pattern of marginal and small farmers selling more through such channels.

In both Haryana and Punjab, majority of lease and control farmers sold though regulated *mandis* and through commission agents to the FCI. Sale through local market and through merchants took place mainly for potato and other vegetable crops in these two states. In Karnataka, all contract farmers (large as well as small) sold their non-contract crops through local market except the marginal farmers, who sold 60 per cent share in the wholesale market. In the case of control farmers, majority of the small as well as large farmers disposed of their produce through local market while some quantity by marginal farmers was sold within the village or in the wholesale market. Thus, on average, marketing channels were found similar among large versus small farmers without any form of discrimination against smaller size of holdings among our selected farmers.

EMPLOYMENT GENERATED BY CONTRACT, LEASE AND CONTROL CROPS

It would be interesting to compare whether CF is able to create better opportunities for employment generation for skilled and unskilled persons, especially unemployed youth in villages, in addition to enhancing agricultural production and providing income support to farm households. From the analysis done in the previous chapters, it was seen that, by and large, value of output as well as net returns were higher from high-value contract crops as compared to traditional food grains, pulses and oilseed crops. In this section, we discuss labour absorption in various activities among our selected contract, leased and control crops.

Labour requirement was higher in horticultural (vegetable) and other high-value crops as compared to traditional cereals, pulses and oilseed crops, irrespective of whether they were grown under CF, leasing or control groups (Table 6.2). For example, in AP, manpower used in one acre chillies production was 184 man-days in contract crops. In gherkin, cotton and jalapeños, the requirement under CF was 167, 156 and 107 man-days, respectively while in lease and control crops, man-days employed varied from 161 to 175 in dry chillies in AP. However, for traditional crops like maize, baby corn, paddy and groundnut under contract or control groups, manpower used was within the range of 30 to 50 man-days.

Similarly in Karnataka, green chillies, tomato, gherkin, and jalapeño employed 159, 151, 139 and 105 man-days per acre, respectively, under CF. Man-days under control farming in the case of red/green chillies and tomatoes were 154 and 139 days and under leased crops, 135 and 104 days respectively. In coconut, groundnut and baby corn in Karnataka, the range of employment was less than 50 man-days per acre. In the case of Punjab and Haryana, the employment absorption in

Table 6.2 *Use of Human Labour in Crop Production (Crop-Wise Man-Days per Acre)*

Name of the Crop	Contract	Lease	Control	Aggregate
AP				
Red/green chilli	184	–	–	184
Dry chilli	–	175	161	168
Gherkin	167	–	–	167
Seed cotton	156	–	–	156
Jalapeño	107	–	–	107
Onion	–	–	68	68
Seed maize	57	–	–	57
Baby corn	53	–	–	53

Commercial cotton	–	68	43	52
Paddy	–	–	51	51
Groundnut	–	–	30	30
Maize	–	–	30	30
Karnataka				
Green chilli	159	135	154	156
Tomato	151	104	139	141
Gherkin	139	–	–	139
Jalapeño	105	–	–	105
Baby corn	49	59	–	49
Ragi	–	–	47	47
Groundnut	–	–	42	42
Coconut	–	–	21	21
Haryana				
Potato	19	23	14	18
Oat	12	12	8	11
Paddy	9	15	10	10
Wheat	4	6	15	9
Mustard	7	10	8	8
Punjab				
Cauliflower	90	–	–	90
Flower	33	–	–	33
Carrot	20	–	–	20
French bean	18	–	–	18
Peas	12	24	–	18
Capsicum	13	–	–	13
Potato	12	10	–	11
Oat	7	7	11	7
Paddy	–	–	6	6
Wheat	5	7	5	5
Radish	5	–	–	5
Cotton	–	–	5	5

all categories was much less as compared to Karnataka and AP, possibly due to heavy mechanization in agriculture. In both these states, the employment absorption was less than 20 man-days per acre for the traditional cereal, pulses and oilseed crops while for vegetables like potato, cauliflower, flower, carrot, etc., it was above 20 man-days per acre. By and large, there was no difference in employment pattern under contract, lease and control crops but the nature of crop determined the extent of absorption of labour force which was mostly unskilled labour.

Comparing across the farm-size holdings, there was no decipherable pattern across different farm-size categories. The labour absorption was random across farm-size holdings as in some crops labour absorption was more either in marginal holdings or in small farmers whereas it was the reverse case in other crops. For example, in AP in the case of CF, labour absorption was more among marginal and small farmers in gherkin and seed cotton whereas in red chillies and baby corn, labour absorption was more among medium and large farmers. The pattern was random in lease and control crops. Same was the case in other states among all the three types of farmers. To sum up, employment creation was high among vegetables and high-value crops and those crops for which value addition was done under CF as compared to traditional cereal crops and other such crops. Therefore, CF should be preferred for bringing in innovations in cropping pattern towards high-value commodities which otherwise farmers do not opt for the lack of technical know-how, lack of seed and technology and scarcity of defined product market which creates post-harvest risk in sowing such crops. All these issues can easily be addressed by the contracting firms.

EARNINGS FROM ALLIED AND NON-AGRICULTURAL ACTIVITIES

As was discussed in Chapter 4, household income consists of earnings from farming, also called farm-business income and earnings from allied and non-farm sources. The aggregate picture of farm and non-farm income was presented in Chapter 4. We discuss here further details of allied activities and non-farm activities that our selected households were engaged in. There were two main allied activities namely animal husbandry and poultry farming. Among other sources, our selected farmers were also engaged in farm and non-farm wages, especially the small and marginal farmers. Some members of the household were engaged in regular-salaried activities either in formal or informal sector. There were also some earnings from self-employment in business and rent from leasing-out land. In the cropping pattern, we also queried about the perennial crops grown by the households. Although we did not include net earnings from perennial crops in the farm-business income because of complications involved in working out the cost of cultivation of such crops as there was significant amount of gestation-period cost involved in such crops.

However, in this section, we have tried to include a rough approximation of such earnings by subtracting from the reference year value of output per household, the reference-year cost borne by the farmers ignoring the gestation-period cost. The crops grown by our selected households belonging to perennial crops were mainly mango, pomegranate, coconut, mulberry and banana in Karnataka; mango, mulberry and beetle nuts in AP and poplar and sugarcane in Haryana and Punjab. Table 6.3 presents details of various sources of income from allied and non-farm activities. On average, allied and non-farm income was measured at ₹80 thousand per household per annum. It varied from ₹51 thousand in AP to ₹62.5 thousand in Punjab, ₹1.0 lakh in Karnataka and ₹1.1 lakh in Haryana. The largest proportion—32 per cent—was contributed by animal husbandry, around 19 per cent by salary and pension and around 25 per cent share contributed by orchards and other perennial and plantation crops. The share of wages from agriculture and non-agriculture sector was around 8 and 5 per cent, respectively. While in AP, farm and non-farm wages constituted the highest share whereas in Karnataka, it was animal husbandry and income from orchards that contributed to the largest share. In Punjab and Haryana, on the other hand, animal husbandry and salary and pension constituted the bigger share.

Among various farm-size categories, the major contribution in earnings from allied and non-farm activities in AP among marginal and small farmers was from farm wages, non-farm wages and salaries and pension, whereas in the case of medium and large farmers, it was comparatively more from farm wages, self-employment and income from orchards, etc. In Haryana, salaries and pension, animal husbandry and self-employment contributed majorly for small and marginal farmers

Table 6.3 *Other Net Income of Cultivating Households (₹ per HH)*

Income Sources	AP	Haryana	Punjab	Karnataka	Aggregate
Milk/dairy or animal husbandry	4,446	25,695	26,158	46,663	25,813
	(8.7)	(23.9)	(41.8)	(46.9)	(32.1)
Poultry	51	795	100	248	306
	(0.1)	(0.7)	(0.2)	(0.2)	(0.4)
Farm wages	22,494	185	48	3,037	6,432
	(43.9)	(0.2)	(0.1)	(3.0)	(8.0)
Non-farm wages	13,030	1,250	240	2,684	4,298
	(25.4)	(1.2)	(0.4)	(2.7)	(5.4)
Salaries/pension	5,101	27,287	23,057	7,180	15,625
	(10.0)	(25.4)	(36.8)	(7.2)	(19.4)
Self-employment/business	2,197	7,338	637	3,637	3,458
	(4.3)	(6.8)	(1.0)	(3.7)	(4.3)

Others	1,919	573	0	6,658	2,304
	(3.7)	(0.5)	(0.0)	(6.7)	(2.9)
Rent (leasing-out land)	133	3,177	3,565	741	1,899
	(0.3)	(3.0)	(5.7)	(0.7)	(2.4)
Income from orchards (including sugarcane in Haryana and Punjab)	1,839	41,220	8,789	28,744	20,200
	(3.6)	(38.3)	(14.0)	(28.9)	(25.1)
Total income	**51,240**	**107,520**	**62,594**	**99,592**	**80,335**

whereas medium and large farmers obtained more income from animal husbandry, salaries and pension and income from orchards. In the case of Punjab, salaries and pension and rent from leasing-out land contributed higher share in the case of small and marginal farmers, whereas animal husbandry, salaried work and income from orchards contributed more for medium and large farmers. Last and least, in Karnataka, income from dairy, salary and orchards contributed to the small and marginal farmers in comparison to more share coming from dairy and orchards in the case of medium and large farmers.

PROBLEMS FACED TOWARDS LAND LEASING

During our interactions with the farmers, we tried to ascertain farmers' opinion on land-leasing and land-sharing practices in the rural areas. In our field questionnaire, we enquired from farmers, who had leased-in or leased-out land during the reference year or in the past, about the problems faced by them and their opinion on how to improve the land-tenure system in the country. We also enquired farmers' responses on development of land-leasing/land-sharing companies and whether such system would benefit the farmers. In this section, we present briefly the findings of our field enquiries on various aspects of land-leasing and land-sharing practices.

To our question, what kind of problems were being faced by the farmers due to absence of a formal lease market, a significant majority of farmers replied that they were facing problem in rent fixation (Table 6.4). Almost all farmers in Karnataka, more than half in Punjab and Haryana and more than one-third of respondents in AP indicated that they were facing this problem. The kinds of problems they face in rent fixation were given as: no possibility for change/modification of rent fixed by the landowner; as rent is fixed pre-hand, loss will have to be borne by tenants alone in the case of low yields or crop loss due to some reasons; rent fixed as per norms of irrigated land but afterwards, landowners do not provide irrigation facility or the facility is not sufficient; lease amount is increased annually; lease amount is to be paid in advance as per agreement; lease amount is fixed irrespective of crop success or failure; lease amount for land with irrigation sources is very high and needs to be brought down; once taken land on lease, it is not

Table 6.4 *Problems Faced Due to Informal Leasing/Sharing (% of HH)*

Problems Faced	AP	Haryana	Punjab	Karnataka	Aggregate
Rent-fixation problem	36.85	54.87	61.00	95.09	62.07
Period of leasing too short	35.26	29.42	31.00	84.87	45.28
Uncertainty for next year	26.29	33.80	39.60	82.32	45.63
Lack of necessary investment	13.75	35.19	44.60	79.76	43.45
Overexploitation of leased land	6.18	51.09	59.80	38.11	38.78
Other problems	10.16	68.59	0.00	33.99	28.25

easy to withdraw; the tenants may be allowed to pay rent in instalments or, at least, on seasonal basis; lease amount is fixed arbitrarily; lease amount is abnormally increased even for ordinary land; lease amount is not properly paid by tenants.

The second most important problem highlighted by the selected households was period of leasing being too short. It is to be clarified that in most of the cases, the lease period was either one season or one year and only in miniscule cases the long-term lease of two years or more was found among the selected farmers. Around 85 per cent farmers in Karnataka and above 30 per cent in all other states pointed out this problem. The specific issues related to short lease period were the following: the required time and energy is not devoted to such land as utilization period is limited; there is insecurity and risk of crop without adequate water facility; it is not viable to apply FYM and make high investment due to short lease period; tenants are not in a position to recover from crop loss in the next season due to shorter lease period, if on the other hand, lease period is longer there is possibility to recover and make out from crop loss in the next season; tenants sometimes are unable to recover even lease amount; landowners, even if willing, do not give land on lease for a longer period due to risk of loss of land;

short duration lease period also restricts tenant from growing more number of crops and more importantly perennial crops; dues may be less in the case of long period lease; tenants are frequently changed or rotated therefore there is a need for written agreement for tenants with two years or more duration.

Uncertainty for the next year was also pointed out by majority of the households. The main issues highlighted were: not sure whether lease period would be extended for the next year; every year, land is available for lease but by a different farmer or different piece by the same farmer (generally single farmer will not give land on lease to same tenant every year); tenants do not make investment in soil fertility because of uncertainty of being not sure for extension of lease next year; lease amount next year will be increased if there is good yields this year; regular payment of lease amount is a concern for farmer while choosing new tenant every time; not sure of decision of farmer for leasing land next year forces tenant to look out for other farmer for lease; uncertainty prevails with increase in lease amount and lack of written agreement; tenant farmer who incurred loss in the previous year opts out of leasing in the next year; due to short-term lease, there remains lack of trust among both the parties; increase in debt burden as land is not given on lease regularly; irregularity of lease payment resulted in termination of lease arrangements for a tenant who had long period lease.

As expressed in the last two paragraphs, due to short-term lease there remains the problem of lack of necessary investment on the lease land. As per farmers' opinion, they are not ready to invest due to the short duration of lease. There are chances of poor crop yield even after investment due to the lack of long-term reform on the land and tenant will lose heavily in such circumstances. For such reasons, tenants opt minimal investment as a coping option as investment for crop is not mobilized in advance; long duration and commercial crops are not grown due to short-term-lease period; they need to borrow loans at higher interest rates to make investment, which is riskier and high lease amount is likely for productive land with better water availability.

Lastly, the short-term lease leads to overexploitation of the land resources. This is evident from the reducing soil fertility and no action is taken by the tenant on preventing depletion of soil fertility. The higher practice of leasing short term also leads to excessive use of ground water as the tenant has to recover not only returns for the labour and investment from the land, but also extra cost as rent which is paid to the land lord. The other problems faced by the tenants were: input subsidy and crop insurance go to landowner and not to tenant; crop-loss compensation is transferred to landowner's account; tenant should not be pressurized for payment of lease amount in the case of crop loss or low yield; landowners think that tenant will get legal right if land is given on lease for long period; owners prefer tenants who are willing to pay lease amount in advance thereby it adds extra cost in terms of high-interest rate as banks do not lend for such money; landowners do not intend to bear maintenance charges that adds extra cost to the tenants; trees are cut and sold/used by tenants without informing the landowner.

FARMERS' OPINION ABOUT DEVELOPMENT OF FORMAL LAND-LEASE MARKET

In our attempt to understand farmers' views on development of formal lease market with set of rules defined for both land lessor and lessee and provision for long-terms lease at least for 10 years with willingness of both the parties, we posed the question to the selected households, 'What would be the advantages and disadvantages if leasing or sharing becomes formal practice with proper rules and regulations and it allows long-term contract, for example, leasing for 10 years period?' The farmers' opinion about advantages and disadvantages are summarized in Tables 6.5a and 6.5b. The farmers' responses on advantages and disadvantages are explained in the following paragraph.

Major advantages highlighted by farmers were: land will be taken care like own land; can plan for the crop and long-duration crops can be sown on such land also; long-term investment like installing a bore or tube well, using land leisure levelling, application of FYM or even organic farming can also be undertaken; new methods of agriculture can be implemented and any crop can be sown on lease land; likely increase in crop yield as a result of better management and better inputs used; for landlord, lease amount will be assured and tenant land will be available for long-term cultivation; local labourers will get more employment;

Table 6.5a How Formal Land Market and Tenancy Can Be Developed in India? (In Support of Land Lease Market, Following Responses Were Obtained from Farmers [in %])

Sl No.	States	AP	Haryana	Punjab	Karnataka	Aggregate
	Total Number of Responses	96	192	97	163	548
	Responses					
1	We will give land on lease if higher lease amount is paid	6.25	51.04	52.58	3.07	29.20
2	Other farmers will learn new technologies of crop cultivation	0.00	34.38	46.39	0.00	20.26
3	Instead of incurring losses by doing agriculture, it is better to earn by doing other activities	30.21	14.58	1.03	15.95	15.33
4	No irrigation facility	25.00	0.00	0.00	5.52	6.02
5	We will lease-out our land as we would not need to invest and face labour problem	0.00	0.00	0.00	15.95	4.74
6	They invest their money and encourage us to do work. It is good to have some or the other crop in the field	4.17	0.00	0.00	10.43	3.83
7	There are not many who are willing to do farming, so it is good to give it to company	0.00	0.00	0.00	11.66	3.47

8	We are assured of annual income	0.00	0.00	0.00	11.04	3.28
9	Land will not be kept fallow; land is cultivated with some crop	17.71	0.00	0.00	0.61	3.28
10	Reduction in transport costs and improved access to marketing services	3.13	0.00	0.00	8.59	3.10
11	We will give our land for lease as cultivation costs have gone up and we arenot getting remunerative price for produce	0.00	0.00	0.00	7.98	2.37
12	Infrastructure for irrigation will be developed and it will increase land value	6.25	0.00	0.00	1.23	1.46
13	We will find some other employment opportunity or activity	6.25	0.00	0.00	0.61	1.28
14	We will give it to company, as agriculture has become unviable	0.00	0.00	0.00	4.29	1.28
15	We want land rights, that is, rights must be with farmers	1.04	0.00	0.00	1.23	0.55
16	Wage employment availability will increase	0.00	0.00	0.00	1.84	0.55

Table 6.5b Following Responses Were Obtained from Farmers for Not Supporting Private Firms to Enter in Agricultural Lease Market (in %)

Sl No.	States / Responses	AP	Haryana	Punjab	Karnataka	Aggregate
	Total Number of Responses	408	320	395	377	1,500
1	We live depending on land. So will not give land to anyone	7.84	69.38	83.04	27.59	45.73
2	We may lose employment/livelihood opportunities	27.21	0.00	0.00	13.00	10.67
3	Small farmers will face labour shortage with company attracting labour	31.37	0.00	0.00	0.27	8.60
4	We can't trust companies	0.00	20.31	8.10	0.00	6.47
5	We may face labour shortage and hike in wage rates	17.40	0.00	0.00	1.59	5.13
6	It may lead to real-estate boom	0.25	10.31	8.86	0.53	4.73
7	We own only small piece of land	0.00	0.00	0.00	16.18	4.07
8	If we give our land to company, we will have to go for wage employment	0.00	0.00	0.00	13.79	3.47
9	I know only agriculture and do not know any other work	0.00	0.00	0.00	10.34	2.60

10	It is difficult to manage agri-allied activities, dairy activities may get affected	0.00	0.00	0.00	9.55	2.40
11	The bondage and relation between farmer and wage-earner will get affected	6.86	0.00	0.00	0.27	1.93
12	Right on land is mine and it will not be transferred to any one	4.41	0.00	0.00	0.27	1.27
13	Our family members will not agree	2.45	0.00	0.00	0.53	0.80
14	There is an agreement and we need to follow conditions	1.96	0.00	0.00	0.27	0.60
15	We depended on agriculture for generations	0.00	0.00	0.00	1.86	0.47
17	We believe/depend on agriculture; we may lose crop in one season; in the next season we will gain	0.00	0.00	0.00	1.59	0.40
18	My social status will be affected if I lease-out my land to company	0.00	0.00	0.00	1.06	0.27

better water facility provision can be made; there will be more crop diversification; this will reduce forced migration; land will not be kept fallow in fear of losing land by the owners; more investment in machinery; increase in market and transport facilities; might lead to higher wage rates; small and marginal farmers can earn more by leasing-out land and entering into wage market; likely to increase price of land as well and cheaper institutional credit will become accessible to tenants.

Major disadvantages highlighted were: it may lead to excessive use of fertilizers; increase in machinery use leading to reduction in work for wage earners; in the event of long-term lease, land may be increasingly used for other than agricultural purposes; small farmers may struggle to get wage labour if dominance of large holdings increases due to rising activities of lease; small farmers' survival and existence may suffer; lease amount may increase and land will not be available for small tenants.

Similarly, we also posed the question to the selected farmers, 'do you support the development of land-leasing and land-sharing companies who will lease land from farmers and cultivate either themselves or on profit sharing basis?' The farmers' responses are summarized as follows: the companies will invest in agriculture and it would be great that they encourage us to do work by paying their money; it would be good to have some crop or other in field rather than keeping the land fallow; this practice will lead to reduction in transport costs and improved access to marketing services; land rights must remain with farmers; infrastructure for irrigation will be developed that will increase land value; due to lack of irrigation facility, it is better to find some other employment opportunity or activity and lease-out land to companies; instead of incurring losses by doing agriculture, it is better to earn elsewhere by doing other activities; leasing-out would be a better option as cultivation costs have gone up and we are not getting remunerative price for produce; we will lease-out our land, as we need not invest and face labour problem; farming is not remunerative any more, therefore it is good if we can give it to company and earn better and wage employment availability will increase.

The farmers who were against such development, they opined the following: right on land is mine and it will not be transferred to any one; small farmers will face labour shortage with company attracting more labour; we may lose employment/livelihood opportunities; the bondage and relation between farmer and wage-earner will get affected; it may lead to real-estate boom; our social status will be affected if we give our land to company; by giving land to lease companies, it may be difficult to manage agri-allied activities like dairy and poultry; if we give our land to company, we will have to go for wage employment; companies might lead to excessive use of fertilizers; increase in machinery use may lead to reduction in work for wage earners; as company people are not known to us, we are not sure whether they will pay the lease amount on time; small farmers may struggle to get wage labour as labourers will be attracted to higher wages paid by companies; small farmers' survival and existence may suffer and traditional crops may be wiped out; crops will be grown without any gap by company and this may suck up all fertility of the soil; fodder for livestock will become a major issue; companies may use land for construction and other activities and farmers will become wage-earners and society cohesiveness and credibility will get affected.

Thus, by and large, farmers favoured a formal system of lease market. Most of the farmers pointed out that they face problems in the informal leasing as lease rate was arbitrary and lease period was too short. The short period of lease does not allow farmers to make reforms on such land and requisite investment is not made by them. As tenants keep shifting, the necessary expenditure on irrigation, land levelling, soil improvement and other such activities are not given any attention on such land. The farmers, in many cases, overuse doses of fertilizer and pesticides in order to fetch more returns from such a land which destroys the soil in the long run. In our analysis, we saw that in many cases, farmers had the least returns from the leased land. The farmers also indicated their desire to lease-out their land to lease companies but they found having lack of trust on such companies. Therefore, any such future provision should be made keeping farmers' interest in mind.

Some changes are being introduced in different states regarding laws on land leasing and land sharing. While doing so, it should be kept in mind that the interest of farmers and not the corporate sector should be given due priority. The right reforms in this direction will go a long way in improving the agriculture system. However, marginal and small farmers should be encouraged and it should be made sure that their situation improves within agriculture, not by converting them from cultivators to landless labourers. They should not end up giving up agriculture, lease out their land to companies and become landless labourers. Land reforms should target to make the land viable for these holders and not making them landless labourers working for the lease companies.

Regarding land-sharing companies, although such examples are rare in India, we posed this question to the farmers to seek their opinion on the same. Most of the farmers expressed their apprehensions that their land will be grabbed by such companies. Majority of the farmers were not comfortable with the fact that their land may be reduced into shareholding in the company, although having shares in the profit of such companies was sumptuous to some of them. Farmers were especially concerned regarding loosing decision making on cropping pattern and resource usage with such share-holding companies. They expressed grave concern of losing ownership of land to such companies and almost all surveyed farmers expressed their denial for the promotion of such land-sharing companies.

SUGGESTIONS ON HOW TO IMPROVE CF

In addition to detailed survey of farmers on various aspects of working of CF that was elaborated in the last chapter, we posed some additional questions to the contract farmers in order to ascertain various aspects of CF, namely delivery of final product to the contracting firms, mechanism of fixation of price, quality of produce demanded by the company, payment system and problem faced during the delivery of the product. The farmers' opinion on these aspects is summarized here. The contract farmers informed that the produce was to be sent to company immediately after harvest, although sometimes there was delay due to unavailability of transport facility. Company asked for delivery to reach the company within stipulated/planned time period. In some cases, company collected produce from the field. For delivery of produce, company generally provided regular guidance mainly in perishable commodities like gherkin, baby corn, tomato, etc. Even in such cases, company guided about the time of harvesting as well.

How the final price of the produce was fixed, replying to this question, farmers informed that generally they did not have any role in fixing up the price that was done by the company, although company gave due attention to the prevailing market price during the reference year or during the previous year. There was also complaint by the farmers that they needed to be involved in this process. Farmers further pointed out that the companies need to provide more remunerative prices as labour cost has increased over the time. Some farmers also opined that the price should be offered as per market price and sometimes market price was more than the price offered by the company. When asked that what kind of quality is preferred by the company, farmers pointed out that, generally, company rejects product based on moisture content but they complained that price offered was uniform and the farmers were not rewarded for premium quality offered. They also pointed out that the company should also make provision of buying the inferior-quality produce at a lower price.

To the question of payment system and whether is it appropriate, farmers pointed out that, generally, payment is made within fortnight or one months' time period. Farmers expressed that the payment should be made at the time of delivery and it should be paid in cash or should be directly transferred to the farmers' account rather than making payment by a cheque. They also pointed out that the payment amount for seed and other inputs should be collected at the time of harvest. Farmers pointed out that if the company has to reject their product due to poor quality, it should be done at the farm gate rather than after the product is delivered at the factory gate so that farmers can sell elsewhere or use it as fodder. The advice given by contracting companies to the farmers is summarized in Box 6.1. The contracting firms provided extension services and advice regarding package of practices to the farmers through their extension staff, albeit only some and not all companies provided the same. The company staff made farmers aware about the practice of sowing, harvesting and care taking of the crop. They made farmers aware about pest management, timely use of various inputs, provided technical know-how on various aspects of farming and also provided some of the inputs on behalf of the company.

Box 6.1 *Kind of Advice Given by Contracting Firms to the Farmers*

- Awareness on pest management information on timely use of pesticides and harvesting
- Guidance about the timing of seed sowing and application of pesticides
- Guidance on various growth aspects of crop
- Guidance on use of farm machinery
- Training about the crossing methods
- Timely weeding and various methods and techniques
- Guidance on seed-sowing methods
- Provided pesticide bottles/spraying bottles
- Extension services provision
- Field officers guide about various aspects of farming to get better yield

Source: Authors' field survey

Finally, suggestions provided by farmers on how to improve CF system are summarized in Table 6.6 and Box 6.2. The major suggestions included—the companies should own farmers like their own staff as they play a significant role in providing raw material to these contracting companies. They should take care of farmer's rights from sowing up to harvesting and disposing of the produce. Among the facilities and inputs, these companies should provide better seeds, fertilizer and pesticides at reasonable prices so that farmers are not cheated by the duplicate inputs available in the market. Company should also make provision of credit and crop insurance at a reasonable interest and premium rate to cover the risk of farmers, especially crops which farmers grow for the first time though CF and other input facilities to the contracting farmers.

Companies should also provide soil testing facility, crop bonus when company earns super normal profits and free extension services. If the company takes care of farmers, they would also devote their full efforts producing and supplying best-quality raw material to the contracting firms.

Table 6.6 Suggestions for Improvement of CF (in %)

Farmer's Response	AP	Haryana	Punjab	Karnataka	Aggregate
Increase price	53.73	48.83	16.05	29.66	38.34
Quality seeds (that are resistant to pests) are to be developed	24.13	55.18	34.11	15.44	31.48
Crop insurance needs to be provided	19.65	46.49	23.41	23.04	27.45
Quality seeds, fertilizers and pesticides are to be supplied by the company at a cheaper rate	12.94	43.81	10.7	19.36	21.00
Provide subsidized inputs on lower prices	40.55	0	2.68	20.34	17.86
Interest-free loans to be given	18.41	0	0	25.74	11.71
Company representative should be available round the clock	12.69	14.05	0	9.8	9.42
Soil testing is to be done	13.18	6.02	2.01	13.73	9.12
Crop bonus as well as crop loans to be provided	0	12.37	0	22.55	8.13
Make advance payment	5.47	16.39	3.68	0.25	6.33
Water facility provision for increasing yield	12.19	0	0	5.88	5.13
Direct agreement with company and not with intermediaries	9.2	0	0	0.98	3.06
Company should buy products at farm gate	0	8.03	2.01	0	2.30

(Table 6.6 Continued)

(Table 6.6 Continued)

Farmer's Response	AP	Haryana	Punjab	Karnataka	Aggregate
Good technical support should be provided by the company	0	0	0	7.11	1.67
Company should provide loan facilities to the contracting farmers	0	7.02	0	0	1.61
All crops should be grown under a contract	0	5.69	0	0	1.30
Harvesting cost to be borne by the company	0	0	0	5.15	1.21
Company should purchase total produce	0	0	0	4.66	1.09

Box 6.2 *Farmers' Suggestions on How to Improve CF*

1. Seed cost to be reduced
2. Quality seeds (that are resistant to pests) should be developed
3. Provision of crop bonus as well as crop loans to contracting farmers
4. Crop insurance should be arranged by the contracting firms
5. Compensation in case of poor germination of seed
6. Quality seeds, fertilizers and pesticides should be supplied
7. Company shall give remunerative price for produce as per agreement
8. Timely supply of seed and fertilizers
9. Soil testing facility should be provided
10. Farmers' meetings should be conducted to meet the requirements of farmers
11. Written agreement is required
12. Interest-free loans should be given
13. Marketing at farm gate (field)
14. Payment to be made immediately after the disposal of product
15. Alternative markets are needed
16. Transparency is required
17. Direct agreement with company and not with organizers or intermediaries, as is the case in South India
18. Distribute vermicompost and organic manure
19. Water facility should be ensured for increasing yield rate
20. Produce price should be fixed following the quality of the produce offered for sale
21. Make advance payments to the needy farmers
22. Company representative should be available round the clock
23. Company should take the responsibility irrespective of crop success or failure
24. Company office should be located in the production area so that farmers are able to approach the company
25. Information on new crops to be given
26. Competition between companies is needed
27. Company shall purchase whole produce and not only a part of the produce

Source: Own field survey

SUMMARY

The crops grown on CF were, by and large, sold through the contracting companies without any exception. Crops grown without CF by the category of contract farmers and other leased and control crops were sold either through wholesale markets, which are known as regulated *mandi*s, or through local markets, which are operating in the peripheral area of production centres, or they were sold through traders or merchants either at the farm gate or a place specified by the buyer. On average, marketing channels were found similar among large versus small farmers without any form of discrimination against smaller size of holdings among our selected farmers.

Employment creation was high among vegetable and high-value crops and those crops for which value addition was done under CF as compared to traditional cereal crops and other such crops. Therefore, CF should be preferred for bringing in innovations in cropping pattern towards high-value commodities, which otherwise farmers do not opt for the lack of technical know-how, lack of seed and technology and scarcity of defined product market, which creates post-harvest risk in sowing such crops. All these issues can easily be addressed by the contracting firms.

There were two main allied activities, namely animal husbandry and poultry farming. Among other sources, our selected farmers were also engaged in farm and non-farm wages, especially the small and marginal farmers. Some members of the household were engaged in regular-salaried activities either in formal or informal sector. There were also some earnings from self-employment in business and rent from leasing-out land.

By and large, farmers favoured a formal system of lease market. Most of the farmers pointed out that they face problems in the informal leasing as lease rate was arbitrary and lease period was too short. The short period of lease does not allow farmers to make reforms on such land and requisite investment is not made by them. As tenants keep shifting, the necessary expenditure on irrigation, land levelling, soil improvement and other such activities are not given any attention on such land. The farmers in many cases overuse doses of fertilizers and pesticides in order to fetch more returns from such land, which destroys the soil in the long run. In our analysis, we saw that in many cases farmers had least returns from the leased land. The farmers also indicated their desire to leaseout their land to lease companies but they found having lack of trust on such companies. Therefore, any such future provision should be made keeping farmers' interest in mind. Regarding land-sharing companies, farmers expressed clear opposition to making such provisions. They expressed fear of losing landownership if such land-sharing companies start working in the field of agricultural activities. Therefore, any decision in this regard should be taken with utmost care. Formal land leasing may benefit farmers but making provision of land sharing may become controversial and need to be averted without having more unanimity at the farmers' front.

Some changes are being introduced in different states regarding laws on land leasing and land sharing. While doing so, it should be kept in mind that the interest of farmers and not the corporate sector should be given due priority. The right reforms in this direction will go a long way in improving the agriculture system. However, marginal and small farmers should be encouraged and it should be made sure that their situation improves within agriculture not by converting them from cultivators to landless labourers. They should not end up giving up agriculture, lease out their land to companies and become landless labourers. Land reforms should target to make the land viable for these holders and not making them landless labourers working for the lease companies.

Chapter 7

Functioning of Contract Farming, Land Leasing and Land Sharing

A predominantly agricultural economy with 182 million ha of cultivable land, India produces more than 290 million tons of food grain. Catering to 65 per cent of the country's more than one billion people, who depend on agriculture for a living, is a tremendous challenge. In addition, a significant percentage of farmers (22.5%) continue to live below poverty line and the average monthly income of agricultural household at all-India level was ₹6,426 against the average monthly consumption expenditure of ₹6,223 (Situation Assessment Survey of Agricultural Households, 2013). Taking this situation into account, the Ministry of Agriculture and Farmers' Welfare in association with NITI Aayog identified a basket of agricultural reforms to create a more conducive environment for the farmers to produce and market and earn enough to improve their well-being.

In the initial phase of planning era, public policy was directed mainly at streamlining the agrarian structure through a series of land reforms, followed by improvements in trade and credit. The interest in contract, lease and land-sharing arrangements was simulated by the perceived importance in either fostering or impeding economic development. In the recent decades, it has been observed that high economic growth, rising per capita income, urbanization and more participation of women in labour force have enforced diversification in agricultural production in India. The dietary pattern of Indian people has shifted from food grains to high-value commodities such as fruits, vegetables, animal products like milk, meat and fish products followed by increase in demand for processed and semi-processed products. This demand-driven production system is opening new opportunities in food retailing and processing. But it raises a major concern of linking different segments of production, value addition and marketing so that interests of various stakeholders are safeguarded. Therefore, it is worthwhile to investigate the nature and progress of CF and other such developments in India in the recent time periods (Gulati et al., 2008).

This chapter seeks to understand the principle key determinants that drive contractual/lease relationships through the examples of various existing arrangements in the country. It is based on the premise that CF/leasing can be an attractive option to policymakers keen on integrating the poor into a more industrialized sector of the economy by helping them access the gains from trade that characterize successful agricultural tenancy arrangements.

CF IN INDIA

CF is a kind of system in which production and supply of agricultural produce is done under forward contracts and the essence of such contracts are commitments made by the farmers/producers to provide an agricultural commodity of specific quality, at a time and a price and in the quantity required by the buyers (Singh, 2002). Contracting system in agriculture had started from the sugarcane sector operating under the cooperative structure in India. Later, the sugarcane industry became dependent on state-government support and needed some political intervention. Similarly, dairy sector also flourished under the cooperative structure and millions of small farmers got benefitted through Operation Flood in the 1970s. Later, private players also followed formation of cooperative structure and started contracting with dairy farmers to source liquid milk from them. Some other corporate firms from poultry industry, basmati rice mills and potato production also applied CF concept and became popular as well as successful. In the early 1990s, some high-value crops such as tomatoes and chillies were brought under CF. Most recently, contracting in exotic vegetables such as baby corn, bell peppers, jalapeños, gherkins, etc., have been started

(Gulati et al., 2009). Most of these companies also have understanding with many banks such as National Bank for Agriculture and Rural Development, ICICI, SBI, Yes Bank, and Unit Trust of India bank that finance these CF arrangements and occasionally have joint ventures.

PROS AND CONS OF CF

It has been observed that several researchers have written about CF in support as well as in critique of these arrangements. CF provides opportunities to both the parties to derive benefit from the use of modern technologies, marketing infrastructure and other services to boost their incomes (Glover & Kusterer, 1990; Grosh, 1994; Little & Watts, 1994; Sahoo, 2010). However, the opponents argue that CF does not bring benefits to smallholders. They say that CF may subjugate the marginal and small farmers to increased control and exploitation by capital and induce a downward social mobility from being employer or self-employed to wage labour by an employer (Feder, 1977; Payer, 1980).

At macroeconomic level, CF can facilitate smooth marketing of produce, capital (credit), land and labour. It can also create positive externalities such as increase in employment, infrastructure improvement and market development (Grosh, 1994; Key & Runsten, 1999). Christensen (1992) says that CF is an institutional arrangement which brings development in agriculture sector through improved inputs, product exchange and product upgradation. The farmers cultivating under CF learn some skillset such as efficient use of farm resources, improved methods of chemical and fertilizer applications, understanding the importance of quality and desirable crop characteristics and demand of products in export market (Eaton & Shepherd, 2001). As farmers get fixed price for their produce, so it reduces price risks for the farmers. Also, technical and extension service offered by agribusiness firms leads to reduction in yield risks (Simmons, 2003).

While there may be empirical literature on CF in high-value and commodity-export sectors, studies on CF in staple-food sectors are very scarce. In this regard, Maertens and Velde (2017) using data from a crosssection of rice-growing-farm households and different propensity score matching estimates found that CF strengthened the domestic-rice value chain in Benin (West Africa) and had positive effects on income, rice production, intensification and commercialization. Well-designed contracts between oil palm companies and smallholder farmers with government support and infrastructural investments in Indonesia were analysed. The results of the panel regression model with village fixed effects showed that these contracts contributed to wealth accumulation in the local communities and reduced inter-village inequalities (Gatto et al., 2017). Contract-design-attribute preferences played a key role in motivating smallholders to participate in CF among potato farmers in Ethiopia, who preferred contracting firm as input providers and technical assistance rather than the State or NGOs that tend to minimize their input-market uncertainty risk (Abebe et al., 2013). Analysis by Bolwig et al. (2009), by controlling a range of factors, found that there were positive revenue effects both from participation in the certified organic coffee CF and from applying organic-farming techniques in Uganda.

On the other hand, the opponents of CF reject these benefits to the parties involved in contracting system including consumers. They state that CF system develops when the state plays a diminished role in agriculture and there is increased demand for specialized agricultural production in the absence of a proper and efficient market, credit and other infrastructure. Other authors state that CF is a mode of capitalist penetration in agriculture sector in which the farming sector undergoes through capital accumulation and exploitation. Once the farmers enter in the contracting system, sometimes they invest fixed resources in the production system or alter their cropping pattern and became dependent on their contract crops. At the end, they face limited exit options and reduced bargaining power which puts them at exploitative position in the contract. Sometimes, there is a possibility of collusion between state and powerful agro-industrial firms which can lead to skew policies and exploit state resources against the benefits of small and marginal farmers (Watts, 1994).

Siddiqui (1998) and Torres (1997) also raised ecological concerns on CF such as overexploitation of ground water, salinity of soil and decline in fertility. As CF involves high-value crop and export-oriented crop production, so this production is at the cost of basic-food crops. This shift in crop production will lead to higher food prices and small farmers and poor section of the society may suffer. Also, CF has some tilt towards large farmers as they are better able to meet contracting requirements, so it can encourage a socially undesirable dual agricultural development (Dunham, 1995; Korovkin, 1992; Little & Watts, 1994; Sachikoyne, 1989). Some evidences are also found that a farmer's risk (production risk, market risk and external capital risk) has increased after participation in CF schemes (Eaton and Shepherd, 2001). Narayan (2014) found that CF arrangements have diverse impacts on income for individual farmers in high-value agriculture (gherkins, papaya, marigold and broiler) from southern India. The average treatment's effect varies widely across contract commodities such as papaya and broiler contracts offer clear net gains whereas marigold contracting leaves participants worse off, while not all contracting firms for gherkins have shown net gains.

A meta-analysis of empirical evidence from five countries (Barrett et al., 2012) also reveals that more research and empirical studies with various approaches is needed to better understand the multifaceted implications of contractual arrangements for sustainable rural development.

INSTITUTIONAL ARRANGEMENTS TO FACILITATE CONTRACTUAL AGREEMENTS

A host of reforms were initiated to spruce up the agriculture sector starting with integration of e-National Agriculture Market (e-NAM) and the Agricultural Produce Market Committee (APMC) Model Act that have had a positive response. So far under e-NAM, 417 markets from 13 States with 39.75 lakh farmers and 88,474 traders have integrated into the online portal.[1] The APMC Model Act is envisioned to improve farmer's capacity to find better prices and avoid any price risks. It caters to reforms with regard to direct marketing, CF, establishment of markets in private and cooperative sectors, single-point levy of market fee, promotion of e-trading and issue of a unified license for traders. The APMC Model Act has provision of issuing permits for CF by registering the parties with them and allows them to purchase the produce directly from farmers and also exempt them from paying any market fee. However, so far only 11 states have applied exemption of market fee on transactions happening under contract agreement. In

---

[1] http://pib.nic.in/newsite/mbErel.aspx?relid=161018

addition, a separate chapter in the model Act specifies that registration of CF companies is compulsory, any disputes arising out of agreement will be resolved in 30 days and producer's ownership title on their land will be safeguarded if any claim arises out of the agreement.[2] Following the issuance of a model APMC Act in 2003, 75 percent of the Indian states were allowed to practise CF in different ways. Only 18 states have amended their respective APMC Act and only 10 states have notified rules to implement the amended provisions. However, there is no homogeneity as shown in the Table 7.1.

Table 7.1 *Progress of Reforms in APMC Act*

Sl No.	Stage of Reforms	Name of States/Union Territories (UTs)
1	States/UTs where reforms to the APMC Act have been legislated to provide for direct marketing, CF and markets in private/cooperative sectors	AP, Arunachal Pradesh, Assam, Chhattisgarh, Goa, Gujarat, Himachal Pradesh, Jharkhand, Karnataka, Maharashtra, Mizoram, Nagaland, Odisha, Rajasthan, Sikkim, Telangana, Tripura and Uttarakhand
2	States/UTs where reforms to APMC Act have been done partially	**1. Direct marketing:** NCT of Delhi, MP, Punjab (in Rule only) and UT of Chandigarh (in Rule only), West Bengal. **2. CF:** MP, Haryana, Punjab (separate act) and Chandigarh (only waiver of market fee and in Rule only) **3. Private market:** Punjab, West Bengal and UT of Chandigarh
3	States/UTs where there is no APMC Act and hence do not require reforms	Bihar (repealed on 1 September 2006), Kerala, Manipur, Andaman and Nicobar Islands, Dadra and Nagar Haveli, Daman and Diu and Lakshadweep.

(Table 7.1 Continued)

---

[2] http://shodhganga.inflibnet.ac.in/bitstream/10603/14594/12/chapter per cent20-v.pdf

(Table 7.1 Continued)

Sl No.	Stage of Reforms	Name of States/Union Territories (UTs)
4	State where APMC Act already provides for the reforms	TN
5	States/UTs where reforms have not yet been initiated	Meghalaya, Jammu and Kashmir, Pondicherry and UP

Source: State of Agriculture, 2015–2016.

Other reforms on which the Ministry has been working on includes promotion of value addition in food-chain and supply-chain management, renewed thrust on Negotiable Warehouse Receipt System (NWRS) and a model Contract Farming Act. The latter has gained traction across the country given the severely fragmented state of farm holdings that has affected farm viability. It is one institutional arrangement that is considered to be useful when transaction costs of direct engagement with the market are high for producers and/or traders. It also expects to enhance farmers' income and facilitate market access of smallholders in high-value supply chains that require specialized inputs for sale of produce in specialized output markets.

Among the study areas, Punjab enacted a separate Contract Farming Act in 2013 and Haryana amended their APMC rules in 2007, respectively. Under the Punjab Contract Farming Act, a registered CF sponsor can enter into an advance agreement with CF producer (farmer) for one-crop season or a maximum of three years. The newly constituted Punjab CF commission ensures proper implementation of the Act as well as provides suggestions to improve the performance of CF in the State. In terms of disputes, the district-level collector is responsible for its resolution and there is also provision for recovery of crop losses or damages as per prior agreement.

Provisions similar to the Punjab Contract Farming Act are expected to be there in the exclusive model law on CF, covering all crops from distribution of seeds to marketing of final produce. A separate comprehensive Act on CF will also ensure that the APMCs do not become arbitrators on CF and not be limited to marketing.[3]

In Karnataka, the APMC Act was amended where the former allowed exemption of 30 per cent of market fee under CF among other amendments to the Act. Karnataka allows CF agreements for a minimum period of one-crop season and the maximum is mutually decided by the contracting parties.[4]

In AP, the Andhra Pradesh (Agriculture Produce and Livestock) Markets Act was amended three times (2005, 2011 and 2015) to incorporate provisions on private markets, CF and e-markets. It has been expressed that the amendment on CF did not attract firms due to non-exemption of market fee, among other reasons.[5] Under CF, CF sponsor has been required to render a bank guarantee for the entire value of the produce.

LAND LEASING

Leasing is a voluntary transaction in which property rights (user and income) are transferred from landowners to tenants on contractual basis. Leasing was believed to have occurred due to particular factors of market imperfections and indivisibilities such as dualism in the labour market, lack of markets for draft power services, land endowments or other imperfectly marketable inputs and prevailing institutional setting, making it difficult to adjust the availability to production requirements (Taslim & Ahmed, 1992). Dasgupta et al. (1999) wrote that the early models of share contracts conveyed Marshallian inefficiency and Reid's postulated that contracts were based on the relative risk aversion, which had limited value. While other models such as incentive contract model were based on principal-agent framework and market-interlinked contracts (with credit), and cooperative contracts were prevalent in

---

[3] http://www.business-standard.com/article/economy-policy/contract-farming-law-may-cover-all-agriculture-commodities-117020400832_1.html

[4] http://krishimaratavahini.kar.nic.in/Acts/KAPMRULES.pdf

[5] http://www.newindianexpress.com/states/andhra-pradesh/2017/apr/01/andhra-pradesh-failed-to-attract-entrepreneurs-sponsors-cag-1588568.html

the USA, however empirical evidence is limited in comparison to the theoretical literature on contracts. Transaction cost theory also offers a basis to understand how land leasing and sharecropping contracts work.

In Brazil, institutional regimes causing insecurity of landownership from the use of land for speculative purposes, non-compliance of terms of contract involving small/poor producers limited land leasing. On the other hand, there also existed experienced tenants/sharecroppers with more capital and better financial and productive conditions in complex and structured agri-industrial chains such as sugarcane, soya, maize and cattle raising (de Almeida & Buainain, 2016).

Therefore, in a nutshell, the bundle of property rights transferred within a lease transaction depends on the type of contractual arrangement between the two parties and the motivation to comply with the agreement emanates from elements such as financial incentives, trustworthiness and institutional framework (Slangen & Polman, 2008).

LAND LEASING IN INDIA

Historically, land was owned by zamindars (landlords) who gave portions of it to tenants on rent or kind. However, this system was abolished by the government owing to the extensive concentration of land under the control of zamindars and consequently in the FYP's land ownership it was recommended to be distributed among the recorded tenants. As a follow-up, land reforms were introduced with a basic objective of abolishing intermediaries and regulation of tenancy. These prohibitive tenancy laws have led to a drastic decline in land lease or area under tenancy and imposed restrictions on land ceilings. Data shows that post these reforms, land leasing declined from 23.34 per cent during 1952–1953 to 10.7 per cent in 1961–1962 and 7.18 per cent in 1983. The NSSO's 45th Round put the percentage of area leased in to the total operational area as 5 per cent in 1957, an underestimate and some opined that it was more than 15 per cent if concealed tenancy was accounted for. These policies also led to drawbacks in the form of informal and insecure tenancy and consequently resulted in no access to credit or any government supportive measures.

Most landowners either left their land fallow or migrated to urban areas concluding that the land reforms proved to be anti-growth and anti-poor. With regard to specific states, Kerala, Jammu and Kashmir and Manipur do not allow leasing of farmland. However, the Kudumbashree mission in Kerala helps the poor by organizing Joint Liability Groups of women and assisting them to lease land informally. While in Punjab, Gujarat and Maharashtra, the tenant has the right to buy the leased land from the owner after tilling it for a certain period of time. Few states like Bihar, Odisha and MP have banned leasing of farmland, with exceptions for widows and handicapped landowners, while West Bengal allows only sharecropping and AP has fixed the lease tenure to a minimum of six years. In the states of Gujarat and Maharashtra, SC/ST tenants cannot be evicted once land is given to them on lease. In ST areas of AP, Bihar, Odisha, MP and Maharashtra, transfer of land from tribal to non-tribal is authorized only by a competent authority to prevent alienation of land from the tribals (Mani, 2016).

In the recent times, the union government has been determined on reversing the order by bringing new legislations. Many farmers in India opted for land lease because the size of landholding is small and has faced fluctuating prices, exploitation by middlemen and traders forced farmers to lease-out farmland. Towards this end, the NITI Aayog had prepared a Model Agricultural Land Leasing Act, 2016 drafted by an expert committee chaired by Dr T. Haque. According to the Act, land can be legally entered into a lease contract with the tenant for use of his/her land for agriculture and allied sectors like fruits and vegetables, floriculture, plantation crops, animal husbandry, prawn culture and poultry farming, agro-processing, breeding and agro-forestry for a specified period and for an amount based on the terms and conditions mutually agreed upon by the owner and the company.

Today, the concept of land leasing and sharing are seen in a different light, namely, as a means to contribute to agricultural inclusion, minimize land disputes and social inequalities and improve the economic efficiency of agriculture. As per the all-India level NSSO's 8th Round, the percentage of area leased-out was estimated at 20.6 per cent and 35–40 per cent of the total cultivated area has been leased-out on the basis of oral or hidden tenancy. The average share of leased-in area showed a sudden increase in 2012–2013 and is possibly due to the declining interest of cultivator farmers on account of declining profitability and better income opportunities outside the agriculture, among other reasons.

The terms of lease have changed with ease against share-of-produce slowly losing importance and fixed money as a term-of-lease increasingly gaining popularity. In Kerala, the prospects of expansion of lease farming by promotion of small-scale lease farming and not large-scale CF was studied by Nair and Menon (2006). They found that with the participation of SHGs and panchayats, the opportunities for improving performance of agriculture, generation of income and employment has widened. However, there is fear that the entry of large farmers into the lease market may further capitalist development in the agricultural sector (Murty, 2004).

BENEFITS OF LAND LEASING

Agricultural land leasing is beneficial on several fronts—improving productivity, access to credit and crop insurance to lease holders and better utilization of land and labour. Second, leasing land would help a company keen on foraying into agriculture or expand their existing business without the high-capital cost of purchasing land. For the land-owner also, it will provide a steady income from land without actually farming. They can engage in non-agricultural activities to get some more income. In addition, small farmers leasing-out land in favour of the medium and large farmers will boost agricultural production and increase employment. A few have also advocated land leasing under the assumption that enterprises would capture the advantages of economies of scale and increase operational holding.

IMPETUS TO ENCOURAGE LAND LEASING

With land acquisition becoming difficult due to stiff political opposition and farmer resistance, land leasing could be one of the best alternatives. As small-scale farming is becoming unviable, leasing farmland by farmers can provide them an assured income. Government's repeated failed efforts to alter the Land Acquisition Act, 2013, passed in Parliament. The negative effects of fragmented smallholdings on production can be avoided with consolidation of holdings, as it is widely practised in Punjab. To promote export and processing, where the lessor and lessee can profit as well as the existing workers, can be absorbed into the processing unit dispelling fears of displacement. Legalization of leasing would increase occupational mobility of people; it would improve the availability of land in the lease market and also poor people's accessibility to land through leasing. It would discourage land being kept fallow and result in better utilization of land and labour and increase farm output. It would promote both farm and non-farm development by improving the landowner's ability and incentives to invest. In recent years, a large number of corporate houses like Essar group, TATA Group, Reliance, ITC have begun investing in the flower sector.

LAND LEASE PRACTICES IN STUDY AREAS

In Karnataka and Telangana, the land leasing is allowed to certain categories of landowners such as those suffering from physical or mental disabilities, widows, unmarried, separated or divorced women, members of the armed forces. In Punjab and Haryana, the land leasing is not explicitly prohibited but the tenant acquires the right to purchase the land from the owner after specified period of creation of tenancy. In AP, there is no legal ban on leasing. But there are several restrictions for leasing. In this state, the leasing is for a minimum period of six years and tenancy can be terminated only by applying to the special judicial officer on any of the specific grounds. In Andhra area of AP, sharecropping tenancy is permitted (Table 7.2).

LAND LEASING IN KARNATAKA

There are no instances of leasing of farmers' land to the companies in a formal way. However, there are quite a number of government agencies taking the land on lease from other departments. For instance, the Karnataka State Warehousing Corporation has taken about 663 acres of land on lease from the agriculture, horticulture and sericulture departments in 72 locations for construction of scientific warehouses

Table 7.2 *Existing Land Lease Policies in Our Selected States*

State	Lease Policies
AP (Andhra Area)	In AP, there is no legal ban on leasing. But there are several restrictions for leasing. In this state, the leasing is for a minimum period of six years and tenancy can be terminated only by applying to the special judicial officer on any of the specific grounds. In 2011, the AP government enacted the Licensed Cultivators Act which made informal tenants eligible for loan eligibility cards with which they get credit, inputs subsidies and crop insurance.
Karnataka and Telangana	The land leasing is allowed to certain categories of landowners such as those suffering from physical or mental disabilities, widows, unmarried, separated or divorced women and members of the armed forces.
Punjab and Haryana	The land leasing is not explicitly prohibited but the tenant acquires the right to purchase the land from the owner after specified period of creation of tenancy.

(Karnataka Agri-Business and Food Processing Policy 2015), Karnataka Public Land Corporation Ltd, a fully government owned company established in 2008, can also lease land to the government.

Karnataka State Horticulture Development (KSHD) is in possession of 410 farms and nurseries spread across the state. The total extent of land under these farms and nurseries was around 5,560 ha out of which only 3,672 ha of land was cultivated and the remaining 1,888 ha remain unused. KSHDA has already bid out 13 of its farms to be developed under a Public-private partnership framework and intends to bid out 43 farms on the same line. In addition, it has identified around 43 sites across 21 districts that have potential for development through Private Sector Participation.

Under section 109 of the KLRA, provision was made to grant exception to acquire land by non-agriculturists for industrial purposes, educational institutions, places of worship, a housing project or horticulture including floriculture or an agro-based industry. At present, there is a provision to lease agricultural land for aquaculture for a period of 20 years in the districts of Dakshina Kannada, Kannada and Uttar Kannada up to 40 units (around 220 acres). Up to 180 acres of D-class land can be leased to a housing project; up to 21.6 acres can be leased for educational institution. Up to 108 acres of D-class-government land can be leased to a housing project. Up to 108 acres of D-class-government land can be leased for horticulture, floriculture and agro-based industries.

In 2012, the state government decided to amend the KLRA, 1974 to allow farmers to lease out their agricultural land to private agro-companies, who in turn adopt innovative technologies to increase yield on the leased land. The proposal was recently cleared by the State Cabinet and an amendment bill tabled in the next legislature session. In 2015, the Land Revenue Amendment Bill was passed empowering the deputy commissioner in the districts to double the area of land that can be acquired by non-agriculturists for industrial, educational, religious, housing and horticulture purposes from the existing 20, 4, 1, 10 and 20 units, respectively.

At present, the KLRA, 1974 bars leasing-out agricultural land. It was not clear whether this bill got the government nod or not. Once the amendments are in place, farmers can lease out their land to agro-companies for a specified period. Cultivation and harvest of the farm produce will have to be taken up by the private players. At the same time, agro-companies entering into the lease will have to utilize value added services in agriculture such as hi-tech cultivation and precision farming to increase the yield on the leased land. On their part, farmers will retain the ownership of land through the agreement period and can also seek fixed rent for the land holding.

The State's latest step towards corporatization of agriculture has been the proposal to amend the KLRA of 1961. The bill also plans to allow 'agro-based industries and agri-infrastructure entities to hold private-agricultural land on long-term lease basis for agribusiness activities subject to certain conditions'. The bill was slated to be tabled in June 2013; however, it was withdrawn owing to pressure from farmers' groups. The bill increases CF, allowing corporate to lease large tracts of land from farmers.

EXAMPLES OF LAND-LEASE PRACTICES IN KARNATAKA

Since 1961, the forest lands were released to the revenue department which subsequently leased those to the Tibetan refugees for taking up agriculture. The extent of land leased out was about 6,142.25 ha. As these forest lands do not have Record of Rights, Tenancy and Crop Information (RTC), cultivators were deprived of agriculture-related subsidies by the state, incentives from the government and loans from banks. Acknowledging the problems faced by Tibetan cultivators, the state government agreed to issue RTC with certain conditions imposed by the revenue department. 'Neither the Central Tibetan Relief Committee nor any of the individual Tibetans would be eligible to transfer, lease, mortgage or pledge the leased lands to any institution or individual. They are also required to pay annual lease amount to the revenue department as decided by the government.

Around Nagarahole forest area, about 350 tribal families living on fringes of the forest were provided four acres of land per family to enable them to shift to agriculture. These farmers have instead leased-out their land for ginger cultivation against the land-granted rules. The lease amount ranged from ₹15,000 to ₹20,000 an acre. The lease is an oral agreement under which money changes hand and ginger is cultivated. Similarly, ginger cultivation has been adopted in HD Kote taluk on 12,000 acres. The Kerala Contractors entered into an oral agreement with the farmers for a fixed rate of rent ranging from ₹60,000 to ₹80,000 per acre per 18 months. The landowner also works on a daily wage for the contractor to whom they have leased-out land to earn extra income.

All categories of farmers including SC and ST were given land on lease even though they were not supposed to leaseout the land as per land grants provided by the government. The practice of this arrange-ment seems to be beneficial as the farmers had earlier experienced uncertainty in growing commercial crops, increasing cost of cultivation and uncertainty of incomes. This informal system has led to several consequences, namely, (a) The tribal people, the SC and ST are not supposed to lease-out the granted land; (b) the crops grown consume large volumes of water and (c) use of heavy, toxic pesticides on the farms and the run-off of water from these lands enter the water bodies affecting the human health, water bodies and ecology downstream. Karnataka Renewable Energy Policy allows leasing of land by farmers for 30 years for making of power generation. In Haryana and Punjab, there are several examples as well; private investors were permitted to set up projects related to renewable sources of energy on farmer-owned land leased for a period of 25 years.

AP LAND LEASING

In 2011, the AP government enacted the Licensed Cultivators Act which made informal tenants eligible for loan eligibility cards (LECs), with which they get credit, inputs, subsidies and crop insurance. In AP, Land Licenced Cultivators Act was introduced in 2011 with an objective of helping the tenant to obtain bank credit. As per the Act, the tenant is entitled to get LECs. The only condition is that the tenant has to enter into a formal contract agreement with the landowner in order to get a loan. However, only a few landowners are willing to sign a tenancy deed with a rent cultivator as they fear loss of their land-ownership in the future. This is clear from the number of lease-licensed cultivators in the state. Of the 17 lakh tenants in the state, only 5.5 lakh (35%) of the tenant farmers received LECs as of 2015.

According to agriculture-department officials, 1.31 lakh tenant farmers are engaged in agriculture in Krishna district and 18,000 LECs have been issued. Towards streamlining land tenancy, the agriculture department and revenue department officials should conduct village-level meets to certify the tenancy and sanction the LEC to eligible farmers. Vijay and Sreenivasulu (2013) investigated the land-lease arrangements in nine villages of AP and found that canal-irrigated areas have a high extent of land under tenancy with fixed rent contracts and the demand for land comes from the poor peasantry, with a significant proportion of landless labour also entering the land-lease market in contrast to non-canal irrigated areas. The presence of non-cultivating peasant households in rural areas and tenancy contracts were witnessed as the dominant institution for resource adjustment which can secure the long-run-agricultural growth and development of the economy.

LAND SHARING

According to Panagariya (2008) and Pitale (2007), land leasing and land sharing systems were favoured, respectively. Under the land sharing, the farmers' land will be given to the company (agricultural holding company) against the shares. Either the company cultivates or the farmer. The company will produce, process the agricultural crops or allied-sector activities. The farmers are the shareholders in the company. If the farmer cultivates, they get fixed rent. Such companies are managed by the board of directors elected by the shareholders or they may also appoint the experts. Each shareholder will receive a share in the profit of the company. The shares are transferable to the successor of the shareholders, not for others and not to be traded in the market otherwise the non-agriculturists buy them.

EVOLUTION OF LAND SHARING IN INDIA

Singh et al. (2015) found some scope of intervention of land-sharing company in agricultural sector in India. However, in reality, land-share concept does not exist in India. It is a viable option for small and marginal farmers who account for more than 80 per cent of land holding to manage agricultural production professionally with their limited capacity and reach. They also state that land-sharing company will not only provide economy of scale but will also facilitate forward and backward linkages to production system. It could also be possible for the farmers to float a land share, agro-processing company in which the farmers will have the option to become a shareholder of that company in proportion to their size of holdings. It is expected that the development of such companies will trigger agricultural and non-agricultural development in rural areas. To promote these companies, some concessional credit and other investment subsidies should be allowed by the local government or NGOs.

CASE STUDIES OF CF FIRMS

In our field survey, we also prepared a questionnaire for the contract companies and canvassed with the companies we selected for our household survey. We approached a number of companies in our selected four states. Despite our repeated visits and persuasion, companies were hesitant in providing information. They initially asked us to mail the questionnaire and promised to send the filled questionnaire later. However, despite repeated request and even continual visits of our field team, most of them refused to divulge with the information asked in the questionnaire. The companies were so hesitant that many of them did not even provide the list of farmers whom we intended to survey later. Somehow on our persuasion, only few of them filled up the questionnaire and handed over to our team.

The information obtained from seven contracting firms reveals that selection of villages by the firms were based on proximity, availability of water, field and crop quality, while selection of farmers was based on their reliability, integrity and economic stability (Tables 7.3 and 7.4). The choice of crops was based on market demand as well as the suitability of soil for the crops that were grown. Some findings of this survey resonated with those from a case study on land leasing in west region of Ireland (Conway, 1986).

The produce procured from the contracting farmers was based on a pre-announced MSP negotiated by taking into account the expected price of processed product and international market price (Global Green). While Technico Agri Sciences Ltd (in Punjab and Haryana) fixed the price based on a pre-announced MSP and their arbitrary information to cover the cost of inputs and extension services provided. None of the companies surveyed provide crop insurance as part of the terms and conditions of the contract. On the positive side, the prices of inputs provided by all the companies were lower than those prevailing in the market, giving the farmers an impetus to participate in contract arrangements rather than independently produced commodities.

Among the interviewed companies, the percentage of breakdown of contract agreements were below 10 per cent and in the event of a breach of contract, the disputes were settled in court (Global Green Co.) mutually between company and farmer (Bharat Agro Hybrid Seeds Co.), at the head office (Technico Agri Science Ltd), etc. Most often, such breakdown in contract agreements occur when the market price is higher than the prior agreed price of purchase. Rejections of produce by the companies were primarily as a result of erroneous or inappropriate grading and not adhering to the standards prescribed or surplus produce supplied. In the latter case, farmers sell their surplus produce at the nearest *mandi*/local-open market.

Common constraints faced by the companies surveyed include—use of non-approved pesticides by farmers; not complying to fertigation schedule; untimely harvesting of crop, not as per stipulated timing; low yield due to poor practices and quality of produce is not given adequate importance by market dealers.

Apart from raw materials, Global Green also partially provided micro irrigation in the terms of contract. Other inputs given to the farmers in 2016–2017 were fertilizers and pesticides to the tune of 58,229 kgs worth ₹10,011,145. The final raw materials purchased by the company in 2016–2017 amounted to 9,632,425 kgs of gherkins worth ₹89,662,993 and 40,070 kgs of jalapeños worth ₹636,024.

In their suggestions, Global Green urged the government to provide support for training farmers on implementation of pesticide protocols as per the package of practices (POP) provided by the company. The common goal stated by the interviewed companies were to expand the area under cultivation given their success.

APPREHENSIONS FROM SMALL FARMERS' PERSPECTIVE

Crop productivity may be limited by geographic or biophysical constraints such as insufficient water for irrigation and limited access to productive assets (e.g., livestock, labour, tools) constraining their capacity to generate a marketable surplus. CF sponsors could be monopsonistic or oligopsonistic and enjoy contractual bargaining power over farmers resulting in firms extracting most of the gains from trade. In extreme cases, firms can also blacklist growers who try to organize resistance against unfair practices. Institutional constraints such as limited access to credit and insurance, insecure land rights and uncertainty regarding new risks could further reduce the feasibility and attractiveness of participation in various tenancy arrangements.

SHORTCOMINGS IN CF ARRANGEMENTS

In the existing models of CF, in the early years, farmers benefit from improved technology and higher productivity, quality and production. However, when the market price is more advantageous than the contract price, farmers have a tendency to renege on the contract and the present legal systems make it impossible to enforce the performance under contract. CF models can sustain in the long run only if the initiative/empowerment comes from the farmers rather than the user (corporate). In the existing models, farmers are largely 'price takers', while the contracting firm 'makes' the price. There is low generation of employment, labour-saving farm practices, low level of commitment of corporate over rural development, lack of transparency and communication, etc. Enforceability of the agreement, and standardization and operationalization of CF agreements are the major bottlenecks plaguing CF ventures in India.

SHORTCOMINGS OF EXISTING LEASE PRACTICES IN INDIA

The following are the shortcomings of existing lease practices in India: Insecurity of landownership, that is, fear of losing ownership of land when leased to corporates; unofficial leasing causing inadequate rental payments as per market values, for example, in states where land leasing is permitted, the farmers were receiving ₹20,000 rent per acre, whereas in UP the farmers were receiving only ₹7,000, as land leasing is not an 'officially formal practice in this state; no benefits to either of the contracting parties, for example, if the value of the land increases during the lease period, the farmers do not derive that benefit and, similarly, when the produce is less than expected, the company incurs losses; intermodal non-compliance of tenancy arrangements by either one of the parties; and large retailers such as Walmart and Tesco have increased the amount of purchases acquired directly from the growers under long-term contracts; and this increase in trade through supermarkets and retail outlet has resulted in drastic damage to ecology.

Table 7.3 Salient Features of Interviewed Contract Firms

Firm	Prabhat Seed Traders	Bharat Agro Hybrid Seeds Co.	Dhariwal Seeds Pvt. Ltd	Hari Bhumi Seeds	Technico Agri Science Ltd	Beauscape	Global Green Co. Ltd
Location	Haryana	Haryana	Haryana	Haryana	Chandigarh (Punjab and Haryana)	Punjab	Telangana, AP and Karnataka
Year of registration	1997	2015	2008	2013	*	2008	1999
Ownership of firm	Partnership	Private Ltd Co.	Private Ltd Co.	Proprietorship	Private Ltd Co.	*	Private Ltd Co.
No. of employees	8	11	*	7	*	36	132
No. of extension staff	10	2	2	7	8	3	32
Total turnover (per annum)	Over ₹10 Crores	₹1.5 crores	*	₹1.5 crores	*	₹7 crores	₹100 crores

Source: Primary data.
Note: *Data not provided.

Table 7.4 *Types of Operational Features*

Firm	Crop Type	No. of Farmers	Area (in Acres)	Contract Area	Seeds/Raw Material	
					Qty (Kgs)	Value (₹)
Prabhat Seed Traders	Mustard	10	50	5	7.5	1,500
	Moong	5	25	*	*	*
	Gwar	3	10	*	*	*
Bharat Agro Hybrid Seeds Co.	Wheat	80	2,000	2,000	86,000	4,500,000
Dhariwal Seeds Pvt. Ltd	Wheat	12	200	*	*	*
Hari Bhumi Seeds	Wheat	50	300	200	40	8,000/kg
	Mustard	5	25	200	1.5	30/kg
	Moong	10	50	60	5	250/kg
	Gwar	10	50	25	5	125/kg
	Arhar	10	50	25	5	125/kg
Technico Agri Science Ltd	Potato	100	1,100	*	*	*
Beauscape	–	–	–	*	*	*
Global Green Co. Ltd	Gherkin	3,635	4,294	4,294	43,037,718	26,145,377
	Jalapeño	51	72	72		

Source: Author's own primary survey data.
Note: * Data not provided.

SUMMARY

The Indian rural economic structure is witnessing changes and to sustain an agrarian economy that ensures food and nutrition security, raw material for its expanding industrial base, surpluses for exports, equitable rewarding system for the farming community, 'commitment-driven' CF and leasing are postulated as viable alternative models of farming.

Unlike the earlier unhealthy relationship that existed between the landlord and tenant, with the latter having no say in the terms of tenancy, today the relationship has evolved into a partnership. Another emerging factor has been that all land-holding categories of farmers from small to medium and large are also leasing-in/leasing-out land to adequately and efficiently use their technical inputs and for optimal utilization of capital resources. In addition, 'occupancy tenancy' has moved to 'tenancy at will' for a fixed period of time and rentals are paid in cash annually.

Several Indian and multinational companies, briefly discussed in the preceding sections, have demonstrated repeated success. These forms of tenancy have provided assured and reliable input service to farmers and desired produce to the contracting firms. The studies also found that contractual design attributes play a key role in farmers' motivation to participate in these land-tenancy arrangements. Therefore, institutional intervention in the input market could induce agribusiness firms to offer attractive contracts for smallholders. In addition, consolidation of farmers through Farmer Producer Organizations (FPOs), cooperatives and SHGs can enhance firm-farm coordination and balance bargaining power between the contracting parties that has been a concern for most farmers.

These successful cases should encourage the rest of the producing and the consuming enterprises to emulate them for mutual benefits. Moving forward, micro assessments across agro-ecological regions need to be conducted to invest in avenues that sustainably utilize human and natural resources with appropriate technologies to improve livelihoods. Subsequently, based on these assessments, policy and legal formulations will incentivize farmers and firms to engage in long-tenure contracts/leases.

Chapter 8

Contract versus Non-contract Agricultural Wage Workers

Literature on CF is mainly focused on the issues of farming households and there is paucity of studies paying attention to issues related to agricultural labourers working on crops produced for CF. This chapter fills this gap as it attempts to look on the agricultural wage workers' side also. The chapter is completely based on primary survey. Data was collected from the four selected states namely, AP (including Telangana), Haryana, Punjab and Karnataka. In the aggregate, 100 agricultural wage-worker households, comprising 50 contract farm wage workers and 50 non-contract, farm-wage workers were selected. Contract-farm-wage workers are those who had worked in contract farms during some months of the year (as less than half of the GCA was under contract for most of the selected farmers) and non-contract agricultural wage workers are mainly involved in the farms which do not have any contract with a company.

To select the sample, it involved some specific steps to reach to the sample population. During the farmers' survey, these wage workers were randomly selected from contract and non-contract farms. This procedure of selecting sample is called 'convenience sampling'. In addition to that, some agricultural workers were contacted through recommendation of peer workers. This process of finding sample population is called 'snowball sampling technique'. It was tried to maintain the 50:50 ratio for contract and non-contract agricultural wage workers but the actual figures are a little different from the original ratio. In the aggregate, 234 were from contract group and 150 were from the non-contract group. Table 8.1 provides the details of numbers of the wage workers.

Table 8.1 Details of Respondents and Household Characteristics of Wage Workers

	AP		Haryana		Punjab		Karnataka		Aggregate	
No. of Respondents/ Households	Contract	Non-contract	Contract	Non-contract	Contract	Non-contract	Contract	Non-contract	Contract	Non-contract
	50	47	77	25	57	28	50	50	234	150
Status of the Respondent										
1. Head of the HH	88.00	87.23	89.61	88.00	73.68	82.14	98.00	90.00	87.18	87.33
2. Member of the household	12.00	12.77	10.39	12.00	26.32	17.86	2.00	10.00	12.82	12.67
Gender of the Head of HH										
1. Male	90.00	95.74	93.51	80	98.25	96.43	80.00	90.00	91.03	91.33
2. Female	10.00	4.26	6.49	20	1.75	3.57	20.00	10.00	8.97	8.67
Respondent's age (years)	40.9	40.8	40.6	38.3	37.0	43.5	47.9	46.4	41.4	42.8
Respondent's Education Status										
1. Non-literate	62.00	63.83	40.26	32.00	49.12	53.57	66.00	70.00	52.56	59.06
2. Up to primary	18.00	12.77	37.66	24.00	31.58	21.43	24.00	10.00	29.06	15.44
3. Up to secondary	20.00	23.40	22.08	44.00	19.3	25.00	8.00	20.00	17.95	25.50
4. Up to graduate	0	0	0	0	0	0	0	0	0	0
5. Above graduate	0	0	0	0	0	0	2.00	0	0.43	0

Respondent's Caste

1. SC	18.00	68.09	72.73	80.00	66.67	60.71	44.00	54.00	53.42	64.00
2. ST	0	0	9.09	0	1.75	17.86	10.00	14.00	5.56	8.00
3. OBC	74.00	27.66	12.99	8.00	26.32	17.86	36.00	18.00	34.19	19.33
4. General	8.00	4.26	5.19	12.00	5.26	3.57	10.00	14.00	6.84	8.67
Average family size	5.08	4.32	5.21	4.84	4.95	5.93	4.24	3.94	4.91	4.58
No. of family members involved in agriculture wage work (per HH)	2.74	2.34	1.43	1.76	1.37	1.68	2.12	2.06	1.84	2.03
No. of family members involved in non-agriculture wage work (per HH)	1.70	2.00	0.25	0.44	0.26	0.82	0.90	1.00	0.70	1.19
No. of family members involved in regular-salaried work (per HH)	0	0.09	0.04	0.04	0.05	0.07	0.22	0.18	0.07	0.11
No. of family members involved in self-business (per HH)	0	0	0.00	0.00	0.04	0.04	0.04	0.04	0.02	0.02
No. of family members involved in other work (per HH)	0.06	0.04	0.03	0.00	0	0	0.04	0	0.03	0.01

This chapter outlines the characteristics and demography of agricultural wage workers and their earning pattern, employment provision under contract and non-contract crops and opinion of labourers about CF as well as their suggestion about the functioning of CF.

CHARACTERISTICS OF AGRICULTURAL WAGE WORKERS

From each state, approx. 100 numbers of wage-worker households were selected. In AP (including Telangana state), 50 were from contract group and 47 were from non-contract group. Similarly, in Haryana, 77 were contract-wage workers and 25 were non-contract-wage workers; in Punjab, 57 and 28 were from contract and non-contract groups, respectively. Karnataka has exactly 50:50 ratio of sample distribution which comprises 50 contract-wage workers and 50 non-contract-wage workers. The status of the respondents indicates that 87 per cent of the respondents in contract group were head of the households and remaining 13 per cent respondents were members of the households. Similarly, in non-contract group also, the percent distribution of the status of respondents was the same.

Across all the states, percentage of head of the household was always above 80 per cent except in Punjab where the status of respondents comprised 74 per cent as head of the household. In the aggregate, gender composition of the respondents comprised 91 per cent male and 9 per cent female in both the groups. In each state, proportion of male respondents was always above 80 per cent. The average age of the respondents was 41.4 years in contract group and 42.8 years in non-contract group. Within each state, age of the respondents was always greater than 40 years, but in the case of non-contract group in Haryana, the average age of the respondents was 38.3 years. In Punjab, the average age of the respondents in contract group was 37 years. The education status of the respondents indicates that 53 and 59 per cent were illiterate in contract group and non-contract group, respectively. Remaining 29 per cent were educated up to primary level and 18 per cent had studied up to secondary level in contract group. Few respondents (0.43%) had studied above graduate level. In non-contract group, 59 per cent of the respondents were illiterate. Remaining 15 per cent had studied up to secondary level and 26 per cent were educated up to graduate level.

Majority of the respondents (more than 80%) belonged to SC and OBC. Contract group consisted of 53.42 per cent of the respondents from SC and 34.19 per cent from OBC category. Similarly, in non-contract group, 64 per cent were from SC and 19.33 per cent from OBC category. The respondents from ST and General category in contract group constituted 5.56 per cent and 6.84 per cent, respectively. In non-contract group, composition of ST and General category constituted 8 per cent and 8.67 per cent, respectively. The average family size in contract group was 4.91 in which 1.84 members were involved in agricultural wage work, 0.70 member were involved in non-agricultural wage work and 0.07 members were involved in regular-salaried work while 0.03 members were involved in self-business and other work, each. Whereas average family size of non-contract group was slightly lower than the contract group. The non-contract group had average family size of 4.58 members in which 2.03 members were involved in agricultural wage work, 1.19 members were involved in non-agricultural wage work, 0.11 members in salaried work, 0.02 members in self-business and 0.01 members were involved in other works. The members involved in different activities are not mutually exclusive and in the case of non-contract group of AP, subtotal of members involved in different activities were slightly higher by 0.15 members as compared to average size of the family.

MAN-DAYS AND EARNING IN CONTRACT AND NON-CONTRACT AGRICULTURAL WAGE WORK

It has been found that the numbers of man-days generated in contract farms in a year are comparatively higher than non-contract farms in AP and Karnataka for male as well as female. In the case of Haryana and Punjab, data for non-contract agricultural wage workers was not collected but these states had higher man-days in contract farms as compared to AP and Karnataka in the case of male labour. Overall, female man-days were lower as compared to male man-days under contract-farm category but under non-contract-farm category female man-days were comparatively higher than male in a year. The above comparison indicates that the contract-farm crops were more labour intensive and it required more male labour.

The wages income earned by the male labourers in a year in the contract farm was almost four times as compared to non-contract agricultural worker's annual wage income. This indicates a great potential in CF to create more employment and income for the agricultural wage workers under CF. Females also earned more wages as compared to non-contract agricultural wage workers but they had less opportunities to work in contract farms as compared to male wage workers. Wage rate for male and female did not vary significantly between contract- and non-contract-farm workers. Male labourers earned lesser wage in contract farms but female labourers earned slightly more wage under contract farms in a year. Table 8.2 shows average man-days and wages earned by male and female labourers in a year under contract and non-contract farms.

MAN-DAYS AND EARNING FROM OTHER ACTIVITIES FOR CONTRACT AND NON-CONTRACT HOUSEHOLDS

It is observed from Table 8.2 that wages earned by contract agricultural wage workers were higher than non-contract-wage workers, but wages earned from other activities were higher among non-contract-wage workers. This is an obvious reason that the non-contract workers would be devoting their time and effort in other activities such as non-agricultural wage work, self-business, jobs in service sector and other activities.

Therefore, it will be interesting to compare whether wages/salary earned in other activities are greater than the wages earned in contract farms. In this study, it is observed that the total income from agricultural and non-agricultural activities of contract-wage workers was higher than non-contract-wage workers. The contract-wage-worker households earned an average annual income of ₹75,017 and non-contract-wage workers earned total income of ₹50,330 per year. It is also interesting to note that whereas in Karnataka and AP, wage work was evenly distributed among sowing, caring/weeding and harvesting activities, in Punjab and Haryana, the major concentration of work was in the case of caring/weeding, etc., as sowing and harvesting work were mainly performed through machines in these two states. Table 8.3 gives details of earning from other activities by contract and non-contract wage-worker households.

Table 8.2 Average Man-Days and Wages Earned by Male and Female Labourers in a Year under Contract and Non-contract Farms

Man-days (per HH) for Agricultural Wage Work for Males in a Year

	AP		Haryana		Punjab		Karnataka		Aggregate	
	Contract	Non-contract	Contract	Non-contract	Contract	Non-contract	Contract	Non-contract	Contract	Non-contract
Sowing/transplanting	36	11	56	0	111	0	23	11	58	11
Caring/weeding, etc.	17	6	166	0	246	0	27	13	124	10
Harvesting/threshing	57	16	9	0	6	0	35	20	24	18
Marketing	2	0	0	0	0	0	7	5	2	3
Others	0	0	0	0	0	0	0	0	0	0
Total man-days	112	34	231	0	364	0	91	48	208	41

Man-days (per HH) for Agricultural Wage Work for Females in a Year

	AP		Haryana		Punjab		Karnataka		Aggregate	
	Contract	Non-contract	Contract	Non-contract	Contract	Non-contract	Contract	Non-contract	Contract	Non-contract
Sowing/transplanting	53	13	4	0	0	0	28	21	19	17
Caring/weeding, etc.	51	9	10	0	0	0	30	23	20	16
Harvesting/threshing	78	13	0	0	0	0	31	24	23	18

(Table 8.2 Continued)

(Table 8.2 Continued)

Man-days (per HH) for Agricultural Wage Work for Males in a Year										
	AP		Haryana		Punjab		Karnataka		Aggregate	
	Contract	Non-contract	Contract	Non-contract	Contract	Non-contract	Contract	Non-contract	Contract	Non-contract
Marketing	0	0	0	0	0	0	0	0	0	0
Others	0	0	0	0	0	0	0	0	0	0
Total man-days	182	35	14	0	0	0	88	67	62	52
Earning (₹/HH) from Agricultural Wage Work for Males in a Year										
Sowing/ transplanting	8,965 (33.47)	2,681 (32.87)	12,990 (24.89)	0	24,453 (36.79)	0	7,200 (25.17)	3,179 (21.43)	13,685 (30.27)	2,938 (25.33)
Caring/weeding, etc.	4,245 (15.85)	1,676 (20.55)	36,740 (70.39)	0	40,789 (61.37)	0	8,280 (28.95)	3,899 (26.28)	24,702 (54.65)	2,822 (24.33)
Harvesting/ threshing	12,913 (48.2)	3,799 (46.58)	2,468 (4.73)	0	1,228 (1.85)	0	10,774 (37.67)	6,187 (41.71)	6,172 (13.65)	5,030 (43.37)
Marketing	666 (2.49)	0 (0)	0 (0)	0	0 (0)	0	2,349 (8.21)	1,570 (10.58)	644 (1.43)	809 (6.98)
Total earning	26,789 (100)	8,155 (100)	52,197 (100)	0	66,470 (100)	0	28,603 (100)	14,835 (100)	45,203 (100)	11,598 (100)

Note: Figures in parentheses indicate % share of income from different activities.

Earning (₹/HH) from Agricultural Wage Work for Females in a Year

Sowing/ transplanting	9,546 (28.52)	2,209 (34.76)	1,052 (33.33)	0	0	4,689 (31.55)	3,422 (30.22)	3,388 (29.81)	2,834 (31.79)
Caring/weeding, etc.	9,272 (27.7)	1,617 (25.45)	2,104 (66.67)	0	0	4,819 (32.43)	3,806 (33.61)	3,703 (32.58)	2,746 (30.8)
Harvesting/ threshing	14,654 (43.78)	2,528 (39.79)	0 (0)	0	0	5,353 (36.02)	4,096 (36.17)	4,275 (37.61)	3,336 (37.42)
Marketing	0 (0)	0 (0)	0 (0)	0	0	0 (0)	0 (0)	0 (0)	0 (0)
Total earning	33,472 (100)	6,353 (100)	3,156 (100)	0	0	14,861 (100)	11,324 (100)	11,366 (100)	8,915 (100)

Note: Figures in parentheses indicate the % share of earning from different activities

(Table 8.2 Continued)

(Table 8.2 Continued)

Male Wage Rate

Sowing/transplanting	248	238	230	0	221	0	319	300	236	269
Caring/weeding, etc.	256	258	222	0	166	0	312	306	200	290
Harvesting/threshing	227	236	286	0	192	0	310	310	257	278
Marketing	282	0	0	0	0	0	320	320	311	320
Average wage rate	239	241	226	0	183	0	314	308	217	281

Female Wage Rate

Sowing/transplanting	181	168	261	0	0	0	166	167	182	167
Caring/weeding, etc.	183	171	216	0	0	0	163	168	182	169
Harvesting/threshing	187	198	0	0	0	0	175	174	184	182
Marketing	0	0	0	0	0	0	0	0	0	0
Average wage rate	184	180	229	0	0	0	168	170	182	173

Table 8.3 *Earning and Man-Days from Other Activities by Contract and Non-contract Wage-Worker Households*

	AP		Haryana		Punjab		Karnataka		Aggregate	
	Contract	Non-contract	Contract	Non-contract	Contract	Non-contract	Contract	Non-contract	Contract	Non-contract
Earning (₹ per HH per Year) for Males in other Activities										
Earning in salaried/ fixed lump-sum work	0	2,299	2,806	2,404	1,054	7,718	11,762	18,842	3,693	8,841
Earning in non-agricultural wage work	14,866	16,963	7,227	13,980	3,667	22,643	12,435	13,870	9,105	16,495
Earning in self-business	0	0	1,558	0	1,754	1,286	1,300	2,520	1,218	1,080
Earning in other activities	3,040	1,191	1,494	720	0	0	600	0	1,269	493
Total earning	17,906	20,454	13,086	17,104	6,475	31,646	26,097	35,232	15,285	26,909
Earning (₹ per HH per year) for Females in Other Activities										
Earning in salaried/ fixed lump-sum work	0	0	0	0	0	0	4,802	0	1,026	0
Earning in non-agricultural wage work	5,050	5,957	1,299	0	1,039	1,679	688	2,180	1,906	2,907

(Table 8.3 Continued)

(Table 8.3 Continued)

Earning (₹ per HH per Year) for Males in other Activities										
	AP		Haryana		Punjab		Karnataka		Aggregate	
	Contract	Non-contract	Contract	Non-contract	Contract	Non-contract	Contract	Non-contract	Contract	Non-contract
Earning in self-business	0	0	0	0	351	0	0	0	85	0
Earning in other activities	0	0	0	0	0	0	680	0	145	0
Total earning	5,050	5,957	1,299	0	1,389	1,679	6,170	2,180	3,163	2,907
Total income (₹/HH) from other activities (including male and female)	22,956	26,411	14,384	17,104	7,865	33,325	32,267	37,412	18,448	29,816
Total income (₹/HH) from agricultural wage work (including male and female)	60,261	14,509	55,353	0	66,470	0	43,464	26,159	56,569	20,514
Total income (₹/HH)	83,217	40,920	69,738	17,104	74,335	33,325	75,731	63,571	75,017	50,330

Man-days (per HH per year) for Males in Other Activities

Man-days in salaried/fixed lump-sum work	0	28	14	15	19	11	46	62	19	34
Man-days in non-agricultural wage work	56	80	25	54	15	98	47	52	34	69
Man-days in self-business	0	0	5	0	6	11	15	14	6	7
Man-days in other activities	16	8	5	2	0	0	7	0	7	3
Total man-days	71	116	49	71	41	120	114	128	66	113

Man-days (per HH per year) for Females in Other Activities

Man-days in salaried/fixed lump-sum work	0	0	0	0	0	0	21	0	4	0
Man-days in non-agricultural wage work	33	39	7	0	17	10	4	14	14	19
Man-days in self-business	0	0	0	0	3	0	0	0	1	0
Man-days in other activities	0	0	0	0	0	0	3	0	1	0
Total man-days	33	39	7	0	20	10	28	14	20	19

Table 8.4 Income from Other Sources and Expenditure of Contract and Non-contract Wage-Worker Households in a Year

Income from Other Sources (₹/HH) in the Reference Year										
	AP		Haryana		Punjab		Karnataka		Aggregate	
Source/item	Contract	Non-contract	Contract	Non-contract	Contract	Non-contract	Contract	Non-contract	Contract	Non-contract
1. Rent from leasing out of land	760	383	0	400	0	79,643	400	0	248	15,053
2. Rent from leasing out of agricultural implements	0	0	0	0	0	0	0	0	0	0
3. Rent from house	0	0	0	0	0	0	0	0	0	0
4. Interest on lending	0	0	0	0	0	0	0	0	0	0
5. Old-age/widow pension	5,400	4,085	2,213	2,304	211	100	2,513	2,088	2,470	2,379
6. Other pensions	0	0	325	768	439	0	120	0	239	128
7. Remittances received	0	0	0	0	0	0	360	0	77	0
8. Any other receipts	0	0	1,558	0	0	0	0	0	513	0
Total income from other sources	6,160	4,468	4,096	3,472	649	79,743	3,393	2,088	3,547	17,560

Expenditure (non-consumption) in ₹/HH

1. Repair of house	3,054 (32.00)	1,723 (30.59)	6,558 (11.46)	8,208 (12.85)	8,070 (18.97)	8,893 (18.95)	710 (5.75)	1,300 (69.15)	4,928 (14.55)	4,001 (18.35)
2. Repair/servicing/ maintenance of agricultural implements	200 (2.10)	21 (0.38)	0 (0)	3,440 (5.38)	0 (0)	0 (0)	0 (0)	0 (0)	43 (0.13)	580 (2.66)
3. Repair/servicing/ maintenance of other productive assets	200 (2.10)	0 (0)	0 (0)	0 (0)	877 (2.06)	0 (0)	0 (0)	0 (0)	256 (0.76)	0 (0)
4. Other heads of expenditure	0 (0)	0 (0)	0 (0)	0 (0)	0 (0)	0 (0)	0 (0)	0 (0)	0 (0)	0 (0)
(i) *Malgujari*/tax	179 (1.88)	205 (3.64)	0 (0)	0 (0)	0 (0)	0 (0)	130 (1.05)	0 (0)	66 (0.19)	64 (0.3)
(ii) Health, education, marriage, vehicle purchase	5,910 (61.93)	3,683 (65.38)	50,672 (88.54)	52,244 (81.77)	33,596 (78.97)	38,036 (81.05)	11,498 (93.19)	580 (30.85)	28,578 (84.37)	17,155 (78.69)
Total expenditure for non-consumption	9,543 (100)	5,633 (100)	57,231 (100)	63,892 (100)	42544 (100)	46,929 (100)	12,338 (100)	1,880 (100)	33,871 (100)	21,800 (100)

INCOME FROM OTHER SOURCES AND EXPENDITURE (NON-CONSUMPTION) OF WAGE-WORKER HOUSEHOLDS

Incomes obtained from different sources are higher in contract-wage workers as compared to non-contract-wage workers except in the case of Punjab. (Table 8.4) In Punjab, rent from leasing-out land contributed to a much higher income as compared to other sources. However, other sources income was not much significant amount as compared to total income coming from agricultural and non-agricultural activities. In the case of contract-farm labourers, it constituted only 4.73 per cent of the total income from agricultural and non-agricultural activities. However, in the case of non-contract-wage workers, the incomes from other sources added up significant amount to the total income coming from agricultural and non-agricultural activities. It added 34.75 per cent of more income to the total income. Comparing the expenditure side, it is interesting to see that contract-wage workers were spending more in non-consumption items such as education, health, marriage, vehicles, etc. They spent ₹33,871 per annum for non-consumption items. It constitutes 84.37 per cent of the total expenditure. Non-contract-wage workers spent ₹21,800 per annum on non-consumption items and 78.69 per cent of it was spent on education, health, marriage, vehicles, etc. Hence, the purchasing power of contract-wage workers was comparatively more than non-contract-wage workers.

AREA DETAILS OF WORKPLACE AND CONTRACT DETAILS

The area of operation of contract farms is found to be closer to the village and city. Also, the villages where contract farm wage workers were residing was closer to the city. Therefore, it indicates that contract farms were operating closer to the city in comparison with non-contract farms. The reason is quite obvious that contracting companies don't want to incur extra cost of transportation by selecting farmers from remote areas. On the other side, contracting farmers also pick up labourers from the nearest possible village so that it will be easier to call them during emergency. Some contract crops such as jalapeño, gherkin, baby corn, tomato, fresh chilli, etc., require intermittent picking to supply fresh products in the market. To commute to the workplace, about 80 per cent of the labourers go by feet in contract as well as non-contract groups. Approximately 10 per cent use bicycle and remaining 10 per cent use motorbike and public transport or either of the means of transport. In contract farms, 44.02 per cent of the respondents said that they have to sign a contract with the contracting farm. In case of Karnataka and AP, all the respondents said that contracts are signed between them and contracting farmer/agency. In Punjab, only 5.26 per cent of the respondents said that they signed contract with the farmer or agency. None of the respondents reported about signing contract in Haryana. The duration of the contract was found to be 12 months in AP and Karnataka and 8 months in Punjab. The average duration of working in the farms was found to be 11 hours and 9.2 hours in contract and non-contract farms, respectively.

As the labourers are closer to the contract farms, farmers extract more work from the labourers. The service of providing credit facility to the workers was not that much prevalent in contracting farms. Only 10 per cent of the respondents in AP reported that they get credit facility by the farmers or contracting agency and the maximum amount they got was ₹12,000 at a time. Table 8.5 gives details of workplace and other details for contract- and non-contract-labour work.

ASSET VALUE OF THE CONTRACT AND NON-CONTRACT WAGE-WORKERS' HOUSEHOLD

Aggregate assets value of contract-farm wage workers was comparatively higher than non-contract-wage workers. Contract-wage workers owned assets value of ₹8,285 and non-contract-wage workers owned assets value of ₹5,829 during the reference year. More than 50 per cent of the households owned semi-pucca house. The house type did not vary across the contract and non-contract group. Also, it was found that contract-wage workers had relatively less number of respondents who owned agricultural land. The data displays that only 18.80 per cent of the respondents in contract group owned land whereas in non-contract group 24 per cent of the respondents owned agricultural land. However, available land per household in contract group was 1.59 acres and non-contract group possessed 1.19 acres per household. This available acre per household is calculated based on the number of households who owned agricultural land. Toilet facilities were still out

Table 8.5 *Details of Workplace and Contract*

Particulars	AP		Haryana		Punjab		Karnataka		Aggregate	
	Contract	Non-contract	Contract	Non-contract	Contract	Non-contract	Contract	Non-contract	Contract	Non-contract
Average distance of village from city	4.08	2.21	1.55	5.48	4.19	9.96	2.48	2.48	2.93	4.29
Average distance of workplace from the city.	4.94	2.98	2.87	8.16	4.64	11.07	3.90	3.90	3.96	5.66
Average distance of workplace from the residence	0.12	0.13	1.35	6.44	0.49	1.32	0.07	0.06	0.60	1.38
Means of Transport to the Workplace										
1. By feet	72.00	91.49	75.32	48.00	84.21	57.14	98.00	98.00	81.62	80.00
2. Bicycle	12.00	2.13	11.69	20.00	12.28	32.14	2.00	2.00	9.83	10.67
3. Motorbike	10.00	0.00	3.90	0.00	0.00	0.00	0.00	0.00	3.42	0.00
4. Public transport	6.00	6.38	9.09	20.00	0.00	7.14	0.00	0.00	4.27	6.67
5. Feet and bicycle	0.00	0.00	0.00	8.00	3.51	3.57	0.00	0.00	0.85	2.00
6. Bicycle and motorbike	0.00	0.00	0.00	4.00	0.00	0.00	0.00	0.00	0.00	0.67

Do you Sign a Contract with the Farmer/Company?

No	0.00	100.00	100.00	100.00	94.74	100.00	0.00	100.00	55.98	100.00
Yes	100.00	0.00	0.00	0.00	5.26	0.00	100.00	0.00	44.02	0.00
Duration of contract (in months)	12.00	0.00	0.00	0.00	8.00	0.00	12.00	0.00	10.67	0.00
Duration of working in farms (in hours/day)	7.64	8.02	11.34	8.96	11.72	9.46	7.78	7.9	11	9.2
Any Credit Facility Provided by Contracting Agency?										
No	90.00	0.00	100.00	100.00	100.00	100.00	100.00	0.00	97.86	100.00
Yes	10.00	0.00	0.00	0.00	0.00	0.00	0.00	0.00	2.14	0.00
Average maximum limit (₹)	10,000	0	0	0	0	0	0	0	10,000	0

of reach to those workers. Only 31.62 per cent of the respondents in contract group had toilet facilities at their home and in non-contract group, the percentage went down to 22 per cent. It was expected that the workers might be getting some produce from farm especially fruits or vegetables which are not marketed and require immediate consumption. The survey results say that 99.15 per cent of the respondents in contract group said that they don't get such produce from farms. About growing fruits and vegetables in their kitchen garden, only 1.28 per cent of the respondents affirmed in positive response. In non-contract group, no one reported of growing fruits and vegetables in the kitchen garden. Table 8.6 provides information about the assets value of contract and non-contract agricultural wage workers.

SOME PERSONAL EXPERIENCE OF CONTRACT-WAGE WORKERS

All the contract-wage workers were asked whether they ever faced any situation of under-paid wages during the reference year. Majority of them (98.25%) said, 'No', they didn't face such situations. The respondents were also asked about doing overtime work in the farms. Only in AP, 30 per cent of the respondents in contract group responded, 'Yes', and on average, they got ₹1,323 per head per year as an overtime payment. More than 60 per cent of the respondents in both groups sent their children to government school. No significant impact was found on the school types of their children belonging to contract and non-contract households. Very few injuries/illnesses were reported by the contract-wage workers while working in the farm. Those injuries/illness were nausea, dizziness, back pain and some skin infection. All the contract-wage workers had accepted that their economic condition has improved after joining contract-wage work. On average, they were earning ₹41,576 per year before joining contract work and now they were earning ₹47,718 per year. To our question about their social status being involved in contract-wage work, only 2.04 per cent of the respondents in Karnataka indicated that somehow they feel superior than non-contract-wage workers while in AP, 24.49 per cent of the contract-wage workers responded that they are feeling somehow good as compared to non-contract-wage workers. In Punjab and Haryana, 57.36 per cent of the contract

Table 8.6 Details of Asset Value in Contract and Non-contract Farms

Particulars	AP Contract	AP Non-contract	Haryana Contract	Haryana Non-contract	Punjab Contract	Punjab Non-contract	Karnataka Contract	Karnataka Non-contract	Aggregate Contract	Aggregate Non-contract
Radio	0	0	13	0	2	0	42	0	14	0
TV	3,670	1,702	835	1,044	1,167	1,036	3,698	2,704	2,133	1,802
Mobile	2,052	945	695	480	1,063	850	2,294	1,680	1,416	1,095
Fridge	0	0	52	0	140	286	0	0	51	53
Bicycle	360	149	573	408	628	729	660	526	559	426
Motorbike	12,240	2,340	623	600	2,456	893	3,060	4,360	4,073	2,453
Air condition	0	0	0	0	0	0	0	0	0	0
Others	0	0	117	0	0	0	0	0	38	0
Total asset value	18,322	5,136	2,908	2,532	5,456	3,793	9,754	9,270	8,285	5,829
Type of House										
1. Kachcha	6.00	10.64	27.27	44.00	45.61	46.43	8.00	10.00	23.08	22.67
2. Semi-pucca	52.00	76.60	53.25	36.00	35.09	28.57	90.00	84.00	56.41	63.33
3. Pucca	42.00	12.77	19.48	20.00	19.30	25.00	2.00	6.00	20.51	14.00
Owned house	96.00	97.87	98.70	92.00	91.23	89.29	98.00	100.00	96.15	96.00
Rented house	4.00	2.13	1.30	8.00	8.77	10.71	2.00	0.00	3.85	4.00

(Table 8.6 Continued)

(Table 8.6 Continued)

Particulars	AP		Haryana		Punjab		Karnataka		Aggregate	
	Contract	Non-contract	Contract	Non-contract	Contract	Non-contract	Contract	Non-contract	Contract	Non-contract
Agricultural Land										
1. No	42.00	42.55	98.70	96.00	100.00	100.00	72.00	84.00	81.20	76.00
2. Yes	58.00	57.45	1.30	4.00	0.00	0.00	28.00	16.00	18.80	24.00
3. Acres/HH	1.84	1.23	0.50	1.00	0.00	0.00	1.16	1.06	1.59	1.19
Toilet Facility										
1. No	86.00	97.87	64.94	48.00	66.67	75.00	58.00	76.00	68.38	78.00
2. Yes	14.00	2.13	35.06	52.00	33.33	25.00	42.00	24.00	31.62	22.00
Produce Received from Farm for Family Consumption										
1. No	100.00	100.00	97.40	100.00	100.00	100.00	100.00	100.00	99.15	100.00
2. Yes	0.00	0.00	2.60	0.00	0.00	0.00	0.00	0.00	0.85	0.00
Growing Fruits and Vegetables in Kitchen Garden										
1. No	98.00	100.00	100.00	100.00	100.00	100.00	96.00	100.00	98.72	100.00
2. Yes	2.00	0.00	0.00	0.00	0.00	0.00	4.00	0.00	1.28	0.00

group respondents reported that non–contract–wage workers are better than them because they don't have to work for long hours in the field and also contract farms need timely availability of labourers. Table 8.7 shows some qualitative responses regarding their feeling of social status after joining contract farms.

Punjab and Haryana wage workers also gave suggestions and remarks on improving their working condition. At the aggregate, 29 per cent of respondents of contract group from both the states said that payment

Table 8.7 *Social Status of Contract-Wage Worker versus Non-contract Wage Worker (in %)*

Particulars	Haryana	Punjab	Aggregate
Contract-wage Worker			
Non-contract workers are good because they don't have to work for long hours	80.82	26.79	57.36
There should be a time limit for work in a day	13.70	23.21	17.83
We get work in most of the time of a year	2.74	26.79	13.18
We have to work strictly as per the time requirement	1.37	16.07	7.75
We are comparatively better than non-contract-wage workers	0.00	5.36	2.33
I am not a contract-wage worker	0.00	0.00	0.78
Contract workers get better wage rate	0.00	1.79	0.78
Non-contract-Wage Worker			
They have to work strictly as per the time requirement	57.14	16.67	31.58
Non-contract workers are good because they don't have to work long hours	42.86	8.33	21.05
I am not contract-wage worker so I can't say	0.00	75.00	47.37

for contract-wage worker should be increased. Also, 26 per cent of them suggested for limiting time duration of work. Other suggestions were creating employment throughout the year, contract should be in written form, employment should be created in their village, etc. The respondents of Punjab and Haryana also talked on how good or bad is contract-wage work for them. In Haryana, only 31 per cent of the contract-wage workers said that contract-wage work is good for them and in Punjab, only 38 per cent of the respondents reported that contract-wage work is good for them. The certain reasons for that are easily available jobs for them, they get money on time and work is available throughout the year. The remaining 69 per cent in Haryana and 56 per cent in Punjab said that contract-wage work is not good because they have to work more. Also, contract is not in the written form so contracting agencies/farmers can breach the contract easily. Sometimes, they are underpaid for their work. There is no time limit for contract-wage workers.

RESPONDENT'S VIEWS ON EFFECT OF CF ON LABOURERS

Every coin has two sides and CF also has positive and negative sides. On the one hand, majority of respondents from all the states had mentioned that due to CF wage workdays have been increased and that has also increased the income of wage workers by providing a greater number of wage work and a higher wage rate. But on the other hand, this increase in wage workdays and income has some costs. These costs are overexploitation of wage workers at low wage rate along with some health hazards. There are other benefits and costs of CF on wage workers. Now contract-wage workers are getting payment on the spot due to commercialization of farms. Some interest-free, advance payments are also made. If some injuries happen to the worker, then the agency takes care of their treatment. Out migration of wage workers has been reduced as they are getting work in nearby villages. Some respondents in Karnataka claimed that their social status has been improved now because of more earning in contract-wage work. The uncultivable land is also brought under CF by making some arrangement of cultivation. Despite these benefits, some undulations need to be addressed. In AP and Karnataka, contract-wage workers reported that they are facing some health problems due to excess use of chemicals and pesticides. Some workers reported that they lost their fingerprints while picking gherkin with bare hands. This resulted in complication of identity verification through fingerprint and they were denied to access bank accounts. CF also created divide among farmers in the village. The farmers who are engaged in CF do not allow the workers to work on other's farm. Also, non-contract farmers are not willing to engage the workers who are working in contract farms. Contract farmers have become more profit oriented; therefore, they deal with workers very strictly. There are other minor positive and negative effects mentioned in Table 8A.1.

SUGGESTIONS FOR MAKING CF MORE BENEFICIAL FOR LABOURERS

There were many suggestions given by farmers from all the four states. In Table 8A.2, suggestions in detail from the four states have been given. There are four major concerns of the contract-wage workers such as creating employment throughout the year from contract farms and contract crops, health risks, stagnant wage rate and exploitation of wage workers by the contract farmers and tenants. In AP, 26 per cent of the respondents suggested to increase wage rate for contract farms as compared to non-contract farms because of higher intensity of work under contract. They also suggested for creating some more opportunities so that labourers will get employment throughout the year. The workplace from which this information has been compiled in AP is a dry belt, therefore workers have suggested to install a shed in the farm to take some rest if they get tired and they also suggested that farmers should make arrangement of drinking water at the farm. Whenever a labourer works for extra hours, he/she should be paid for overtime work. Some other suggestions such as providing credit facilities to the workers by the company were given. They also suggested for giving some liberty to the workers if they get some emergency call during the work hours.

In Haryana, 61 per cent of the respondents reported that there should be contract and the same should be in written form. Also, they suggested for limiting the working hours of contract-farm workers. They also suggested to increase wage rate and payment of overtime work. There were other minor suggestions such as following minimum-support wage rate in contract wages, to make payment system more efficient and also asked involvement of government to design the contract and other terms and conditions of work. In Punjab, 64 per cent respondents pointed out that they want contract in the written form. Around 60 per cent of them raised concern for overtime payment. They also feel that wage work hours should be clearly defined while doing a contract. They were expecting higher wage rate for the efforts they put in contract-wage work. Other minor suggestions given by the respondents were creating employment throughout the year, care should be taken for the worker's transport, a minimum-support wage rate should be followed in contract farms, payment should be done every day, transparency in payment, etc.

In Karnataka, 39 per cent of the respondents said that their wage rate should be increased as compared to wages paid by non-contract farmers. It is interesting to observe that 37 per cent of the respondents asked to provide transport facilities by the contracting firm. It indicates that workers in Karnataka have to travel larger distances as compared to other three states. Also, they raised concern for providing credit facilities by the contracting farm. As they don't have easy access to the credit in their village, they are expecting that contracting farm should take initiatives in this direction. They also demanded that safety kits, drinking water, mid-day meal, shade/shelter to take rest during working hours, health insurance, etc., should be provided by the contracting farms.

SUMMARY

To sum it up, total number of 234 contract-wage workers and 150 non-contract-wage workers were selected from four states, namely AP, Karnataka, Punjab and Haryana. Summing up the observations on agricultural labourers, the number of man-days generated in contract farm was higher than non-contract farms consisting mainly of male labourers. There was no significant increase in number of man-days for females after the introduction of CF. The wages earned by the male labourers in a year in the contract farm was almost four-times higher than the non-contract agricultural male worker's annual wage income. This indicates a great potential in CF to create more employment and income for the agricultural-wage workers.

Females also earn more wages as compared to non-contract agricultural female-wage workers but they had less opportunities to work in contract farms as compared to male-wage workers. However, wage rate did not vary significantly across contract and non-contract group but increase in man-days entails more income to contract group. Adding up income from other activities to the wage income, contract group still earn more annual income than non-contract wage worker. The contract-wage worker earns ₹75 thousand per year and non-contract wage worker earns₹50 thousand per year. Also, it has been seen that expenditure for non-consumption items in contract group was higher than non-contract group. Contract-wage workers spent ₹34 thousand per year on non-consumption items whereas non-contract group wage worker spent ₹22 thousand per annum.

Area of operation of contract farms was found closer to village and city as compared to non-contract farms. Approximately 80 per cent of the respondents went to the workplace by feet in both the cases of contract and non-contract groups. Among the remaining, 10 per cent used bicycle and other 10 per cent used motorbike and public transport or either of the means of transport. In Karnataka and AP, contract was signed between them and contracting farm but in Punjab, only 5.26 per cent of the respondents said that they signed contract with the farmer or agency. None of the respondents reported about signing contract in Haryana. The duration of the contract was found to be 12 months in AP and Karnataka and 8 months in Punjab. The average duration of working in the farms was found to be 11 hours and 9.2 hours in contract and non-contract farms, respectively.

The aggregate asset value of contract farm wage workers was comparatively higher than non-contract-wage workers. More than 50 per cent of the respondents in both groups owned semi-pucca houses. Greater number of respondents in non-contract group owned land as compared to contract group. Toilet facilities were still out of reach to those workers. Only 31.62 per cent of the respondents in contract group had toilet facilities at their home and in non-contract group, the percentage went down to 22 per cent. No significant advantage of receiving farm produce from contract-farm was reported.

Only in AP, 30 per cent of the respondents in contract group responded, 'Yes', that they have to work overtime and on average, they got ₹1,323 per head per year as overtime payment. More than 60 per cent of the respondents in both groups sent their children to government school. Very few injuries/illnesses were reported by the contract-wage workers while working on the farm. Among those who reported such incidences, these injuries/illnesses were nausea, dizziness, back pain and some skin infection. However, after joining contract farm, economic conditions of contract-wage workers have been improved. On average, they were earning ₹42 thousand per year before joining contract work and now they were earning ₹48 thousand per annum.

CF definitely increased the wage workdays and wage worker's income but it happened at some cost. They described these costs as over-exploitation of wage workers at low wage rate along with some health hazards. There are other benefits and costs of CF on wage workers. Now contract-wage workers are getting payment on the spot due to commercialization of farms. Some interest-free, advance payments were also made. If some injuries happen to the worker, then the agency takes care of their treatment. Out migration of wage workers has been reduced as they are getting work in nearby villages. Despite these benefits, some costs have occurred to the wage workers. In AP and Karnataka, contract-wage workers reported that they were facing some health problems due to the excess use of chemicals and pesticides. Some workers reported that they lost their fingerprints while picking gherkin with bare hands. This resulted in complication of identity verification through fingerprint and they were denied access to bank accounts. CF also created divide among farmers in the village. The farmers who are engaged in CF do not allow the workers to work on other's farms. Also, non-contract farmers are not willing to engage the workers who are working on contract farms. Contract farmers have become more profit oriented; therefore, they deal with workers very strictly.

Some valuable suggestions were given by the wage workers to make CF more beneficial. There are four major concerns of the contract-wage workers which are—creating employment throughout the year from contract farms, health risks, stagnant wage rate and overexploitation of wage workers by the tenants. Majority of respondents reported for increasing their wage rate, define clear timing of the wage work, create more employment in their villages, covering their health risk by the contracting farmers and some credit facilities should be provided by the contracting farmers.

Chapter 9

Promotion of Contract Farming and Land Tenancy

MAIN ISSUES FACED BY CF IN INDIA

One common problem among all existing CF models in India is the absence of common legally binding contractual agreements. In almost all cases, contracts are done on the basis of mutual trust. As a result, both the parties sponsor and producer try to take advantage of open-market prices or product grades, whenever is profitable for them. Under the present CF system, sponsoring companies face a big problem of insecurity of contract termination at any time and uncertain land-use tenure. In such circumstances, it becomes difficult for the companies to go for long-term investment in the contracted land. Companies, while making contract with the producers, are selectively biased as they prefer large and medium farmers who are comparatively more educated and have better access to credit than the marginal and small farmers. Some cases of monopsony are observed in CF in which a large buyer procures raw materials from hundreds and thousands of farmers. This kind of market structure is disadvantageous to farmers because of lack of adequate information about the market which results into asymmetric information issues.

Pricing, under the present CF system, is mostly as per the convenience of the sponsoring company, who either prefix contract price or fix it at the time of harvest given the open-market price. Whatever may be the case, the price fixation is unilateral, often not involving the producers in such activity. Sometimes sponsoring companies reject the farmer's produce based on quality grounds, especially when they see that market price is lower than the contracted price. Delay in payment by sponsoring companies is also another issue faced by farmers. In most of the existing models, the contracts mainly safeguard companies' interest at the cost of producers and do not protect the latter from production risks, especially during crop failure. The company retains the right to change price and generally offer prices which are based on the open-market prices. The firms also manipulate provisions of the contracts in practice, especially in those cases where farmers make contract-specific, fixed investments, for example, in dairy, poultry and plantation crops.

In many of the states, the present APMC Act still restricts the processors/manufacturers from entering into direct contract with farmers as the produce is required to be canalized through regulated markets only. In the absence of the system of registration of contracts with any authorized agency of the state for the verification of the credentials/track record of the sponsoring companies, there are reported cases of farmers becoming victims of the unscrupulous operators. This was highlighted by some farmers during our survey in Punjab where many companies in the past assigned buy-back contract with farmers but ran away after the crash of price in the open market. There is low level of awareness about CF amongst different stakeholders. The lack of information about CF has probably kept CF sponsoring companies away from a vast area in the country.

It has been observed that absence of legal framework impedes the CF system to flourish in the country. At present, there is only one law, that is, Contract Act for CF but provisions of the Contract Act do not suffice the requirements in the contractual agreement. Also, complex procedure and delay in court proceedings as well as distance from courts discourage farmers to knock the door of courts when time needs. There are several possible disputes which are expected to arise from the CF system and that can be attributed to: delayed payment received by the farmers, undefined discounting of payments, returning the delivered goods without giving any proper reason, deliberate reduction in price, making it mandatory for subcontractors to purchase inputs from the parent firms and forcing the subcontractors to pay in advance for the inputs purchased from parent firms.

The nature of contract varies across different crops or different activities. A contact covering plantation crops, for example, oil palm, tea or fruit crops like mango, orange, etc., where significant long-term investment is required from all parties, will be different from a contract covering annual field crops such as cereals or vegetables for local supermarket. Similarly, the produce which are to be exported may have very strict guidelines in terms of pesticide residue and product quality as well as packaging quality and its appearance. These guidelines are mainly developed by the corporate bodies, government agencies and individual developers. However, it will be more feasible if farmers or their representatives are also invited to contribute while drafting the guidelines. Generally, the drafting responsibility stems only with the contracting firms. Management should make sure that each and every terms and conditions are fully understood by the farmers and it should be circulated to the farmers' representative for independent examination.

The legal framework of the agreement should comply with the minimum legal requirements of the Indian Contract Act, local practices must be taken into account and arrangements for arbitration must be addressed. Usually, written agreement specifies the responsibilities and obligations of each contracting parties, how the agreement will be enforced and what remedies can be followed if the contract breaks. In most cases, agreements are made between the sponsor and the farmer, although in the case of multipartite arrangements, the contracts can be between the sponsor and farmer associations or cooperatives. In majority of cases, it is well predicted that sponsors will take any legal action against a traitor (in this case, farmers). In most cases, cost involved in litigation is more expensive than the amount to be claimed. Also, legal conrtract bitters the relationship between sponsors and farmers against whom the case has been filed as well as his fellow farmers. On the other hand, legal action by a farmer is also very improbable. None of them seek a legal remedy through the courts, so they find easy and quick ways of resolving the disputes identified in the agreement. So, the above incidents necessitate a legal provision in the law that will govern marketing of agricultural produce and make it mandatory for all the agreements to be registered and quick redressal of disputes arising from the contract.

The fixed price contracts generally protect the farmers well, but if the market collapses or in the case of crop failure, sponsors should also shoulder the loss. On the other hand, if the contracts are based on a flexible spot price, farmer's stability of income will always be at a risk. In order to protect the farmers from volatile price risks, a risk analysis should be done to determine the economic advantage of insurance against specific risk applicable to a certain crop. In addition to the above conditions of the agreement, sponsors of large volume of produce may also provide few more services as part of the agreement which will facilitate the coordination of production. They can identify suitable production areas; enforce farmer's group formation; provide extension services on new cultivation practices, appropriate use of fertilizers, insecticides and pesticides; cropping schedules and conduct training and awareness programmes for the success of CF.

Farmers' intermediary bodies are required to negotiate between management/sponsors and farmers for all contracts. By making farmer-management coordination, a sponsor can negotiate the contract with the farmers either directly or through their representatives. The farmers' management includes different forms of associations such as farmers association, farmers cooperatives, farmers group or any other group they form. Quality control and monitoring system must be clearly defined in each contract agreement for a particular operation. Monitoring procedures must be prioritized by the sponsors and they should decide about schedule, location and people for monitoring.

A typical feature of CF is an agreement between two unequal parties. On one side, it involves large number of marginal, poor and illiterate farmers and on the other side, it comprises big agribusiness firms. In current situation, these farmers have limited access to courts for resolution of disputes arising between them and the sponsoring agency. It is also equally challenging for the sponsoring agencies to take legal action against farmers violating contract agreements through present mechanism of civil court. Therefore, it is necessary to set up a dispute resolution mechanism near to the farmers which will facilitate quick and easy settlement of disputes. A situation can also arrive when farmers may invest heavy amount of fixed assets to raise the contracted crops and may go into huge debt during crop failure which may result in forceful displacement of farmers from their land by the sponsors. So, a provision in CF law must be included to protect the ownership title of the land.

The sponsoring companies should discharge some social responsibilities for the farmers in respect of health, hygiene, education and long-term training in good agricultural practices, hygiene practices, marketing practices, etc. This would help in the sustenance of long-term relationship between the farmers and the sponsoring companies. There is a need for widespread awareness for CF through campaigns, media, etc. To sum up, amendment of agricultural laws to promote CF and to provide for dispute redressal mechanism coupled with institutional arrangements for recording of CF agreement would provide a framework for introducing an effective, speedy and inexpensive method of resolving legal disputes.

WAYS TO PROMOTING CF

Government of India has drafted a promotional and facilitative Model Contract Farming Act entitled The—State/UT Agriculture Produce and Livestock Contract Farming (Promotion and Facilitation) Act, 2018[1] after consultation with stakeholders including CF and value chain promoting companies, FPOs and progressive farmers. The proposed Model Contract Farming Act still has scope for improvement. Following are some guidelines proposed in the draft. Based on the findings of this study, some italicized suggestions have been put forth by authors to further improve the draft.

Registration of Agreement

- The first and the foremost requirement in CF for legally binding agreement is its registration with the Registering and Agreement Recording Committee. More than 90 per cent of farmers in the study area are practicing CF on oral agreement. To maintain a

---

[1] For details see http://www.agricoop.nic.in/sites/default/files/Model%20Contract%20Farming%20Act%202018.pdf

formal record of CF, it is necessary to make all the contracts registered with the committee. This is more desirable, given the fact that in official parlance hardly there is any record of the existing contracting companies, the contract crops, contract farmers and the numbers of acres grown under CF.

- The committee should constitute officials from the departments of agriculture, horticulture, animal husbandry, marketing, rural development cooperation, fisheries/poultry and allied fields not exceeding five members headed by an officer as nominated by the government/administration. Under the Act, there is no representative from the farmers' front. There is dire need to have a member from the producer organizations if such organization exists or from the farmers' union if so exists or at least a member from the farmers' commission as the same exists in Punjab, Bihar and many other states.

- The agreement should be written in local and simple language so that each and every term and condition should be clearly understandable to the producer and shall be in such legally acceptable 'form(s)' containing all particulars (terms and conditions) unambiguously and explicitly mentioned.

- The producers can enter into contract with one or more sponsors without any overlap.

- The agreement should be made exclusively for the purchase of the agricultural produce and/or livestock or its product. It can also include supply of material inputs including soil reclamation, levelling, feed and fodder and technology or any other activity.

- The period of agreement should be at least one-crop season and maximum period should not exceed five years to maintain the soil quality and land structure. The provision for continuity of the contract after one season and up to five years subject to agreement by both the parties should be entailed in the Model Act to provide durability to prevailing contract among both the parties.

- In the case of plantation crops, the TOR should be different from the field crops. In the latter case, the gestation period does not materialize any return to the producer. The sponsor should support the producer during this period which can later be deducted from the emoluments obtained by the producer once plantation crops start yielding.

Information Dissemination of the Produce

- Once the agreement is registered with Registering and Agreement Recording Committee, a dashboard of contracted produce should be made to track the acreage and production (area) and supply (quantity and price) of the agricultural produce in the market.
- Daily updates of the dashboard should be done to reflect the area, production and price of the contracted crop produce.
- This information will help to take decisions on crop production by the farmers or setting up quota for different crops under different climatic conditions to ensure environmental sustainability.

Sponsor's Right on Erecting Permanent Structure on Producer's Land or Premise

- Sponsors should be prohibited from raising any permanent structure or creating any kind of leasehold rights or asking any payment for the restoration of land for production or dismantling previous structure which will place cost on the producer. However, sponsors should be allowed to raise temporary structure related to production processes of produce, rearing of livestock or marketing if desired by the producer. Farmers had raised concern about some structural changes on their land if they give their land to CF companies. If a company leaves the land in uncultivable state, then the producer will have to face some restoration cost of the land. Therefore, this issue should be taken very seriously to formulate any policy on CF.

Input Supply by the Sponsor

- In case of buy-back and input supply contract, company/government should provide quality seeds, fertilizers and pesticides at subsidized rate. Farmers gave second priority for the quality input supply.
- Farmers had demanded to provide reasonable interest-based crop loans from/through the sponsors for the crops grown under contract. This will help to reduce financial pressure on the farmers and will facilitate participation of financially weak farmers.

- Farmers also demanded for providing crop-insurance facilities by the companies. The insurance of the contracted crop can be linked to Pradhan Mantri Fasal Bima Yojana (PMFBY) through the sponsors. The insurance premium can be paid by the sponsor and later, it can be deducted from the total value of sold crops.
- One company representative (especially the extension agent) should be available round the clock in his jurisdiction. The area of jurisdiction should not exceed 10 villages per extension agent.

Quality Grade Standards of the Produce

- Although the quality grade standards are mutually accepted by the contracting parties but ensuring correct price for their produce based on their quality standards is a big challenge. In case of seed production, company itself gives certification of germination percentage of seeds which gives a scope of either misguiding farmers by the company or applying inappropriate means by the company and farmers get underpaid for their produce. Therefore, certification of agri-products should be done by the third party (government or NGO) who will give more transparent report of the quality standards of the commodities.
- Quality parameters should be defined by considering generic and specific use of produce.

Role of Government in Fixing Pre-agreed Price of the Produce

- Pre-agreed price of the produce should be determined in collaboration with farmers, sponsors and government/administration. Sponsors should not be the only agent to decide the price of the produce. Increasing price of produce has been given third priority by the farmers in this study.
- Sometimes, in certain crops, there is a single buyer who encourages monopolistic tendencies when the farmers are locked into a fairly sizeable investment such as plantation crop. In that case, farmers cannot easily change to other crops. Therefore, farmers will remain at receiving position for the price of crop produce. In order to protect those farmers, government should intervene in determining the price of the produce.

- Make the price fixation more transparent. The agreement should include minimum and maximum range of prices rather than only one price. For fixation of price, past values of low and high range of prices as well as the cost of production and normal profit for the farmers should be the guiding principal. The Model Act is salient on introduction of grading system under CF. Farmers deserve premium for the high-quality produce.

Buying and Selling of Produce

- It will be facilitative for the contracting parties if the buying and selling of contracted products are kept outside the ambit of regulation of State/UT Agricultural Marketing Act. The contract will be already registered with the committee so it should be regulated as per committee's directives to keep it simple and straight.
- The company should buy the pre-agreed quantity of produce to the extent commensurate to fair average quality, as mentioned in the agreement explicitly but not less than fixed percent of such pre-agreed quantity, as may be prescribed. The sponsor should also buy rest of the pre-agreed quantity at a slightly lower rate mutually acceptable to both if the quality of produce is not as per the standards prescribed. Farmers, in the study, said that sometimes companies are not willing to take bigger size of gherkin and farmers do not have any alternative option to sell those rejected products because of unavailability of domestic market. Hence, the company should arrange alternatives to sell those products in case of export-oriented products.
- Farmers had also talked about providing crop bonus or higher price for premium quality to sustain their interest in CF.
- Weighing of produce should be done by electronic instruments as prescribed by the Standard of Weights and Measures Act, 1976. Farmers suggested that their produce should be weighed at farm gate in case of fruits and vegetables, to avoid moisture loss.
- Payment for the purchased produce should be done on the spot. In some cases, especially seed crops, it takes time of 1–2 weeks to get the result of germination rate and then payment is cleared. Therefore, the crops in which it requires certification for assured quality, the sponsor should make half of the expected payment

on the spot and remaining amount should be paid after getting certification result. Once the company accepts the produce, then it cannot be retracted to reject it.

- If the payment is not done on the spot, then a penal interest should be levied on sponsor for late payment up to 30 days. If the sponsor fails to pay within 30 days, it shall be recovered as an arrear of land revenue with interest as prescribed, till such time as it is recovered and paid to the producer.

Promoting FPO

- Promoting FPOs/Farmer Producer Companies (FPCs) to mobilize small and marginal farmers to benefit from scales of economy. To incentivize FPOs/producer companies to opt for CF, they should be given tax concessions. Provisions should be made under the Model Act to promote group CF to reduce information asymmetry between firms and growers and to raise bargaining power by the smallholders. Promote new generation cooperatives of small and marginal farmers who can deal with CF agencies.

Crop Insurance

- The crop grown under CF should be insured against crop loss (like the case of farmers with loans). It should be covered under production-linked agricultural insurance scheme in operation such as PMFBY. Farmers have given fourth priority on having crop insurance of the contracted crops in this study. However, in the present PMFBY, most of the horticultural crops are not covered for insurance and thereby there is need to have specific insurance schemes for such crops.

Details of Other Parties in the Contract

- It should be mandatory to mention roles and services of other parties such as insurance company, banking institution, agri-input supplier, extension agent and buyers of produce in the agreement.

Alteration and Termination of Contract

- The agreement can be altered or terminated based on the mutual consent and due approval of the authority or the officer authorized in this behalf. 'In the present CF, no such provisions exist.
- There may be cases of impact of macro changes at micro level. In that case, the affected party shall not be bound to honour the contract and can accordingly alter the terms with mutual consent or terminate the contract with the approval of the authority or the officer authorized in this behalf.

Recommendation for Promoting Land Leasing

The study recorded response of the farmers on supporting land-leasing companies in which only 25 per cent of the farmers gave positive response for supporting land-leasing companies and remaining 75 per cent of the farmers completely opposed entry of companies in lease market. The major dilemma of the farmers who are not supporting companies to enter in land lease market are: their dependency on agricultural land for their livelihood; fear of losing employment or livelihood opportunities as they are not skilled in other work; they may face labour shortage as big companies will attract labourers to their farms; no trust on companies, etc. Although many points have been discussed in Model Land Leasing Act 2016 (draft prepared by NITI Aayog[2]), but still this draft has some lacuna which need to be modified. Based on findings of this study, following points should be considered while framing Land Leasing Act.

- The Model Act has not clearly defined agricultural and allied activities. Companies may start using land for commercial purposes rather than crop cultivation (Mani, 2016). The farmers in the study have rightly pointed out that it may lead to real estate boom on agricultural land.

---

[2] For details see http://niti.gov.in/writereaddata/files/document_publication/ Final_Report_Expert_Group_on_Land_Leasing.pdf

- Losing employment/livelihood opportunities is the second major concern of the farmers if companies enter in the land-lease market. It can be difficult for the smallholders to compete with big companies in terms of product quality and price. Therefore, marketing of products produced under lease contract should be taken care of in such a way that local smallholders should not face much competition by the leasing companies.

- Leasing companies will have more paying capacity for wage workers than smallholders. It may attract labourers to work in the leasing company farms rather than on smallholder's farm. Hence, it will lead to increase in wage rate to which smallholder will find it costly to cultivate labour-intensive crops.

- It has been mentioned in the Model Land Leasing Act that the lease agreement can be written or oral. In case of oral agreement, farmers will not have trust on companies to deal with them. Trust on companies is the fourth concern raised by the farmers. Therefore, it should be made mandatory for the companies to lease land on written agreement.

- The lease price should be fixed in more transparent manner and there should be upper limit which may vary from state to state. The Model Act is silent on sharecropping and many other such local systems as bhagidhari (labour tenancy) and water tenancy (cases in Gujarat) that still is prevalent among many states.

- More than 90 per cent of the leasing farmers are practicing short-term lease in the study. The reason behind this is the fear of losing ownership title of the land. It is well protected in the Model Lease Act 2016. Once it is assured for the lessor that they will not lose ownership title, then it will increase the duration of lease period and it will help the lessee to compensate the losses in the next season by retaining the same cultivable land and owner.

Mani (2016) also gave some suggestions for improvement of Model Land Leasing Act 2016. He mentioned that adopting the Model Land Leasing Act in the proposed form will encourage the shift of agricultural land from crop cultivation to commercial use because the proposed act has mentioned that the agricultural land can be leased in for agriculture and allied activities. Therefore, the companies will lease in land for high return agricultural activities such as plantation crops, animal husbandry and dairy, poultry farming, stock breeding, fishery, agro-forestry, agro-processing and other related activities. Also, he found that there is lack of clarity on the definition of lessee cultivator. In the proposed Act, it is not clear whether corporate and absentee landlords can be allowed to cultivate leased-in agricultural land through their employees/representatives or it is restricted to farmers/group of cultivators (SHGs/joint liability groups/FPOs) including landless cultivators. However, he has raised concern about food security of the country if the use of leased land is solely motivated by profit. The act has provision of cancelling the lease agreement if the lessee causes any damage to soil health. Perspective of damage to soil health varies from person to person and it may give rise to disputes between the lessor and lessee. Mani (2016) suggested relooking on the issues of change of landownership. He proposed that if the ownership of land is changed on account of sale or gift, lease contract should be terminated unless the new landlord and lessee agree to continue the contract for the rest of the agreed period. Also, he raised a question about keeping the leased-out land for mortgage or not, keeping in view that the lessee might be interested in availing crop loans or term loans in case of allied activities. The act has completely ignored that why not lessor should terminate the lease contract if the lessee keeps or intends to keep the contracted land fallow in a normal case due to his loss of interest in cultivation (except in case of natural calamities when the land becomes uncultivable). Also, he opined that endorsement of renewal of lease contract by third party will help to avoid any undue pressure/influence from lessee to lessor. The study concludes that there are two vital issues which are missing in the proposed Land Leasing Act 2016. First one relates to the ceiling on ownership of land holding. In normal cases, states have stipulated that leased-in land is also included to calculate operational land holding. But for joint liability group or producer's organization, no restrictions should be placed if they lease land. Second issue relates to fragmentation of land holding. Most land parcels/holdings are quite small in size in India, leasing out only a part/portion of the land plot at a particular location will only lead to further fragmentation. If the lessor leases out entire parcel of land available at a particular location, it will not lead to fragmentation of land. But the lessor may consider leasing out their land to more than one lessee if the parcel of land is quite big (say more than one acre). To solve the issue of leasing by large or very-large farmers, the Act can include ceiling of land holding for owned land including the leased land thereby land leased plus owned land should be allowed only up to the upper limit set under the ceiling of land holding in every state.

Recommendation for Land-Sharing Companies

Land sharing is a relatively new concept and the central government mooted a proposal to adopt it in India's agrarian land system which hoped to be a midway between CF and direct corporate farming. It was favoured based on experiments of these formats in other countries and its success in achieving growth and equity. Particularly, China experimented with a land-stock share system in some of its provinces, Russia passed a law to facilitate such experiments, while Vietnam liberalized its agricultural land-leasing system. Subsequently, the concept of land-share companies was also included as part of the policy note prepared by the working group Land Policy and Globalization for the 11th FYP.

Structurally, land-share companies could either be producer companies, joint-stock companies or a company-farmer partnership, where the farmers collectively mobilize their resources, gain access to modern technology and employ professional managerial personnel. It aimed at not only providing economies of scale but would also help in the establishment of forward and backward linkages to production systems. For example, by floating a land share agro-processing company, farmers of all categories may have the option to become shareholders in proportion to their land-holding size which will be treated as the farmer's equity and receive a share in the company's profits. Farmers may also lease land including their own from the company for a fixed rent. Thereby gaining from both farming as well as a share in the agro-processing company. Such enterprises are also eligible to receive concessional credit and other investment subsidies allowed for the promotion of agro-processing enterprises (Haque, 2003; Mishra et al., 2018).

Another option was that the land-share company be operated on a commercial basis and the management vested on an elected board of directors, where the voting rights are on the basis of cooperative principles (one member, one vote) irrespective of the value of shares held by each member. In this format, a farmer can sell their share to other farmers, but the shares cannot be traded through public issues as there might be a risk of a takeover by corporate houses or other entities. In case of liquidation, the shareholders' land rights are returned to them and not alienated of their land (Bansil, 2011). There are only a few land-share companies that exist without a legal framework governing them. The ITC Group grows tobacco in AP. PepsiCo grows potatoes, tomatoes, chillies and rice in Punjab, Maharashtra, Karnataka and West Bengal. The Mittal Group in collaboration with UK Bank-Rothschild cultivate multiple crops. Narendra Murukumbs of Shree Renuka Sugar Mills in Karnataka also runs as a shareholding company. As early as 2002, the TN and Gujarat State Governments also leased-out wasteland to corporates to grow crops like cotton, flowers, fruits, vegetables and spices.

Although Singh et al. (2015) indicated some scope of intervention for land-sharing companies in the agricultural sector in India, the concept has not gathered significant pace in its adoption and still remains relatively unknown and underused as alternatives to promoting access to land. However, there have been apprehensions among farmers because they view the promotion of land sharing as encouraging corporate-sector control over farmland ownership, losing control over land use decisions and eventual outright alienation of their rights and attachment. Although the government plans to incorporate safeguards by restricting access to shares to only farmers and their successors, there have been very few takers. Therefore, under the current circumstances, the feasibility of operationalizing land-sharing policies in India is improbable and more emphasis may be placed on promoting CF and leasing options. The positive factors in land sharing may be inherently utilized by promoting FPOs which have most of the advantages of land-sharing companies but it retains farmer's ownership and resource usage decision with the farmers without an external inference. The government may opt to promote collective farming rather than land sharing though corporate sector which will be opposed tooth and nail by the farming community and other stake holders.

Conclusively, apart from addressing equity and efficiency parameters (Baumann, 2000; Birthal et al., 2009) that have been adequately incorporated in the new model policies, there is scope for integrating sustainability across the popular land-institutional arrangements that have been suggested as policy recommendations in the report.

Legal Framework and Regulatory Mechanism in Case of CF and Land Leasing

In the proposed Model Contract Farming Act, 2018, total 12 salient features have been mentioned which include setting up of an appropriate and unbiased state-level agency called Contract Farming (Development and Promotion) Authority, constituting Registering and Agreement Recording Committee at district/block/taluka levels, enabling production support, keeping CF outside the ambit of respective Agricultural Produce Marketing Act of the states/UTs, prohibiting sponsors from raising permanent structure, promoting FPOs/FPCs, no transfer of rights, title ownership or possession, ensuring buying of entire pre-agreed quantity, provision to guide the contracting parties to fix pre-agreed price, providing Contract Farming Facilitation Group at village/panchayat levels, purchasing of agricultural produce, livestock and/or its produce based on quality parameters as per CF agreement and catering to a dispute-settlement mechanism at the lowest level. The proposed Model Act, as is indicative from the title, only intends to promote and facilitate CF. It, however, ignores the role of state as regulatory authority in CF. The biggest flaw of present CF is that the proposed Model Act did not accord environmental and social sustainability in the Act. Deininger (2011) pointed out five policy areas where attention needs to be focussed while formulating policies on farmland investment. Those five policy areas include recognition of existing rights, provision of voluntary land transfer, technical and economic viability of investment, environmental and social sustainability.

Deininger (2011) mentions that to prevent investments from generating negative externalities, areas not suitable for agricultural expansion need to be protected from encroachment, environment polices clearly defined and adhered to and social safeguards (including provisions on gender and worker welfare) defined and implemented. In the proposed Act, no limitations on contracting with farmers have been put based on the availability of natural resources such as water, soil fertility status, etc. Companies might start contracting with farmers which can give maximum profit irrespective of type of crops selected and availability of natural resources. Some areas might have critical natural-resource status but for short run it may give maximum profit to the companies. This situation will lead to depletion of natural resources. Therefore, area and location of crop production should be based on the assessment of natural-resource status. Same is the case with Land Leasing Act.

The proposed Model Contract Farming Act, 2018, also misses to incorporate social sustainability of the policy initiatives. Nothing has been talked about gender and caste issues while participating in CF. The study has found that only 1 per cent of the respondents belonged to women-headed household in case of CF and land leasing. There should be provision of encouraging women headed-households to participate in CF and land leasing. Singh (2002) believes that the labour issues in CF has not been addressed in research and hence in policy formulation. Since contract production is primarily carried out with female labour-adult and increasing child-labour there is a need to address the whole question of changing the agrarian production structure under CF from a gender perspective with focus on issues of transfer of skills, choice of technology, organization of labour, working conditions and terms of work. Although it has been found in the study that CF and land leasing are operating across different caste and communities, but still 80per cent of the participants were from OBC and General caste. SC and ST participants were sharing 20 per cent of the sample population. So, special attention should be given to promote SC and ST people to participate in CF and land leasing.

Singh (2002) argues that firms are the only beneficiaries of surplus generated through value addition which they do not share with the farmers. Farmers in the study also pointed out that there should be provision of crop bonus or incentives for premium quality and high production of the produce. It will motivate farmers to sustain their participation in CF. The Model Act has not mentioned such provision for the farmers who participate in CF.

Some opponents of CF argue that promotion of CF as an inclusive alternative to land grabbing attends to (justified) fears over the consequences for small-farming households who are alienated from their land. Li (2011) opines that agribusiness firms, whether engaging in land acquisition or CF, are always beholden to the profit motive and are unlikely to implement schemes that produce a better outcome for farmers at the expense of profit margin. Vicol (2015) found similar results in a case study of potato CF in a village in Maharashtra. While potato CF provided some material livelihood benefits but it did not represent a 'win–win' solution for all the households. The intersection of the dynamics of the contract scheme and local livelihood patterns produces a particular pattern of participation that excludes the most economically backwards households, while also not providing any significant livelihood benefits to the households who are enrolled in the scheme. Economically backward households are confined to precarious wage-labour pathways; the majority of middle-farmer households continue to struggle to reproduce themselves through agriculture (including CF), sometimes getting ahead but also frequently going backwards; while the best-off households continue to increase their advantage in the non-agricultural economy. Therefore, the Model Act needs to safeguard marginal and small farmers by making it mandatory for the companies to share percentage of total contracting farmers with them.

Role of Government in Facilitating CF

Eaton and Shepherd (2001) opine that government has to play an important role if CF is to be successful. It requires a relevant legal framework and an efficient legal system. Moreover, government can foster success of CF by developing linkages between investors and farmers and can play an important role in protecting farmers by ensuring the financial and managerial reliability of potential sponsors. The role of government can be divided into

1. Enabling and regulatory role
2. Developmental role.

As CF depends on either legal or informal arrangements between the contracting parties, it should be backed up by appropriate laws and efficient legal system. The relevant laws can be grouped into three categories: enabling functions, economic regulatory functions and constraining functions. In the context of CF, enabling aspect of the law is most important. Government needs to be aware of the implications of all laws and policy decisions on agribusiness development and how those policies influence CF. For example, in the Philippines, fast-food chains were importing frozen French fries and that particular variety of potato could be grown in the Philippines. The Philippines government imposed import restriction on those seed potatoes, resulting in the unavailability of the required variety. Later, by approach of the companies, government lifted the ban and this permitted the establishment of two CF ventures to supply the rapidly growing fast-food industry. Thus, a simple policy reform ultimately benefited the sponsors as well as farmers.

There are other enabling activities where government can help to sustain CF. Those activities include—provision of training in technological and managerial skills at all levels if sponsors do not provide those services; facilitation of research studies in collaboration and consultation with the sponsors and provision of agricultural extension services to ventures where small-scale developers cannot afford the luxury of their own extension service. The regulatory role involves constituting legislation that specifically regulates CF. In most countries, there is no legislation that regulates CF. Sometimes, government tries to overregulate if the sponsor is a parastatal or other government agency. For example, legislation in Kenya authorized the parastatal sponsor of contract tea farming to issue licences to farmers on rigid conditions on uprooting tea bushes, pest and disease controls, unauthorized planting of tea, failure to cultivate in the approved manner and the right of the parastatal to grant or refuse a license to plant tea. These strict regulations create insecurity to the farmers entering in the contract. The government should enact legislation to protect farmers as they are the weaker party in the contract system. The PAFC contract model in Punjab tried to facilitate CF in a set number of crops by providing per acre payment facility to contracting firms, namely, Mahindra Shubhlabh, Hariyali Kisan Bazar, Tata Chemicals and so on but ultimately ended up only making payment without any real CF taking place at the ground. Therefore, the role of government should remain only facilitating and not participating directly in CF (Kumar, 2006).

Government also plays developmental role in reallocating development resources towards promotion of CF. For example, the Philippines government with assistance from an FAO project, promoted CF for small-scale farmers who were allocated land under the agrarian reform programme. Government organized a 'market matching' exercise by facilitating agribusiness entrepreneurs and farmers' meeting to discuss their requirements. This resulted in establishment of contractual relationships between 27 companies and the farmers. Apart from this, government can disseminate market information, highlighting products which have a commercial demand that can be satisfied through CF operations. The agrarian department can also act as arbitrator in the case of disputes.

SUMMARY

Government of India has taken a big step towards uplifting the agrarian economy by formulating Model Land Leasing Act, 2016 and Model CF Act, 2018. The Land Leasing Act aims to permit and facilitate leasing of agricultural land, to improve agricultural efficiency and equity, access to land by the landless and semi-landless poor, occupational diversity and for accelerated rural growth and transformation; provide recognition to farmers cultivating agricultural land on lease for enabling them to access loans through credit institutions, insurance, disaster relief and other support services provided by government, while protecting fully the land rights of the owners; and matters connected therewith or incidental thereto. On the other hand, the Model Contract Farming Act aims to integrate farmers with agro-industries so as to ensure better price realization for their produce, reduce post-harvest losses and create job opportunities in rural areas. Both the acts are at initial phase of implementation. It requires some more improvement in terms of social and environmental sustainability.

The Model Land Leasing Act in the proposed form will encourage the shift of agricultural land from crop cultivation to commercial use because the proposed Act has mentioned that the agricultural land can be leased in for agriculture and allied activities. In long term, that can challenge food security of the country. Some aspects such as lessee cultivator, soil health, ceiling of ownership are not clearly defined, which may subject to social unrest. Overall, the Leasing Act will benefit both lessors, who prefer to enter into a lease agreement without the fear of losing ownership rights, and lessees, who require protection from premature termination of lease contracts.

Similarly, Model Contract Farming misses to accord environmental and social sustainability in the Act. In the long run, this form of Act can cause environmental and social un-sustainability because the Act did not consider the assessment of natural resources to put restrictions on encroachment of CF companies. It also misses the gender and caste issues to incorporate in formulating the act. However, the Act will foster capital investment by sponsors and increase farmer's income, doubling farmer's income by 2022. The study also found that the value of crop output per acre was highest in the case of CF crops—₹52 thousand, followed by leased-in crops—₹43 thousand and least was control crops—₹38 thousand. Considering the type of crop grown in CF, it seems quite achievable to double the farmer's income by 2022. Farmers should integrate high-value crop in their cropping system apart from cereal crops.

Government will play a vital role in making CF successful by setting up legal framework and an efficient legal system. Government can control CF regime through two mechanisms: (a) by enabling a regulatory role and (b) by developmental role. Enabling and regulatory role will smoothen the system of CF and development role will provide platform for negotiation between different actors.

Chapter 10

Conclusions and Policy Suggestions

Indian economy is growing at a faster pace in the post-liberalization era. High economic growth, rising per capita income, urbanization and more participation of women in labour force have enforced diversification in the consumption basket. The dietary pattern of Indian people is shifting from food grains to high-value commodities such as fruits, vegetables, meats and fish products followed by increase in demand for processed and semi-processed products. The fast-changing consumption pattern is putting pressure on Indian agriculture to make adjustments in the cropping pattern to adjust with changing consumption basket. This demand-driven production system is opening new opportunities in food retailing and processing. But it is also raising a major concern of linking different segments of production, value addition and marketing so that interests of various stakeholders are safeguarded. Thus, Indian agriculture is gradually opening up on lines of the global pattern and is fast becoming internationalized through various developments taking place in the recent period.

A host of reforms have been initiated to spruce up the agriculture sector starting with integration to e-NAM and the APMC Model Act that have had a positive response. The APMC Model Act is envisioned to improve price discovery and reduce the risks farmers face due to price volatility. It caters to reforms with regard to direct marketing, CF, establishment of markets in private and cooperative sectors, single-point levy of market fee, promotion of e-trading and issue of a unified license for traders. The APMC Model Act has provision of issuing permits for CF by registering the parties with them and allows them to purchase the produce directly from farmers and also exempt them from paying any market fee. In addition, a separate chapter in the Model Act includes compulsory registration of CF sponsors. Other reforms on which the ministry has been working on includes promotion of food-value chain and supply-chain management, renewed thrust on NWRS and a Model Contract Farming Act. The latter has gained traction across the country given the severely fragmented state of farm holdings that has affected farm viability. It is one institutional arrangement that is considered to be useful when transaction costs of direct engagement with the market are high for producers and/or traders. It also expects to enhance farmers' income and facilitate market access of smallholders in high-value supply chains that require specialized inputs for sale of produce in specialized output markets.

This study seeks to understand the principle key determinants that drive contractual/lease relationships through the examples of various existing arrangements in the country. It is based on the premise that CF/leasing can be an attractive option to policymakers keen on integrating the poor into a more industrialized sector of the economy by helping them access the gains from trade that characterize successful agricultural tenancy arrangements. CF is a kind of system in which production and supply of agricultural produce is done under forward contracts and the essence of such contracts are commitments made by the farmers/producers to provide an agricultural commodity of specific quality, at a time and a price, and in the quantity required by the buyers. In the early 1990s, tomatoes and chillies were brought under CF which expanded later into multiple products. Most recently contracting in exotic vegetables such as baby corn, bell peppers, jalapeños, gherkins, etc., has been started.

The present study systematically analyses CF in the broader framework of existing land- and lease-market system. It examines CF, vis-à-vis, land leasing and land sharing (farmer to farmer and companies to farmers) to find out the pros and cons of the above system from the point of view of different farm categories. The specific objectives of this study are:

- To analyse the merits and de-merits of promotion of CF, land leasing and land sharing
- To assess the impact of CF, land leasing and land sharing on various stakeholders including agricultural cultivators
- To document the legal framework and regulatory mechanism required to deal with disputes and issues arising from the proposed policy
- To document best practices and models adopted in India and abroad

The study is primarily based on a primary survey. Two states in the North and two states in the South were selected for conducting this study. In the North, Punjab and Haryana and in the South, Karnataka and AP (including Telangana) were selected for carrying out this study. In the aggregate, 500 farm households, comprising 400 farmers belonging to the category of contract farmers, land-leasing farmers and sharecropping farmers and 100 farmers from the control group, not belonging to any of the above-mentioned categories, were selected in each state.

In order to study the institutional and governance mechanism, company's perspective was construed directly by the guided interviews and informal discussions with company management, officials and other field employees of the company indulging in contract, lease or land sharing. Further, international experiences of successful models of CF, land-leasing and land-sharing companies are documented through the literature review, whereas the best practices are captured during the field survey as well as through the literature review. The summary of findings is outlined in the following paragraphs.

HOUSEHOLD CHARACTERISTICS, CROPPING PATTERN, PRODUCTIVITY AND RETURNS FROM FARMING

A total number of 2,014 households were selected in all the four states. Majority of the selected farmers belonged to CF as that was the design of the study proposed. In most of the cases, tenancy existed only in terms of cash payment on seasonal or yearly basis and tenancy in terms of sharecropping was almost non-existent. On average, operated area was highest among the tenant farmers who in addition to their own area also leased-in area to make their holdings more economical. The leased-in farmers operated 13.8 acres per household followed by contract farmers who operated 11 acres, whereas the control group farmers operated only 5.6 acres per household. Operational holding size was highest in Punjab—19.7 acres, followed by Haryana—16.5 acres, AP—4.2 acres and Karnataka with lowest holding size of 3.2 acres per household. The household size varied from less than five members to around eight members in different states. Generally, contract farmers were younger in age as compared to other categories and they were also more educated as compared to other two category in all the four states.

CF was observed existing among the SC and ST categories as well, albeit their percentage was slightly less among the SC farmers. Thus, contrary to the general thinking that CF exists only among upper-caste farmers, we observed that CF was widespread across various social class structures. The cropping intensity was almost two crops in a year, per acre in Haryana and more than two crops in Punjab as compared to much less than two crops in Karnataka and near one crop in AP.

The proportion of net leased-in land was much higher in Punjab and Haryana as compared to other two selected states. The sharecropping existed in small quantity only in Haryana. Most of the leasing-in land was in terms of short-term lease, not exceeding one year, while miniscule cases were found of long-term lease of two years or more. The rent paid for leasing-in per acre on average was ₹14 thousand in AP, ₹16 thousand in Karnataka, ₹34 thousand in Haryana and as high as ₹41 thousand per acre in Punjab for the cultivation of land for one year. There existed reverse tenancy in all the four states possibly to economize their size of holdings and making appropriate use of existing machinery with them, the medium and large farmers leased-in more land than marginal and small farmers.

Although long-term lease was only in miniscule cases, but it did exist and has important implications for this study as rent for long-term lease was significantly lower as compared to short-term lease. The long-term rent was around 66 percent that of short-term rent in AP, less than half in Haryana and around 58 per cent in Karnataka. This has long-term implication for the tenants as with the rise in the duration of tenancy there is a decline in rent which gives opportunity to smallholders to make their holding size more economical by leasing-in land if provisions are made for long-term lease. The possible reason for decline in land rent at longer interval of lease could be such long-term lease gives landlords more security for their holdings and they can plan alternate options for themselves.

Regarding land transaction, not only during the reference year but also past three years indicated only a few abysmal cases in all the four states. This indicates that land market in terms of sale and purchase is almost absent. The existing nature of land tenancy laws and complete absence of land markets makes it impossible for cultivators to move away for alternate employment, especially the small and marginal farmers who find it very difficult to endure in agriculture with their small-holding size.

Regarding access to credit, the wedge between contract farmers, leased farmers and control group was too wide. Whereas contract farmers borrowed above ₹4 lakh per household, the amount was slightly less in the case of lease farmers—₹3.9 lakh, while control group had less than half of this amount, around ₹1.1 lakh only. However, huge difference in access to credit per household between the three categories of farmers was partly on account of differences in operated area. Among different sources, institutional sources constituted almost 80 per cent, whereas moneylenders, commission agents and friends and relatives constituted rest of 20 per cent while contracting firms provided almost negligible amount (to contract farmers). The less institutional credit availability to leased farmers in Haryana and AP indicates lack of banking credit on the basis of leased-in land as there is no legal sanctity of leasing-in in the country as yet. Possibly after proposed land-tenancy reforms, there would be higher access to credit based on leased-in land as well. Credit access (per acre) was scale neutral in Punjab and Haryana whereas it had inverse relation with holding size in AP and Karnataka.

By and large, contract farmers were sowing a greater number of crops as compared to other two categories indicating that CF was helping farmers diversify their crops. This disproves the literature which indicates that CF leads to unification of cropping pattern. Among our selected farmers, the major contract crops grown in AP were groundnut, paddy, gherkin, green and red chilli/jalapeño, cotton and maize seed and baby corn. In Karnataka, the major crops grown under contract were baby corn, ragi, tomato, gherkin and chilli/jalapeño. In Punjab and Haryana, the contract crops were mainly the seed crops of most of the cereals like paddy, wheat, jowar, bajra, maize and vegetables like potato, peas, carrot, radish, French beans and cotton.

In the aggregate, output of all the crops grown by the selected farmers averaged at ₹8 lakh per household, per annum. The value of output per household was highest among the leased farmers—₹9.3 lakh, followed by contract farmers—₹8.5 lakh and it was lowest—₹4.1 lakh—in the case of control farmers. Across the four states, the value of output per household, as expected, was highest in Punjab—₹16.5 lakh, followed by Haryana—₹10.4 lakh, Karnataka—₹3.1 lakh—and AP—₹2.3 lakh per annum. Productivity value (per acre) was highest among the contract farmers—₹76 thousand, followed by control farmers—₹73 thousand—and it was least among the leased farmers—₹67 thousand. The comparison across four states reveals interesting trends. The highest farm productivity was observed in Karnataka—₹98 thousand, followed by Punjab—₹83.5 thousand, Haryana—₹63 thousand and it was least once again in AP—₹55 thousand per acre. Whereas in Punjab and Haryana, paddy and wheat were the predominant crops among both control and contract-farmer groups, it was baby corn, gherkin and tomato in Karnataka and dry chilli and cotton in AP, specifically among leased and control-group farmers. The productivity and gross returns for the cereal crops are much less as compared to high-value commodities, especially the case of gherkin, baby corn and chilli/jalapeño.

The cost of production including both material cost and labour cost was also not significantly different among the three categories of contract, lease and control farmers. It was almost the same—₹30 thousand per acre—among contract and control farmers and slightly less—₹26 thousand—for leased farmers. Across the four selected states, the cost was highest in Karnataka like that of value of output, ₹50 thousand per acre, followed by Punjab—₹30.5 thousand, AP—₹30 thousand—and Haryana—₹23 thousand per acre. On average, net returns (value of output – cost of production) per household had similar trends as that of value of output per household (gross returns). Net returns per acre averaged at ₹45 thousand and its value was highest for contract farmers—46 thousand, while it was almost the same—₹42–₹43 thousand—for the other two categories of leased and control farmers. Across the four states, unlike gross returns that were highest in Karnataka, net returns per acre were highest in Punjab—₹53 thousand, followed by Karnataka—₹48 thousand, Haryana—₹40 thousand and lowest in AP—₹25 thousand per acre. The aggregate household income including farm-business income and non-farm income aggregated at ₹5.5 lakh and it was highest—₹6.3 lakh—for leased farmers and lowest, around ₹3 lakh, for control group while contract farmers lied in between with an amount of ₹5.7 lakh.

Among four states, aggregate income was highest, around ₹11 lakh, in Punjab for which the contribution of non-farm income was less than 5 per cent only. Punjab was followed by Haryana with ₹7.2 lakh average-household income in which non-farm income share was around 9 per cent. Karnataka followed Haryana with average household income of ₹2.2 lakh with contribution of non-farm income by almost one-third. AP lied at the bottom with per household income of ₹1.6 lakh whereby non-farm income contributed one-third, like in the case of Karnataka. Thus, non-farm income provided support to farm income and its share was inversely related to farm income. With decreasing farm income, share of non-farm income increased, although absolute amount of non-farm income does not support this hypothesis.

NATURE OF CF AMONG THE SELECTED FARMERS

Out of our total 2,014 households selected, a sum of 1,408 farmer were engaged in CF, thus making our sample of almost 70 per cent doing CF. On average, all farmers had more than four years of experience with CF. In is interesting to note that while more than two-thirds of the farmers in Punjab and Haryana were engaged in fixed-price contract without provision of extension and other services, whereas almost 90 per cent farmers in AP and Karnataka were engaged in contract with provision of inputs and buy-back facility. In Punjab and Haryana, many farmers were engaged in contract with seed firms for crops like paddy, wheat, potato, mustard, etc., who were mainly providing buy-back facility, while in AP and Karnataka, CF consisted of commodities meant for export purpose like gherkin, jalapeño and baby corn in which case contracting firms closely monitored the quality of crops to meet the requirements of exports.

The contract was mostly oral except in Punjab, where majority of the farmers had written contract in English (and not in local language). However, the written contract in Punjab also was mostly on a plain paper without any legal sanctity. On average, contract farmers were having only one crop under CF in a year except in the case of Haryana, where farmers indicated growing more than one crop under CF in a year. In Haryana, farmers were growing seed crops under CF whereby they covered both kharif (paddy) crop and rabi (wheat) crop under contract but the nature of contract was only provision of buy-back arrangements. Thus, although farmers in the selected states were mostly producing two crops or more than one crop in year, as cropping intensity of the sample was 1.9, but only one crop was covered under CF. The average size of area under CF was only 4 acres, whereas the average operated area of the sample was around 11 acres and GCA was 21 acres. It indicates that only less than 20 per cent of the GCA of a particular household was under CF.

Around 85 per cent of the contracting farmers pointed out that contracting companies or firms provided seed for the contracted crop. In addition to seed, around 35 per cent selected contract farmers also pointed out that they were provided with fertilizer facility with the exception of Haryana, where very few farmers pointed out that they were provided fertilizer. Similarly, around one-fourth of the selected farmers also indicated provision of pesticides and other plant-protection chemicals, once again with exception of Haryana state. Farm-advisory services were indicated by around 38 per cent farmers. Crop loan, crop insurance and soil testing facility were almost negligible among the selected contract farmers. A large number of farmers in Punjab and Karnataka indicated that they were provided farm machinery and implements by the contracting firms.

As per farmers' opinion, the necessary requirements for farmers entering into CF include assured irrigation, labour availability and having reasonable size of holdings. Around two-thirds of the majority of selected farmers indicated that for implementation of any successful contract with the companies require assured irrigation and farmers without having assured irrigation might not have successful participation in CF. Similarly, a thin majority of farmers also indicated that easy access of labour is required as CF involves more labour-intensive crops like gherkin, baby corn and other vegetable cultivation. Reasonable size of holding might help CF but does not seem to be a necessary condition. Similarly, tractor ownership and having social contacts was not found as a necessary requirement for CF. All the selected farmers indicated that the contracted produce was being procured. All farmers doing CF in AP and Karnataka indicated that the produce was procured by the companies from the farm gate, while two-thirds of the majority of farmers in Punjab and Haryana pointed out that the companies asked the farmers to deliver the produce at the company gate. Only a handful of farmers indicated very small quantity of produce being rejected in all the four states. Similarly, breach of contract by the farmers was also almost negligible.

Assured income, superior price based on quality product supplied and hassle-free marketing were the main advantages of CF as per majority of the farmers engaged in CF. However, good farm practices advised by the experts of the companies as a benefit to the farmers was expressed only by 5 per cent of the selected contract farmers. Similarly, provision of crop loan, crop insurance and coping mechanism of farm risk through CF was not preferred as a benefit by the contracting farmers. A clear majority of the contract farmers (58%) expressed that they were satisfied with CF and another 24 per cent expressed as somewhat satisfied while only 7 per cent of the farmers expressed very much satisfied. Only 10 per cent were not satisfied and less than half a per cent expressed totally dissatisfied.

RESOURCE-USE PRODUCTIVITY AND PROFITABILITY: CONTRACT, LEASE VERSUS CONTROL CROPS

In the aggregate, only 20 per cent area of the contract farmers was under contract while 80 per cent area was under non-contract crops. Similarly, only one-third area by leased farmers was actually leased-in for which they paid rent and cultivated it as tenant farmer and rest of the two-thirds of area was their owned area. Comparing all contract crops, leased crops and control crops, on average, value of crop output per acre was highest in the case of CF crops—₹52 thousand, followed by leased-in crops—₹43 thousand—and least was of control crops—₹38 thousand. The value of output per cropped area under CF was highest—₹91 thousand in AP, followed by Karnataka—₹68 thousand, Punjab—₹51.5 thousand and it was least in Haryana—₹41 thousand per acre. Thus, these results are completely opposite from what was seen in the case of total value of output of all the crops per acre of net sown area as presented in the previous section. The reason for high value in AP and Karnataka as compared to Punjab and Haryana under CF and against the general trends of high productivity in the latter green revolution states lie in the nature of crops grown under CF.

The two southern states were growing high-value commodities under CF like gherkins, baby corn, jalapeño and green chillies. In comparison, cereal crops like paddy and wheat were grown in Haryana and wheat and potato were grown in Punjab, albeit cereal crops were grown for seed under buy-back arrangements with seed companies. Except potato, most of the other crops grown in these two states had only low returns as compared to high-value crops which occupied major share in the southern states.

It is especially mentioned here that in AP and Karnataka, new crops like gherkins, jalapeño and baby corn were grown by the farmers because of the initiatives of contracting firms like Global Green, Namdhari and Indo-Spanish companies. These firms not only provide seed to the farmers and ensure the buy-back facility, but they also provided training to the farmers, gave technical know-how, mechanical implements and provided package of practices for the successful implementation of contract with the farmers. Therefore, these trends indicate the importance of CF in bringing diversification of cropping pattern towards high-value crops for which demand is rising at a faster pace with the rising living standard, especially among the urban masses.

The value of crop productivity in the case of leased-in crops was not much different from that of contract crops. The value of output per cropped area was ₹91 thousand in Karnataka, ₹70 thousand in AP,

₹50 thousand in Punjab and only ₹30 thousand in Haryana. The reason for the difference across two regions was same as that of contract crops. In Karnataka, tomato, baby corn, green chillies and carrot were grown while in AP, dry chillies and cotton were grown on the leased area. Although these crops were not covered by the assured buy-back under CF and they had high price and market risk, but at the same time these crops entail much better profitability. In comparison, in both Punjab and Haryana, farmers were growing paddy and wheat for assured MSP but with average returns. Thus, assured MSP only yielded average returns to Punjab and Haryana farmers, whereas market-based risky crops entail high returns to AP and Karnataka farmers.

In the case of control crops, the difference in productivity was much less across these four states probably because of coverage of low-value cereals and oilseed crops in all the four states. For these reasons, average value of output per cropped area of control crops was also low, ₹41 thousand in AP, ₹40 thousand in Punjab, ₹33 thousand in Haryana and ₹31 thousand in Karnataka. Comparing the cost of cultivation, excluding rent charges, the cost was highest for the contract crops, followed by leased-in and control group farmers, however, the wedge between the three was much less, ₹27 thousand, ₹20 thousand and ₹17 thousand per acre of cropped area, respectively for contract, leased and control-group farmers.

On average, value of net returns followed the same order, that is, contract crops followed by leased-in and control crops but their values varied from ₹24 thousand per acre for contract crops to ₹22.5 thousand per acre for leased crops and ₹21 thousand per acre for control crops. Its value for contract crops once again was highest in AP—₹46 thousand, followed by Karnataka—₹26 thousand, Punjab—₹25 thousand and Haryana—₹22 thousand. In the case of leased crops, net returns were highest—₹38 thousand—in Karnataka followed by Punjab and AP both at ₹26 thousand and Haryana at ₹17 thousand. In control crops, Punjab and Haryana led the other two states with value of ₹23 thousand per acre in Punjab, ₹19 thousand in Haryana, ₹15 thousand in AP and least was Karnataka with per acre value of ₹9 thousand only.

Thus, whereas in contract and leased crops, AP and Karnataka realized higher returns on account of growing high-value crops, but

Punjab and Haryana gained more returns in the control group as in this category, cropping pattern was more similar across the four states and Punjab and Haryana had better economies of scale in growing these crops. The above analysis highlights the fact that diversifying cropping pattern towards high-value crops like fruits, vegetables and animal products and paying more attention towards changing consumer pattern can help achieving the target of doubling farmers' income in a set time period. The role of CF in helping farmers adopting such a cropping pattern and disseminating information and technical know-how is highlighted by the above results.

Whereas in Punjab and Haryana, large farmers enjoy economies of scale in their productivity because of more mechanized agriculture, the same was true for contract and leased crops in Karnataka and AP against the general trends observed in control crops. This also indicates the natural inclination of CF towards large and medium farmers as compared to small and marginal farmers. However, against the favourable trends in value of output realized by contract and leased farmers across all the four states, no such disadvantage was seen in the case of cost of production. Cost per acre for contract and leased crops in AP, in the case of marginal farmers was higher as compared to medium farmers. Similarly, cost was higher for marginal farmers as compared to medium and large farmers for contract crops in Haryana and Karnataka and leased crops in Punjab.

MARKETING PATTERN FOLLOWED BY CONTRACT, LEASE AND CONTROL FARMERS

The crops grown on CF were, by and large, sold through the contracting companies without any exception. Crops grown without CF by the category of contract farmers and other leased and control crops were sold either through wholesale markets, which are known as regulated *mandis*, or through local markets, which operate in the peripheral area of production centres, or they were sold through traders or merchants either at the farm gate or a place specified by the buyer. In AP, the output produced under non-contract crops and leased and control crops was disposed of thorough regulated *mandis* while rest of the half was disposed though local markets, through merchants and intermediaries who lifted the produce at the farm gate. In Haryana and Punjab, a part of the non-contract produce was also sold through pre-arranged contract with the same companies or other companies, as in both these states, CF was mainly there for seed purpose in traditional crops. The other channels were mainly regulated *mandis* and government agency though MSP system as government procurement was high in these two states. In Karnataka, non-contract produces by contract farmers as well as leased and control crops were sold through local markets and a small proportion was sold through wholesale or regulated markets. On average, marketing channels were found similar among large versus small farmers without any form of discrimination against smaller size of holdings among our selected farmers.

EMPLOYMENT GENERATED BY CONTRACT, LEASE AND CONTROL CROPS

Labour requirement was higher in horticultural (vegetable) and other high-value crops as compared to traditional cereals, pulses and oilseed crops, irrespective of whether they were grown under CF, leasing or control groups. In AP, manpower used in one acre chillies production was 184 man-days in contract crops. In gherkin, cotton and jalapeño the requirement under CF was 167, 156 and 107-man-days, respectively, while in lease and control crops, man-days employed varied from 161 to 175 in dry chillies in AP. However, for traditional crops like maize, baby corn, paddy and groundnut under contract or control groups, manpower used was within the range of 30 to 50 man-days.

Similarly, in Karnataka, green chilli, tomato, gherkin, and jalapeño employed 159, 151, 139 and 105 man-days per acre, respectively, under CF. Man-days under control farming in the case of red/green chillies and tomatoes were 154 and 139 days and under leased crops—135 and 104 days, respectively. In coconut, groundnut and baby corn in Karnataka, the range of employment was less than 50 man-days per acre. In the case of Punjab and Haryana, the employment absorption in all categories was much less as compared to Karnataka and AP, possibly due to heavy mechanization in agriculture. In both these states, the employment absorption was less than

20 man-days per acre for the traditional cereal, pulses and oilseed crops while for vegetables like potato, cauliflower, flower, carrot, etc., it was above 20 man-days per acre. By and large, there was no difference in employment pattern under contract, lease and control crops but the nature of crop determined the extent of absorption of labour force which was mostly unskilled labour.

There was no decipherable pattern across different farm-size categories. The labour absorption was random across farm-size holdings as in some crops, labour absorption was more either in marginal holdings or in small farmers whereas it was a reverse case in other crops. To sum up, employment creation was high among vegetable and high-value crops and those crops for which value addition was done under CF as compared to traditional cereal crops and other such crops. Therefore, CF should be preferred for bringing in innovations in cropping pattern towards high-value commodities which otherwise farmers do not opt for the lack of technical know-how, lack of seed and technology and scarcity of defined product market which creates post-harvest risk in sowing such crops. All these issues can easily be addressed by the contracting firms.

EARNINGS FROM ALLIED AND NON-AGRICULTURAL ACTIVITIES

There were two main allied activities namely, animal husbandry and poultry farming. Among other sources, our selected farmers were also engaged in farm and non-farm wages, especially the small and marginal farmers. Some members of the household were engaged in regular-salaried activities either in formal or informal sector. There were also some earnings from self-employment in business and rent from leasing-out land. On average, allied and non-farm income was measured at ₹80 thousand per household, per annum. It varied from ₹51 thousand in AP to ₹62.5 thousand in Punjab, ₹1.0 lakh in Karnataka and ₹1.1 lakh in Haryana. The largest proportion—32 per cent—was contributed by animal husbandry, around 19 per cent by salary and pension and around 25 per cent share contributed by orchards and other perennial and plantation crops. The share of wages from agriculture and non-agriculture sector was around eight and five per cent, respectively.

PROBLEMS FACED TOWARDS LAND LEASING

To our question, what kind of problems were being faced by the farm- ers due to absence of a formal lease market, a significant majority of farmers replied that they were facing problem in rent fixation. Almost all farmers in Karnataka, more than half in Punjab and Haryana and more than one-third of respondents in AP indicated that they were facing this problem. The nature of problems was like rent has no rela- tion with profitability from land, rent is fixed arbitrarily and there is no sharing of risk by landowners in the event of crop failure or in case of any natural hazards. The second most important problem highlighted by the selected households was period of leasing being too short. Around 85 per cent farmers in Karnataka and above 30 per cent in all other states pointed out this problem. The specific issues related to short lease period were that tenants cannot make long-term investment on leased land and they cannot apply FYM due to short lease period. Uncertainty for the next year was also pointed out by majority of the households. Owing to short-term lease there remains the problem of lack of neces- sary investment on the leased land. As per farmers' opinion, they are not ready to invest due to short duration of lease. The short-term lease leads to overexploitation of the land resources. The higher practice of leasing short term also leads to excessive use of ground water as the tenant has to recover not only returns for the labour and investment from the land, but also extra cost as rent which is paid to the landlord. The other problems faced by the tenants were that input subsidy and crop insurance go to landowner and not to tenant and that crop-loss compensation is transferred to landowner's account.

FARMERS' OPINION ABOUT DEVELOPMENT OF FORMAL LAND-LEASE MARKET

Major advantages of formal land-lease market highlighted by farmers were as: land will be taken care like one's own land; can plan for the crop and long-duration crops can be sown on such land also; long term-investment like installing a bore or tube well, using land leisure levelling, application of FYM or even organic farming can also be undertaken; likely increase in crop yield as a result of better manage- ment and better inputs used; local labourers will get more employment;

there will be more crop diversification and it will reduce forced migration; land will not be kept fallow in fear of losing land by the owners; small and marginal farmers can earn more by leasing-out land and entering into wage market and cheaper institutional credit will become accessible to tenants.

Major disadvantages highlighted were: it may lead to excessive use of fertilizers; increase in machinery use leading to reduction in work for wage earners; in the event of long-term lease, land may be increasingly used for other than agriculture purposes; small farmers may struggle to get wage labour if dominance of large holdings increases due to rising activities of lease; small farmers' survival and existence may suffer; lease amount may increase and land will not be available for small tenants.

Similarly, we also posed the question to the selected farmers, 'do you support the development of land-leasing and land-sharing companies who will lease land from farmers and cultivate either themselves or on profit-sharing basis'? The farmers' responses were: the companies will invest in agriculture and it would be great that they encourage us to do work by paying their money; it would be good to have some crop or other in field rather than keeping the land fallow; this practice will lead to reduction in transport costs and improved access to marketing services; land rights must remain with farmers; infrastructure for irrigation will be developed that will increase land value; instead of incurring losses by doing agriculture, it is better to earn elsewhere by doing other activities and wage employment availability will increase.

The farmers who were against such development they opined that small farmers will face labour shortage with company attracting more labour; the bondage and relation between farmer and wage earner will get affected; it may lead to real-estate boom; by giving land to lease companies, it may be difficult to manage agri-allied activities like dairy and poultry; companies might lead to excessive use of fertilizers; increase in machinery use may lead to reduction in work for wage earners; small farmers' survival and existence may suffer and traditional crops may be wiped out; crops will be grown without any gap by company and this may suck up all fertility of the soil; fodder for livestock will become a major issue and companies may use land for construction and other activities.

Regarding land-sharing companies, although such examples are rare in India, we posed this question to the farmers to seek their opinion on the same. Most of the farmers expressed their apprehensions that their land will be grabbed by such companies. Majority of the farmers were not comfortable with the fact that their land may be reduced into shareholding in the company, although having shares in the profit of such companies was sumptuous to some of them. Farmers were especially concerned regarding losing decision making on cropping pattern and resource usage with such shareholding companies. They expressed grave concern of losing ownership of land to such companies and almost all surveyed farmers expressed their denial for the promotion of such land-sharing companies.

FEEDBACK FROM THE CONTRACTING COMPANIES IN THE STUDY AREA

Common constraints faced by the companies surveyed include the following:

- Use of non-approved pesticides by farmers
- Not complying to fertigation schedule
- Untimely harvesting of crop, not as per stipulated timing
- Low yield due to poor practices
- Quality of produce is not given adequate importance by market dealers

Shortcomings in CF arrangements:

- In the existing models of CF, in the early years, farmers benefit from improved technology and higher productivity, quality and production. However, when the market price is more advantageous than the contract price, farmers have a tendency to renege on the contract and the present legal systems makes it impossible to enforce the performance under contract.
- CF models can sustain in the long run only if the initiative/empowerment comes from the farmers rather than the user (corporate).
- In the existing models, farmers are largely 'price takers', while the contracting firm 'makes' the price.

- There is low generation of employment and labour-saving farm practices.
- Low level of commitment of corporate over rural development, lack of transparency and communication, etc.
- Enforceability of the agreement, and standardization and operation-alization of CF agreements are the major bottlenecks plaguing CF ventures in India.

Shortcomings of existing lease practices in India:

- Insecurity of landownership: Fear of losing ownership of land when leased to corporate
- Unofficial leasing causing inadequate rental payments as per market values. For example, in states where the land leasing is permitted, the farmers were receiving ₹20,000 rent per acre. Whereas in UP, the farmers received only ₹7,000, as land leasing is not an 'officially formal practice in this state'.
- No benefits to either contracting parties. For example, if the value of the land increases during the lease period, the farmers do not derive that benefit and similarly, when the produce is less than expected, the company incurs losses.
- Intermodal non-compliance of tenancy arrangements by either one of the parties.
- Large retailers such as Walmart and Tesco have increased the amount of purchases acquired directly from the growers under long-term contracts. This increase in trade through supermarkets and retail outlet has resulted in drastic damage to ecology.

AGRICULTURE WAGE WORKERS: CONTRACT VERSUS NON-CONTRACT FARMING

A total number of 234 contract-wage workers and 150 non-contract-wage workers were selected from four states namely, AP, Karnataka, Punjab and Haryana. Summing up the observations on agricultural labourers, the number of man-days generated in contract farm was higher than non-contract farms consisting mainly of male labourers. There was no significant increase in number of man-days for females after the introduction of CF. The wages earned by the male labourers in a year in the contract farm was almost four times higher than the non-contract agricultural male worker's annual wage income. This indicates a great potential in CF to create more employment and income for the agricultural wage workers.

POLICY RECOMMENDATIONS BASED ON OBJECTIVES

Merits and De-merits of Promotion of CF, Land Leasing and Land Sharing and Their Impact on Various Stakeholders

The Indian rural economic structure is witnessing changes and to sustain an agrarian economy that ensures food and nutrition security, raw material for its expanding industrial base, surpluses for exports, an equitable rewarding system for the farming community, 'commitment-driven' CF and leasing are postulated as viable alternative models of farming. Unlike the earlier unhealthy relationship that existed between the landlord and tenant, with the latter having no say in the terms of tenancy, today the relationship has evolved into a partnership. Another emerging factor has been that all land-holding categories of farmers from small to medium and large are also leasing/leasing-out land to adequately and efficiently use their technical inputs and optimally utilize capital resources. In addition, 'occupancy tenancy' has moved to 'tenancy at will' for a fixed period of time and rentals are paid in cash annually. Overall, these arrangements need to be given an institutional shape to make a high degree of chain coordination possible.

The study reiterates literature that shows that positive income effects are likely a precondition for farmers to give up part of their autonomy in marketing, production and quality control. Assured income was the primary reason farmers participated in CF following the system's ability to obtain superior prices based on the quality of produce. Hassle-free guaranteed marketing was also a beneficial attribute that induced farmers to enter to these contracts. Employment creation was also high among vegetable and high-value crops and those crops for which value addition was done under CF as compared to traditional cereal crops and other such crops. A small proportion of farmers also considered that via contracts/leases they have access to new cutting-edge production knowledge, inputs and upgraded technical support that small and marginal farmers were unable to acquire due to lack of financial capacity. Diversification of cropping pattern towards high-value crops for which demand has been rising at a fast pace is another credible attribute of CF.

The issues that were found disadvantageous and of serious concern to the farmers in the study were problems of rent fixing that might have been related to the issue of power imbalances which is a conspicuous concern across other studies as well. For example, Vicol (2017) pointed out the tendency for unequal power relations between companies and farmers would skew the benefits towards the firm and render farmers vulnerable to loss of autonomy over land and livelihood decisions and indebtedness. The study also revealed that a majority of the arrangements were short-term lease/contracts resulting in uncertainty in the year following the expiry of contract period. Also, both firms and farmers face risks; for example, farmers may side-sell products after having received the services from the firm due to better market prices at the time of honouring the contract. Short-term contracts have also resulted in overexploitation of leased land especially loss of soil quality, excessive use of groundwater resulting in a low environmental foot-prints witnessed by the contract farmers, while tenants are unable to make long-term investments and input subsidies, crop insurance and crop loss compensation were transferred to landowner's account were among the other demerits stated by the farmers.

Therefore, institutional interventions can induce agribusiness firms to offer more attractive and equitable contracts through a negotiation process between the parties to the contract. The most effective being contractual arrangements that would include price premiums at the onset. Further, having witnessed from the study that large holdings earn high profitability, better per acre net returns on account of economies of scale, there is a need to attract more small and marginal farmers via consolidation of small/marginal farmers and boost economies of scale. FPO and producer companies can provide more favourable returns from CF given their better combined bargaining power as compared to individual marginal and small farmers.

Document Legal Framework and Regulatory Mechanisms for Promotion of a Fair and Just Environment for CF, Land Leasing and Land Sharing and Redressal of Disputes/Issues, Safeguards for Contract Farmers

Promotion

- The Expert Committee Report on land leasing chaired by Dr T. Haque provides pointers for the promotion of land leasing and protection of small and marginal farmers through Model Land Leasing Act, 2016.
- Some cases of unsuccessful CF points to the problem of enforceability of contracts. This issue should be addressed by providing transparent price determination mechanism and quality verification.
- Farmer's production risk should be covered/shared in the contract.
- In many states, the present APMC Act still restricts the processor/manufacturer, etc., from entering into direct contract with farmers. They should also be allowed to enter in the contract system (Jain, 2008).

Disputes

Although breach of contracts among the farmers from the study was negligible, following steps could help formally address disputes arising from such issues.

- 'CF can help combine the assets of investors and smallholders in mutually beneficial relationships, where the only limiting factors are ensuring well-defined property rights and a 'proper regulatory framework' are in place' (Deininger, 2011).
- Any imbalances in the CF relation can be addressed through governance and institutional design (FAO, 2013).
- The intersection of the dynamics of the contract scheme and local livelihood patterns produces a particular pattern of participation that excludes the poorest households, while also not providing any significant livelihood benefits to the households who are enrolled in the scheme—a case of potato farmers in Maharashtra (Vicol, 2017).

- 'Firms are the only beneficiaries of surplus generation through value addition which they do not share with farmers' (Singh, 2012).
- Cohen (2013) also situates CF as a corporate strategy of capital accumulation, rather than as an inclusive tool of smallholder development in West Bengal.
- There should be minimum safeguard for the farmer's income in the wake of unnatural events like total crop loss due to pests and disease, drought, flood or price fall due to excess production, etc., either in terms of farmer's crop/income insurance or in terms of compensation shared through the contracting company or the state/central government.

Safeguards

A law on CF in Haryana was on the anvil in 2003. The bill had following characteristics (Tribune India, 2003):

1. Provide an institutional arrangement for registration of sponsoring and recording of the Contract Farming Agreement, indemnity to farmer's land.
2. The regulatory authority will resolve the dispute within 30 days after giving the parties a reasonable amount of time to be heard. If the party is not pleased with the decision of the regulatory body, an appeal can be made within 30 days from the day of the decision. The appellate authority's decision will be treated as a decree of the civil court. The appellate authority should be the concerned district collector and magistrate. Disputes arising out of CF cannot be brought before any civil court to avoid lengthy and costly process of litigation.

Constraints

- In the present system, there is no security of continuity of CF or tenure of land use. So, this barrier should be removed by allowing sponsors and lessee for long-term contract.
- The companies prefer large and medium farmers as compared to the small farmers. It should be made compulsory for the companies to include small farmers to certain extent.

- Monopsony market causes asymmetry of information among farmers. So, there should be intervention by government for information dissemination and alternate market creation.
- There should be a regulatory authority who should register all CF taking place in the state. At present, there is no authority who keeps records of CF and as a result there is complete information gap on which companies and farmers are engaged in CF, which crops and how much area, at present, is under CF.

Document Legal Framework and Regulatory Mechanism for Land-Sharing System

Some changes are being introduced in different states regarding laws on land leasing and land sharing. While doing so, it should be kept in mind that the interest of farmers and not the corporate sector should be given due priority. The right reforms in this direction will go a long way improving the agriculture system. However, marginal and small farmers should be encouraged and it should be made sure that their situation improves within agriculture, not by converting them from cultivators to land-less labourers. They should not end up giving up agriculture, lease out their land to companies and become landless labourers. Land reforms should target to make the land viable for these holders and not making them landless labourers working for the lease companies.

By and large, farmers favoured a formal system of lease market. Most of the farmers pointed out that they face problems in the informal leasing as lease rate was arbitrary and lease period was too short. The short period of lease does not allow farmers to make reforms on such land and requisite investment is not made by them. As tenants keep shifting, the necessary expenditure on irrigation, land levelling, soil improvement and other such activities are not given any attention on such land. The farmers in many cases overuse doses of fertilizer and pesticides in order to fetch more returns from such land which destroys the soil in the long run. The study showed that in many cases, farmers had least returns from the leased land. The farmers also indicated their desire to lease-out their land to lease companies but they hesitated due to lack of trust on such companies. Such cases were found in a plenty in Punjab, where large farmers whose descendants have already shifted abroad and they wish to lease out their land on long-term tenure basis either to fellow farmers or lease companies provided there is legal system of leasing which protects their ownership right on the land. The preference of such farmers is to lease out at least for a period of five to ten years, given the provision under the law. Therefore, future provisions in the contract should be made keeping farmers' interest in mind and based on sound contractual arrangements.

Document Best Practices in the Field within India and Successful Models Adopted Abroad

Several Indian and multinational companies have demonstrated repeated success. These forms of tenancy have provided assured and reliable input service to farmers and desired produce to the contracting firms. The studies also found that contractual design attributes play a key role in farmers' motivation to participate in these land tenancy arrangements. Therefore, institutional intervention in the input market could induce agribusiness firms to offer attractive contracts for smallholders. In addition, consolidation of farmers through FPOs, cooperatives and SHGs can enhance firm-farm coordination and balance bargaining power between the contracting parties that has been a concern for most farmers. These successful cases should encourage the rest of the producing and the consuming enterprises to emulate them for mutual benefits.

Local communities involving small farmers and companies have been successful in decreasing inter-village inequality and contributed to wealth accumulation with the help of public sector support and infrastructure investments in the oil palm cultivation in Indonesia. However, more research needs to be conducted in terms of addressing the multi-faceted implication of oil palm in sustainable rural development (Gatto et al., 2017). A framed field experiment conducted by Saenger et al. (2016) evaluated the impact of two incentive instruments, namely, a price penalty for low quality and a bonus for consistent high-quality milk, on farmers' investment in quality-improving inputs in Vietnam. The analysis revealed that penalty drove farmers to use higher inputs that resulted in better output quality, while bonus payments generated even better-quality milk.

There are also positive revenue effects for small farmers from certified organic CF with the adoption of organic agriculture farming methods (Bolwig et al., 2009). In addition, a comparison of contract and non-contract horticulture growers (apples and green onions) in China found that CF helped raise small-farm incomes and there was scant evidence that indicated firms preferred to work with large farms (Miyata et al., 2009). In India, the backward integration traceability project for red chillies is a market linkage scheme by AVT McCormick co-owned by US spices multinational McCormick & Co. that procures chillies under a farm to fork traceability regime for the export market where India is the world's largest exporter of chillies. It is an example of managing risk, given the geographical diversity of farmers, and illustrated the importance of understanding grounded contexts while CF in India, thereby leveraging a change in the agrarian landscape (Pritchard & Connell, 2011).

In terms of governance of the contract, the following points need to be considered:

- To ensure rules and regulations related to contract formation and terms are adhered to, such as quality requirements, timing, payment procedures, the provisioning of technical support, extension and inputs. While the farmers should agree to deliver all products to the contracting company based on the pricing terms.
- A confrontationist approach to increase procurement price may not only dissuade companies but may also not resolve the issue of monopsonistic exploitation. Therefore, negotiation of a higher price and simultaneously assuring buyers, supply of contracted output should be incorporated in the negotiating strategy of farmer groups.
- Enforcement and monitoring of compliance to the rules such as local government support to legitimize the interests of both firms and contracting farmers by taking mediation measures.
- The local authorities and external developmental agencies, farmer groups can also support CF by including it as a market arrangement in supporting policies for district planning/development programmes on value chains.
- Adopt a system of sanctions and incentives to promote adherence to the rules and regulations such as provision of transportation and credit schemes.

- Altogether, contract-enforcement mechanism is largely dependent on the code of conduct of the company and its ability to maintain a long-term partnership with the farmers/community.
- On the farmer's front, cooperation and collaboration and their ability to organize themselves would go a long way in empowering them to manage their contracts through training and group management.
- A model by Huh et al. (2012) showed that granting farmer the option to renege the contract if market prices were sufficiently high may improve the company's expected profits keeping in mind a long-term sustainable solution.

To Suggest Recommendations for Promotion of CF, Land-Leasing and Land-Sharing Companies and Other Issues Incidental to These Measures

CF is an institutional innovation that balances agricultural modernization and capitalist development taking into consideration the needs of organized small farmers in the face of substantial advocacy against land grabbing. Therefore, incorporating suggestions provided by farmers based on their needs can further promote CF. Some of these suggestions from the study have been listed as follows:

- Seed cost to be reduced
- Provision of crop bonus as well as crop loans to contracting farmers
- Crop insurance should be arranged by the contracting firms
- Compensation in case of poor germination of seed
- Quality seeds, fertilizers and pesticides should be supplied ona payment basis
- Company shall give remunerative price for produce as per agreement
- Timely supply of seeds and fertilizers
- Soil testing facility should be provided
- Farmers meetings should be conducted with the company officials from time to time to thrust farmers' requirements to the company
- Written agreement through a proper registration process is required. The written agreement may be used by farmer and company to seek bank loan as a form of bank pledge

- Marketing at farm gate (field)
- Payment to be made immediately after the disposal of product
- Transparency is required
- Direct agreement with company and not with organizers or intermediaries as is the case in South India
- Distribute vermi compost and organic manure
- Water facility should be facilitated for increasing yield rate
- Produce price should be fixed following the quality of the produce offered for sale
- Make advance payments to the needy farmers
- Company representative should be available round the clock and company office should be located in the production area so that farmers are able to approach the company
- Information on new crops given to the farmers
- Competition between companies is needed
- Company shall purchase whole produce and not only a part of the produce

Moving forward, micro assessments across gender power dynamics in CF and agro-ecological regions need to be conducted to invest in avenues that sustainably utilize human and natural resources with appropriate technologies to improve livelihoods. Azumah et al. (2017) confirmed from their primary survey that CF can also enhance the adoption of climate change adaptation strategies and this forms a viable policy instrument to consider in climate change adaptation for a sustainable agricultural forward-looking agenda for India. Therefore, based on these assessments, policy and legal formulations will incentivize farmers and firms to engage in long tenure contracts/leases. To conclude, following points should be given due attention while finally framing Contract Farming and Land Leasing Act by different states.

- Under the draft Act, there is no representative from the farmers' front in the Registering and Agreement Recording Committee. There is dire need to have a member from the producer organizations, if such organization exists, or from the farmers' union, if so exists, or at least a member from the farmers' commission as the same exists in Punjab, Bihar and many other states. The provision for continuity of the contract after one season and up to five years subject to agreement by both the parties should be entailed in the Model Act to provide durability to prevailing contract among both the parties. In the case of plantation crops, the TOR should be different from the field crops. In the latter case, the gestation period does not materialize any return to the producer. The sponsor should support the producer during this period which can later be deducted from the emoluments obtained by the producer once plantation crops start yielding.

- In case of buy-back and input-supply contract, company/government should provide quality seeds, fertilizers and pesticides at subsidized rate. Farmers gave second priority for the quality input supply.

- Farmers had demanded to provide reasonable interest crop loans from/through the sponsors for the crops grown under contract. This will help to reduce financial pressure on the farmers and will facilitate participation of financially weak farmers.

- Farmers also demanded for providing crop insurance facilities by the companies. The insurance of the contracted crop can be linked to PMFBY through the sponsors. The insurance premium can be paid by the sponsor and later it can be deducted from the total value of sold crops.

- One company representative (especially the extension agent) should be available round the clock in his jurisdiction. The area of jurisdiction should not exceed 10 villages per extension agent.

- Although the quality grade standards are mutually accepted by the contracting parties but ensuring correct price for their produce based on their quality standards is a big challenge. In case of seed production, company itself gives certification of germination percentage of seeds which gives a scope of either misguiding farmers by the company or applying inappropriate means by the company and farmers get under paid for their produce. Therefore, certification of agri-products should be done by the third party (government or NGO) who will give more transparent report of the quality standards of the commodities.

- Pre-agreed price of the produce should be determined in collaboration with farmers, sponsors and government/administration. Sponsors should not be the only agent to decide the price of the produce. Increasing price of produce has been given third priority by the farmers in this study.

- Make the price fixation more transparent. The agreement should include minimum and maximum range of prices rather than only one price. For fixation of price, past values of low and high range of prices as well as the cost of production and normal profit for the farmers should be the guiding principal. The Model Act is salient on introduction of grading system under CF. Farmers deserve premium for the high-quality produce.

- It will be facilitative for the contracting parties if the buying and selling of contracted products are kept outside the ambit of regulation of State/UT Agricultural Marketing Act. The contract will be already registered with the committee so it should be regulated as per committee's directives to keep it simple and straight.

- Farmers, in the study, said that sometimes companies are not willing to take bigger size of gherkin and farmers do not have any alternative option to sell those rejected products because of unavailability of domestic market. Hence, the company should arrange alternatives to sell those products in case of export-oriented products.

- Payment for the purchased produce should be done on the spot. In some cases, especially seed crops, it takes time of 1–2 weeks to get the result of germination rate and then payment is cleared. Therefore, the crops in which it requires certification for assured quality, the sponsor should make half of the expected payment on the spot and remaining amount should be paid after getting certification result. Once the company accepts the produce then it cannot be retracted to reject it.

- To incentivize FPOs/producer companies to opt for CF they should be given tax concessions. Provisions should be made under the Model Act to promote group CF to reduce information asymmetry between firms and growers and to raise bargaining power by the smallholders. Promote new generation cooperatives of small and marginal farmers who can deal with CF agencies.

- The agreement can be altered or terminated based on the mutual consent and due approval of the authority or the officer authorized in this behalf. In the present CF no such provisions exist.

- The Model Leasing Act has not clearly defined agricultural and allied activities. Companies may start using land for commercial purposes rather than crop cultivation. The farmers in the study have rightly pointed out that it may lead to real estate boom on agricultural land.
- Losing employment/livelihood opportunities is the second major concern of the farmers if companies enter in the land lease market. It can be difficult for the smallholders to compete with big companies in terms of product quality and price. Therefore, marketing of products produced under lease contract should be taken care of in such a way that local smallholders should not face much competition by the leasing companies.
- It has been mentioned in the Model Land Leasing Act that the lease agreement can be written or oral. In case of oral agreement farmers will not have trust on companies to deal with them. Trust on companies is the fourth concern raised by the farmers. Therefore, it should be made mandatory for the companies to lease land on written agreement.
- The lease price should be fixed in more transparent manner and there should be upper limit which may vary from state to state. The Model Act is silent on sharecropping and many other such local systems as *bhagidhari* (labour tenancy) and water tenancy (cases in Gujarat) that still is prevalent among many states.
- Although Singh et al. (2015) indicated some scope of intervention for land-sharing companies in the agricultural sector in India, the concept has not gathered significant pace in its adoption. There have been apprehensions among farmers because they view the promotion of land sharing as encouraging corporate-sector control over farmland ownership, losing control over land use decisions and eventual outright alienation of their rights and attachment. The feasibility of operationalizing land-sharing policies in India is improbable and more emphasis may be placed on promoting CF and leasing options. The government may opt to promote collective farming rather than land sharing though corporate sector which will be opposed tooth and nail by the farming community and other stake holders.

References

Abebe, G.K., Bijman, J., Kemp, R., Omta, O., & Tsegaye, A. (2013). Contract farming configuration: Smallholders' preferences for contract design attributes. *Food Policy, 40,* 14–24.

Akter, S., Farrington, J., Deshingkar, P., Sharma, P., & Rao, L. (2006, 12–18 August). *Land rental markets in India: Efficiency and equity considerations.* Paper presented at the annual meeting of the International Association of Agricultural Economists, Queensland, Australia.

Anseeuw, W., Lay, J., Messerli, P., Giger, M., & Taylor, M. (2013).Creating a public tool to assess and promote transparency in global land deals: The experience of the land matrix. *The Journal of Peasant Studies, 40*(3), 521–530.

Appu, P.S. (1975).Tenancy Reform in India. *Economic & Political Weekly, 10*(special issue), 1339–1375.

Ashby, R., and Ashby, D. (2011). *Successful land leasing in Australia.* (RIRDC Publication No. 11/052). Rural Industries Research and Development Corporation.

Ashok, K.M., Anjani, K., Pramod, K.J., & Alwin, D. (2016). Impact of contracts in high-yielding varieties seed production and profits and yield: The case in Nepal. *Food Policy, 62,* 110–121.

Awasthi, M.K. (2009). Dynamics and resource use efficiency of agricultural land sales and rental market in India. *Land Use Policy, 26,* 736–743.

Ayako, A.B., & Glover, D.G. (Eds.). (1989). Special issues on contract farming and smallholder outgrower schemes in eastern and southern Africa. *Eastern Africa Economic Review, 50*(2, August), 194–204.

Azumah, S.B., Samuel A. Donkoh & Isaac Gershon K. Ansah (2017). Contract farming and the adoption of climate change coping and adaptation strategies in the northern region of Ghana; *Springer,* 19(6), 1387-585X.

Banerjee, A.V., Gertler, P.J. & Ghatak, M. (2002). Empowerment and efficiency: Tenancy reform in West Bengal. *Journal of Political Economy, 110*(2), 239–280.

Banga, M.S. (2001). Food revolution—A win-win for farmer and consumer (Anabridged version of the HLL chairman's speech). *Economic & Political Weekly, 36*(29, 21 July), 2733–2736.

Bansil, P.C. (2004). Farmers in lease market. *Economic & Political Weekly, 39*(35), 3955–3956.

Bansil, P.C. (2011). *Bihar agriculture: A perspective.* Concept Publishing Company.

Barrett, C.B., Bachke, M.E., Bellemare, M.F., Michelson, H.C., Narayanan, S., & Walker, T.F. (2012). Smallholder participation in contract farming: Comparative evidence from five countries. *World Development, 40*(4), 715–730.

Baumann, P. (2000). *Equity and efficiency in contract farming schemes: The Experience of Agricultural Tree Crops* (Working Paper No. 139).Overseas Development Institute.

Bellemare, M.F. (2010). As you sow, so shall you reap: The welfare impacts of contract farming. *World Development, 40*(7), 1418–1434.

Bellemare, M.F. (2015).Contract farming: What's in it for smallholder farmers in developing countries? *Choices: Magazine of Food, Farm and Resource Issues, 30*(3).

Besley, T. (1995). Property rights and investment incentives: Theory and evidence from Ghana. *The Journal of Political Economy, 103*(5), 903–937.

Besley, T., & Burgess, R. (2000). Land reform, poverty reduction and growth: Evidence from India. *The Quarterly Journal of Economics, 115*(2), 389–430.

Besley, T., Leight, J., Pande, R., & Rao, V. (2013). *Long-run impacts of land regulation: Evidence from Tenancy Reform in India.* CEPR Discussion Paper Series. https://pdfs.semanticscholar.org/d334/d6ea063963c63f4c71a696c6bae-3deb7bf55.pdf

Bidinger, R.D., Walker, T.S., Sarkar, B., Murty, A.R., and Babu, E. (1991). Consequences of mid-1980s drought: Longitudinal evidence from Mahbnhnagar. *Economic & Political Weekly, 26,* A105–A114.

Bijman, J. (2008). *Contract farming in developing countries: An overview* (Working Paper). Wageningen University.

Birthal, P.S., Joshi, P.K., & Ashok, G. (2005). *Vertical coordination in high value commodities: Implications for smallholders.* (Markets, Trade and Institutions Division Discussion Paper No.85). International Food Policy Research Institute.

Birthal, P.S., Jha, A.K., Tiongco, M.M. & Narrod, C. (2008). *Improving farm-to-market linkages through contract farming.* (MTID Discussion Paper No. 85). International Food Policy Research Institute.

Blaug, M. (1978). Ricardo's system. In *Economic theory in retrospect* (3rd ed; pp. 91–112). Cambridge University Press.

Boehlje, M., Akridge, J., & Downey, D. (1995). Restructuring agribusiness for the 21st century. *Agribusiness, 11*(6), 493–500.

Bolwig, S., Gibbon, P., & Jones, S. (2009). The economics of small holder organic contract farming in tropical Africa. *World Development, 37*(6), 1094–1104.

Brouwer, F. (Ed.), (2004). Edward Elgar, Cheltenham, UK, Northampton USA.

Buch-Hansen, M., & Marcussen, H. S. (1982). Contract farming and the peasantry: Cases from western Kenya. *Review of African Political Economy, 23.*

Bulow, D.V. & Sorensen, A. (1993). Gender and contract farming: Tea outgrower schemes in Kenya. *Review of African Political Economy, 23.*

Cain, M.(1981). Risk and insurance: Perspectives on fertility and agrarian change in India and Bangladesh. *Population and Development Review, 7,* 435–474.

Carney, J. and Watts, M. (1990). Manufacturing dissent: Work, gender and the politics of meaning in a peasant society. *Africa, 60*(2), 207–241.

Chakraborty, D. (2006). Contract farming in India: Prospect and retrospect. In B. Debroy and A.U. Khan (Eds.). *Agri business and the small farmer* (pp.117–128). Angus and Grapher.

Cheshire, P., & Vermeulen, W. (2009). Land markets and the irregulation: The welfare economics of planning. In H.S. Geyer (Ed.). *International Handbook of Urban Policy, Vol.II: Issues in the Developed World*. Edward Elgar Publishing. ISBN 9781847204592

Chitrambigai, K., Pandian, A.S.S., & Shree, J.S. (2013). Perception analysis of the factors influencing the farmers to get into contract Japanese quail farming. *Indian Journal of Applied Research, 3*(6).

Christensen, S. (1992). The role of agribusiness in Thai agriculture: Toward a policy analysis. *TDRI Quarterly Review, 7*(4), 3–9.

Ciaian, P., d'Artis K., Swinnen, J., VanHerck, K., Vranken, L., (2012). *Institutional factors affecting agricultural land markets*. (Factor Markets, Discussion Paper No. 16). Centre for European Policy Studies.

Cianin, P., d'Artis, K., Swinnen, J., Herck, K, V., & Vranken, L. (2012). *Rental market regulations for agricultural land in EU member states and candidate countries*. (Factor Markets Working Paper). Centre for European Policy Studies.

Clapp, R.A.J. (1988). Representing reciprocity, reproducing domination: Ideology and the labour process in Latin American contract farming. *The Journal of Peasant Studies, 16*(1), 5–39.

Clemente, F., & Silva d.J, A.G. (2013, February). Contracts between small-scale soybean farmers and the biodiesel industry in Brazil: An application of the principal-agent model. *System dynamics and innovation in food network*. Proceedings of 15th International European Forum (Igls Forum) (177th EAAE Seminar), Garmisch-P, Germany.

Cohen, A., (2013). Supermarkets in India: Struggles over the organization of agricultural markets and food supply chains. *University of Miami Law Review, 68*(19), pp.19–86.

Conway, A.G. (1986). Land leasing: Findings of a study in the west region of the Republic of Ireland. *Irish Journal of Agricultural Economics and Rural Sociology, II*, 1–17.

Cotula, L. (2012). The international political economy of the global land rush: A critical appraisal of trends, scale, geography and drivers. *The Journal of Peasant Studies, 39*(3), 1–32.

Czyżewski, B., & Matuszczak, A. (2016). A new land rent theory for sustainable agriculture. *Land Use Policy, 55*, 222–229. https://doi.org/10.1016/j.landusepol.2016.04.002.

Dantwala, M. L. (1950). India's Progress in Agrarian Reforms; Far Eastern Survey. *Agrarian Reform in India, 19*(22), 239–244.

D'Silva, C.A.B. (2005). *The growing role of contract farming in agri-food systems development: Drivers, theory and practice*. Agricultural Management, Marketing and Finance Service. http://www.fao.org/fileadmin/user_upload/ags/publications/AGSF_WD_9.pdf

Dale, P., & Baldwin, R.(2000). Emerging Land Markets in Central and Eastern Europe. (World Bank Technical Paper No.456). In C. Csaki, & Z. Lerman (Eds.), *Structural Change in the Farming Sectors in Central and Eastern Europe.* World Bank.

Daly, H., (2007). *Ecological economics and sustainable development, selected essays of Herman Daly.* Edward Elgar Cheltenham.

Dasgupta, S., Knight, T.O., & Love, H.A. (1999). Evolution of agricultural land leasing models: A survey of the literature. *Review of Agricultural Economics, 21*(1), 148–176.

deAlmeida, P. J., & Buainain, A.M. (2016). Land leasing and sharecropping in Brazil: Determinants, modus operandi and future perspectives. *Land Use Policy, 52,* 206–220.

Deininger, K, & Feder, G. (2001). Land institutions and land markets. In B. L. Gardner & G.C. Rausser (Eds.). *Handbook of agricultural economics* (pp. 287–331). Elsevier.

Deininger, K. (2011). Challenges posed by the new wave of farmland investment. *The Journal of Peasant Studies, 38*(2), 217–247.

Deininger, K., & Nagarajan, H.K. (2009). Land reforms, poverty reduction and economic growth: Evidence from India. *India Policy Forum,* 225–279. http://testnew.ncaer.org/image/userfiles/file/IPF-Volumes/Volume%20 6/5_Klaus%20Deininger%20and%20H%20K%20Nagarajan.pdf

Deininger, K., & Jin, S. (2003). *Land sales and rental markets in transition: Evidence from rural Vietnam* (Working Paper 3013). World Bank.

Deininger, K., Ali, D.A., & Alemu, T. (2008). Assessing the functioning of land rental markets in Ethiopia. *Economic Development and Cultural Change, 57*(1), 67–101.

Deininger, K., Byerlee, D., Lindsay, J., Norton, A., Selod, H., Stickler, M. (2011). *Rising global interest in farm land: Can it yield sustainable and equitable benefits?* World Bank.

Deininger, K., Jin, S., & Nagarjan, H.K. (2007). Efficiency and equity impacts of rural land rental restrictions: Evidence from India. *European Economic Review,* 892–918.

Deininger, K., Jin, S., Adenew, B., & Gebre-Selassie, S. (2002). *Tenure security and land- related investment: Evidence from Ethiopia* (Research Paper).World Bank.

Dev, S.M., & Rao, N.C. (2005). Food processing and contract farming in AP: A small farmer perspective. *Economic & Political Weekly, XL*(26, June–July), 2705–2713.

Dileep, B.K., Grover, R.K., & Rai, K.N. (2002). Contract farming in tomato: An economic analysis. *Indian Journal of Agricultural Economics, 57*(2, April–June), 199–210.

Dunham, D. (1995). Contract farming and export horticulture: Can agribusiness revitalise the peasant sector in Sri Lanka? (Research Studies Agricultural Policy Series No.3). Institute of Policy Studies.

Dutta, A., Dutta, A., & Sengupta, S. (2016). A case study of Pepsico contract farming for potatoes. *Journal of Business and Management,* 75–85.

Eaton, C., & Shepherd, A.W. (2001). *Contract farming: Partnerships for growth* (FAO, AGS Bulletin No. 145). Food and Agriculture Organization of the United Nations.

Eswaran, M. & Kotwal, A. (1985). A theory of contractual structure in agriculture. *American Economic Review, 75*(3), 352–367.

FAO. (2011). The state of the world's land and water resources for food and agriculture: Managing systems at risk. The Food and Agriculture Organization of the United Nations and Earthscan.

FAO. (2013). FAO Strategy for partnership with private sector; food and agriculture organisation. UNO, Rome.

Fałkowski, J., (2010). Wielofunkcyjno´s´crolnictwajakoprzedmiotanalizyekon omicznej. In:J. Wilkin (Ed.), *Wielofunkcyjno´s´c Rolnictwa. KierunkiBada´n, Podstawy Metodologiczne IImplikacje Praktyczne* (pp. 53–58). Instytut Rozwoju Wsii Rolnictwa Polskiej Akademii Nauk.

Feder, E. (1977). Agribusiness and the elimination of Latin America's rural proletariat. *World Development, 5*(5–7), 559–571.

Feder, E. (1980). The new agrarian and agricultural change trends in Latin America. In D.A. Preston (Ed.), *Environment, society and rural change in Latin America*. John Wiley.

Fulton, A.L.A. & Clark, R.J. (1996). Farmer decision making under contract farming in Northern Tasmania. In D. Burch, R.E. Rickson, & G. Lawrence (Eds.), *Globalisation and agri-food restructuring perspectives from the Australasia region* (pp.219–237). Avebury.

Gandhi, V.P. (2006). Economic liberalization and rural land and labour markets in India: A study (W.P. No. 2006-09-02). Indian Institute of Management.

Gatto, M., Wollni, M., Asnawi, R., & Qaim, M. (2017). Oil palm boom, contract farming, and rural economic development: Village-level evidence from Indonesia. *World Development, 95*, 127–140.

Giovannetti, G., & Ticci, E. (2016). Determinants of biofuel-oriented land acquisitions in sub-Saharan Africa. *Renewable and Sustainable Energy Reviews, 54*, 678–687.

Glover, D. (1990). Contract farming and outgrower schemes in East and Southern Africa. *Journal of Agricultural Economics, 41*(3), 303–315.

Glover, D., & Kusterer, K. (1990). *Small farmers, big business: Contract farming and rural development*. Macmillan.

Grosh, B. (1994). Contract farming in Africa: An application of the new institutional economies. *Journal of African Economies, 3*(2), 231–261.

Grossman, M.R. (1992).Agricultural leases: Some issues in the landlord-tenant relationship. *Journal of Agribusiness, 10*(1), 65–79.

Gulati, A., Ganguly, K., & Landes, M.R. (2009). *Toward contract farming in a changing agri-food system*. International Food Policy Research Institute.

Gulati, A., Ganguly, K. & Landes, M.R. (2008). Toward contract farming in a changing agri-food system. *Contract farming in India: Are source book*. ICAR, IFPRI, USDA.

Gurumurthy, G. (2002, 15 April). Reaping a rich harvest on foreign soil. *The Hindu Business Line.*

Hakizimana, C., Goldsmith, P., Nunow, A.A., Ruba, A.W., & Biashara, J.K. (2017). Land and agricultural commercialization in Meru county, Kenya: Evidence from three models. *The Journal of Peasant Studies, 44*(3), 555–573.

Hanumantha Rao, C.H. (1971). Uncertainty, entrepreneurship, and sharecropping in India. *Journal of Political Economy, 79*(3), 578–595.

Haque. T. (2001). *Impact of tenancy reforms on productivity improvement and socio-economic status of poor tenants* (Policy Paper No.13). National Centre for Agricultural Economics and Policy Research.

Haque, T. (2003). Land reforms and agricultural development: Retrospect and prospect. In S. Pal et al (Eds.), *Institutional Change in Indian Agriculture* (pp. 267–284). NCAP.

Haque, T. (2012). *Impact of land leasing restrictions on agricultural efficiency and equity in India.* Council for Social Development and Rural Development Institute.

Haugerud, A. (2017). Land tenure and agrarian change in Kenya. *Journal of African Institute, 59*(1), 61–90.

Hill, B. E., & Ingersent, K.A. (1982). *An economic analysis of agriculture.* Heinemann.

Huha, W.T., Stergios, A., and Lal, U. (2012). Contract farming with possible reneging in a developing country: Can it work? Indian Institute of Management Bangalore, http://dx.doi.org/10.1016/j.iimb.2012.06.003.

Hüttel, S., Wildermann, L., & Croonenbroek, C. (2016). How do institutional market players matter in farmland pricing? *Land Use Policy, 59*, 154–167.

Jackson, J.C. & Cheater, A.P. (1994). Contract farming in Zimbabwe: Case studies of sugar, tea, and cotton. In P.D. Little & M.J. Watts (Ed.), *Living under contract: Contract farming and agrarian transformation in sub-Saharan Africa* (pp.140–166). University of Wisconsin Press.

Jain, R.C.A. (2008). Regulation and dispute settlement in contract farming in India. In A. Gulat, P.K. Joshi and M. Landes (Ed.), *Contract Farming in India: A Resource Book.*

Jaeger, W.K. (2013). Determinants of urban land market outcomes: Evidence from California. *Land Use Policy, 30*(1), 966.

Jayadev, A., & Ha, H. (2015). Land reforms in Kerala: An aid to ensure sustainable development. *Land and Disaster Management Strategies in Asia*, 15–28.

Johl S.S. (1986). Diversification of Agriculture in Punjab. Report of Expert Committee, Government of Punjab, Chandigarh.

Johl, S.S. (2002). Agricultural Production Pattern Adjustment Programme in Punjab for Productivity and Growth. Government of Punjab, Chandigarh.

Johl, S.S. (1996). Future of agriculture in Punjab: Some policy issues. *Journal of Agriculture Development and Policy, 7*(1), 1–21.

Kadrolker, V.M. (2016). An empirical study on contract farming in India. *Indian Journal of Research, 5*(7).

Kaggere, N. (2015, 4 November). Karnataka to allow Tibetan refugees to lease land in their names. *Bangalore Mirror.*

Kaur, P. (2014). Contract farming of potatoes: A case study of Pepsico plant. *International Journal of Scientific and Research Publications, 4*(6), 1–5

Kaur, P., & Singla N. (2016). Contract farming in India: Models and impact. *Voice of Research, 5*(1).

Key, N., & Runsten, D. (1999). Contract farming, smallholders and rural development in Latin America: The organisation of agro-processing firms and the scale of outgrower production. *World Development, 27*(2), 381–401.

Kirk, C. (1987). Contracting out: Plantations, smallholders and transational enterprise. *IDS Bulletin, 18*(2), 45–51.

Klaiber, H.A., Salhofer, K., & Thompson, S.R. (2017). Capitalization of the SPS into agricultural land rental prices under harmonization of payments. *Journal of Agricultural Economics, 68*(3), 710–726.

Korovkin, T. (1992). Peasants, grapes and corporations—The growth of contract farming in a Chilean community. *The Journal of Peasant Studies, 19*(2), 228–254.

Krishna Kumar, R. (2015, 21 February). Farm owners work for whom they lease the land and earn extra income. *The Hindu.*

Krishna Kumar, R. (2016, 13 March). Tribal families 'illegally' lease land for ginger cultivation. *The Hindu.*

Krishnan, K.P., Panchapagesan, V., & Venkataraman, M. (2016). *Distortions in land markets and their implications to credit generation in India* (WP-2016-005). Department of Land Resources, Government of India.

Kumar, J., & Kumar, P.K. (2008). Contract farming: Problems, prospects and its effect on income and employment. *Agricultural Economics Research Review, 21*, 243–250.

Kumar, P., Pradhan, B., & Subramanian, A. (2005). Farmland prices in a developing economy: Some stylised facts and determinants. *Journal of International and Area Studies, 12*(2), 93–113. http://www.jstor.org/stable/43107123

Kumar, P. and Sarkar, S. (2012). *Economic reforms and small farmers: Implications for production, marketing and employment.* Academic Foundation.

Kumar, P., & Sharma, A. (2005). Exports of value added products from the agricultural sector: Impediments and strategies for the future. (Mimeo) NCAER.

Kumar, P. (2006). Contract farming through agribusiness firms and state corporation: A case study in Punjab. *Economic & Political Weekly, 41*(52), 5367–5375.

Kung, J.K.S. (2002). Off-farm labor markets and the emergence of land rental markets in rural China. *Journal of Comparative Economics, 30*(2), 395–414.

Li, T.M. (2011). Centering labor in the land grab debate. *The Journal of Peasant Studies, 38*(2), 281–298.

Lin, J.Y. (1992). Rural reforms and agricultural growth in China. *American Economic Review, 82*, 34–51.

Little, P.D. & Watts, M.J. (Eds.). (1994). *Living under contract: Contract farming and agrarian transformation in sub-Saharan Africa.* University of Wisconsin Press.

Little, P.D. (1994). Contract farming and the development question. In P.D. Little, & M.J. Watts (Ed.), *Living under contract.* University of Wisconsin Press.

Lobo, L., & Kumar, S. (2009). *Land acquisition, displacement and resettlement in Gujarat* (pp. 1947–2004). SAGE Publications.

MacDonald, J., Ahearn, J. M., Banker, D., Chambers, W., Dimitri, C., Key, N., Nelson, K., & Southard, L. (2004). *Contracts, markets, and prices: Organizing the production and use of agricultural commodities* (Agricultural Economic Report No. 837). United States Department of Agriculture.

Maertens, M., & Velde, K.V. (2017). Contract-farming in staple food chains: The case of rice in Benin. *World Development, 95*, 73–87.

Mahoney, R., Dale, P., & McLaren, R. (2007, 13–17 May). Land markets— Why are they required and how will they develop? Paper presented at FIG Working Week 2007, Fédération Internationale des Géometrès, Hong Kong SAR, China.

Majida, R. B. and Hassan, S. (2014). Performance of broiler contract farmers: A case study in Perak, Malaysia. *In International Agribusiness Marketing Conference, IAMC 2013*, Selangor, Malaysia, 22–23 October.

Mallika, M., Suresha, S. V., & Raghuprasad, K.P. (2013). Impact of contract farming on economic status of farmers in Karnataka. *Journal of Rural Development, 32*(2), 201–212.

Malpezzi, S., Chun, G.H., & Green, R.K. (1998). New place-to-place housing price indices for U.S. metropolitan areas, and their determinants. *Real Estate Economics, 26*(2), 235–274.

Manas, C. (2015). An empirical study on contract farming in India. *International Journal of Informative and Futuristic Research, 2*(5), 1464–1475.

Manarungsa, S., & Suwanjinder, S. (1992). Contract farming outgrower schemes in Thailand. In D. Glover & L. T. Ghee (Eds.), *Contract Farming in Southeast Asia: Three Country Studies.* University of Malaya.

Mani, G. (2015). *Agricultural tenancy in India: Some dimensions, rural pulse* (Issue–XII). NABARD.

Mani, G. (2016). Model Agricultural Land Leasing Act, 2016: Some observations. *Economic & Political Weekly, 51*(42).

Mansur, K., Tola, M., & Ationg, R. (2009). *Contract farming system: A tool to transforming rural society in sabah* (MPRA Paper No. 13271). Munich Personal RePEc Archive. http://mpra.ub.uni- muenchen.de/13271/

Manzoor, H. (2014). Contract farming in India: An economic partnership for agricultural development. *International Research Journal of Marketing and Economics, 1*(3).

Melly Maitrey, M.L. (2015, 19 October). Not even 10 pc of tenant farmers get bank loans. *The Hindu.*

Melese, A.T. (2010). *Contract farming in Ethiopia* (Report No. VC4PD No.2). Wageningen University & Research Centre.

Melese, A.T. (2011). Contract farming: Business models that maximise the inclusion of and benefits for smallholder farmers in the value chain. Paper presented on Promoting Investment in Agricultural Production: Private Law Aspects at UNIDROIT colloquium, Rome, Italy.

Minot, N. (1986). *Contract farming and its impact on small farmers in LDCs.* Michigan State University/USAID.

Mishra, A.K., Vairam, A. and Patnaik, D. Ed. (2018); Current Issues in the economy and finance of India ICEF 2018. Springer Proceedings in Business and Economics.

Misra, N. (2009, 13 November). Biggest land grab after Columbus. *Hindustan Times*.

Miyata, S., Minot, N., & Hu, D. (2009). Impact of contract farming on income: Linking small farmers, packers, and supermarkets in China. *World Development, 37*(11), 1781–1790.

Murty, C.S. (2004). Large farmers in lease market: Are marginal farmers affected. *Economic & Political Weekly, 39*(29), 3270–3279.

Nagaraj, N., Chandrakanth, M.G., Chengappa, P.G., Roopa, H.S. & Chadakavate, P.M. (2008). Contract farming and its implications for input-supply, linkages between markets and farmers in Karnataka (Conference Issue). *Agricultural Economics Research Review, 21*, 307–316.

Nair, K.N., & Menon, V. (2006). Lease farming in Kerala: Findings from micro level studies. *Economic & Political Weekly, 41*(26), 2732–2738.

Narayanan, S. (2014). Profits from participation in high value agriculture: Evidence of heterogeneous benefits in contract farming schemes in Southern India. *Food Policy, 44*, 142–157.

Newbery, D.M.G. (1977). Risk sharing, sharecropping and uncertain labor markets. *Review of Economic Studies 44*, 585–594.

NSSO. (2013). Assessment survey of agricultural households, NSS 70th Round: Jan–Dec. National Sample Survey Office, M/o Statistics and Programme Implementation (MOSPI), Government of India (GOI).

OECD. (1997). *Review of Agricultural Policies*. OECD.

Patrick, I. (2004). Contract farming in Indonesia: Smallholders and agribusiness working together (Working paper). Canberra, Australia: The Australian Centre for International Agricultural Research.

Paty, B.K. (2005). *Contract farming in India—Progress and potential, agricultural marketing, directorate of marketing and inspection* (pp. 13–19). Ministry of Agriculture, GoI.

Payer, C. (1980). The World Bank and the small farmer. *Monthly Review, 33(36)* (6), 30–47.

Panagariya, A. (2008). Building a modern India. *Democracy, 9*, 1.

Pandit, A., Pandey, N.K., Rana, R.K. & Lal, B. (2009). An empirical study of gains from potato contract farming. *Indian Journal of Agricultural Economics, 64*(3), 497–508.

Phillips, J., & Goodstein, E. (2000). Growth management and housing prices: The case of Portland, Oregon. *Contemporary Economic Policy, 18*(3), 334–344.

Pitale, R.L. (2007). *India rich agriculture poor farmers: Income policy for farmers*. Daya.

Planning Commission of India. (2002–2007). *Tenth Five Year Plan*. (Vol. 2, p. 301). Planning Commission of India.

Planning Commission of India. (2007–2012). *Eleventh Five Year Plan*. (Vol. III, p. 33). Planning Commission of India.

Planning Commission of India. (2012–2017). *Twelfth Five Year Plan*. (Vol. III, p. 168). Planning Commission of India.

Porter, G. & Phillips-Howard, K. (1995). Farmers, labourers and the company: Exploring relationships on a Transkei contract farming scheme. *The Journal of Development Studies, 32*(1), 55–73.

Prasad, V.D.H., Singh, P., Kumar, S., & Singh, B.K. (2013). Performance and constraints of gherkin contract farming. *Indian Research Journal of Extension Education, 13*(1).

Press Trust of India. (2009, 3 September). Formulate land leasing Act for contract farming: CII to Centre. *Business Standard.*

Pritchard, B. and Connell, J. (2011). Contract farming and the remaking of agrarian landscapes: Insights from South India's Chilly Belt. *Singapore Journal of Tropical Geography, 32*(3), 236–252.

Punjabi, M. (2015). *The potato supply chain to PepsiCo's FritoLay, India.* FAO, United Nations.

Rangi, P.S. & Sidhu, M.S. (2000). A study on contract farming of Tomato in Punjab. *Agricultural Marketing, 42*(4), 15–23.

Quigley, J.M. (2007). Regulation and property values in the United States: The high cost of monopoly. In G.K. Ingram, & Y.H. Hong (Eds.), *Land policies and their outcomes.* Lincoln Institute.

Ramaswami, B., Birthal, P.S., & Joshi, P.K. (2009). Grower heterogeneity and the gains from contract farming—The case of Indian poultry. *Indian Growth and Development Review, 2*(1), 56–74.

Rangi, P.S. & Sidhu, M.S. (2000). A study on contract farming of tomato in Punjab. *Agricultural Marketing, 42*(4), 15–23.

Rangi, P.S. & Sidhu, M.S. (2003). Contract farming in Punjab. *Productivity, 44*(3, October–December).

Roy, E.P. (1972). *Contract farming and economic integration.* Interstate.

Rao, P., Joshi, P.K., Ashok, G., Kavery, G., & Kumar, S. (2007). *Agricultural diversification in AP, India: Patterns and determinants.* Manuscript submitted to IFPRI, New Delhi.

Rao, R. C. H. (1971). Uncertainty, entrepreneurship, and sharecropping in India. *Journal of Political Economy, 79*(3, May–June).

Reddy, G.P., Meena, P.C., & Kumar, R.V.P. (2010). Institutional innovations for contract poultry farming in AP—A case study of Suguna Foods. *Agricultural Economics Research Review, 23.*

Ricardo, D. ([1817]1821). *Principles of political economy and taxation* (3rd ed.). John Murray.

Roy, N.V.P. (2016). Land reforms, land markets and urban transformation: Identifying some long run impacts of land reforms from Kerala, India. *Journal of Land and Rural Studies, 4*(2), 1–17.

Runsten, D., & Key, N. (1996). *Contract farming in developing countries: Theoretical aspects and analysis of some Mexican cases* (Research Report No. 3). United Nations Economic Commission for Latin America and the Caribbean.

Saenger, C., Torero, M. & Qaim, M. (2016). Impact of third-party enforcement of contracts in agricultural markets—A field experiment in Vietnam.

IFPRI book chapters, In Devaux, André, Torero, Maximo, Donovan, Jason & Horton, Douglas E. (Ed.), *Innovation for Inclusive Value-chain Development: Successes and Challenges* (pp. 343–374). International Food Policy Research Institute (IFPRI).

Sachikoyne, L.M. (1989). The state and agribusiness in Zimbabwe: Plantations and contract farming (Series: Leeds Southern African Studies, No. 13). African Studies Unit, Department of Politics, University of Leeds.

Sahoo, B. B. (2010). Global market and local players: A value chain system of collaborative strategies. *Agricultural Economics Research Review, 23,* 535–543.

Sarkar, M.A.R., Rashid, M.H.A. & Sarker, M.R. (2011). Contract farming in tomato seed production in Rangpur district of Bangladesh: A financial analysis. *Progressive Agriculture, 22*(1 & 2), 169–179.

Sathe, D. (2011). Political economy of land and development in India. *Economic & Political Weekly, XLVI*(29, 16 July).

Sathe, D. (2016). Land acquisition: Need for a shift in discourse? *Economic & Political Weekly, LI*(51, 17 December).

Sapa, A. (2009, 23–24 April). Food security in the developing countries within the globalization process. In *10th International Scientific Conference on Economic Science for Rural Development*, Jelgava, Latvia, April 23–24, pp. 288–293.

Scott, C.D. (1984). Transnational corporations and asymmetries in the Latin American food system. *Bulletin of Latin American Research, 3*(1), 63–80.

Sharma, A. (2006, 1 September). Lease farming catches on in Punjab. *Business Standard.*

Sharma, V.P. (2008). India's agrarian crisis and corporate led contract farming: Socio-economic implications for smallholder producers. *International Food and Agribusiness Management Review, 11*(4), 25–48.

Sharma, N., & Singh, S.P. (2013). Agricultural diversification and contract farming in Punjab. *Journal of Economic & Social Development, 9*(1).

Shi, Y.J., Phipps, T.T., & Colyer, D. (1997). Agricultural land values under urbanizing influences. *Land Economics, 73*(1), 90–100.

Shiva, V. (2011, 7 June). The great land grab: India's war on farmers. *Al Jazeera.*

Siddiqui, K. (1998). Agricultural exports, poverty and ecological crisis – case study of Central American countries. *Economic & Political Weekly, 33,* A128–A136.

Simmons, P. (2003). *Overview of smallholder contract farming in developing countries.* FAO. ftp://ftp.fao.org/docrep/fao/007/ae023e/ae023e00.pdf

Singh, S. (1997). Multinational enterprises and agribusiness sector in developing economies: A case study of Pepsi in India. In K.J. Azam (Ed.), *Economic Liberalisation in India—Implications for Indo-US Relations* (pp. 202–217). Delta.

Singh, S. (2000). Contract farming for agricultural diversification in the Indian Punjab: A study of performance and problems. *Indian Journal of Agricultural Economics, 55*(3, July–September), 283–294.

Singh, S. (2002). Contracting out solutions: Political economy of contract farming in the Indian Punjab. *World Development, 30*(9), 1621–1638.

Singh, S. (2003). *Contract farming in India: Impacts on women and children workers* (Gatekeeper Series No. 111). IIED.

Singh, G., & Ashokan, S.R. (2003). *Contract farming in India: Text and cases.* Centre for Management in Agriculture, Indian Institute of Management.

Singh, S. (2004). Crisis and diversification in Punjab Agriculture: Role of state and agribusiness. *Economic & Political Weekly, 39*(52), 5583–5590.

Singh, S. (2005a). *Political economy of contract farming in India.* Allied Publishers.

Singh, S. (2005b). Contract farming for agricultural development and diversification in Punjab: Problems and prospects. *Journal of Punjab Studies, 12*(2, Fall), 251–269.

Singh, S. (2006, November).*Corporate farming in India: Is it must for agricultural development?* (Working Paper No. 2006-11-06). Ahmedabad, India: Indian Institute of Management.

Singh, S. (2007). Leveraging contract farming for improving supply chain efficiency in India: Some innovative and successful models. *Acta Horticulture, 794*, 317–324. http://www.actahort.org/

Singh, S. (2012). New markets for smallholders in India: Exclusion, policy and mechanisms. *Economic & Political Weekly, 47*(52).

Singh, A. K., Dagar, J.C., Arunachalam, A., Gopichandran, R., & Shelat, K.N. (2015). *Climate change modelling, planning and policy for agriculture* (pp. 119–140). Springer.

Slangen, L.H.G., & Polman, N.B.P. (2008). Land lease contracts: Properties and the value of bundles of property rights. *NJAS–Wageningen Journal of Life Sciences, 55*, 397–412.

Social Scientist. (1974). Economic Crisis in India and the Fifth Five-Year Plan: Conclusions of the Third All India Conference of the Indian School of Social Sciences. *Author, 3*(5), 61–88.

Sriboonchitta, S., & Wiboonpongse, A. (2005). Analysis of contract farming in Thailand. *MU Journal, 4*(3), 361.

Stiglitz, J. (1974). Incentives and risk sharing in sharecropping. *Review of Economic Studies, 41*, 219–255.

Taslim, M.A., & Ahmed, F.U. (1992). An analysis of land leasing in Bangladesh agriculture. *Economic Development and Cultural Change, 40*(3), 615–628.

Tripathi, R.S., Singh, R. & Singh, S. (2005). Contract farming in potato production: An alternative for managing risk and uncertainty. *Agricultural Economics Research Review, 18*, 47–60.

Torres, G. (1997). *The force of irony: Power in the everyday life of Mexican tomato workers.* Routledge.

Väth, S. and Kirk, M. (2014). *Do contract farming and property rights matter for rural development? Evidence from a large-scale investment in Ghana* (Joint Discussion Paper Series in Economics No. 16-2014). The Universities of Aachen, Gießen Göttingen Kassel, Marburg Siegen.

Vatn, A. (2010, 2–3 July). Transaction costs and multifunctionality. In *Directorate for food, agriculture and fisheries workshop on multifunctionality,* OECD, Paris, 2001. http://www.oecd.org/dataoecd/27/36/37633999.pdf.

Vermeulen, S., & Cotula, L. (2010). *Making the most of agricultural investment: A survey of business models that provide opportunities for smallholders.* IIED/FAO/IFAD/SDC.

Vicol, M. (2015). *Corporatisation of rural spaces: Contract farming as local scale land grabs in Maharashtra, India.* BRICS Initiatives for Critical Agrarian Studies (BICAS).

Vijay, R., & Sreenivasulu, Y. (2013). Agrarian structure and land lease arrangements. *Economic & Political Weekly, 48*(26/27), 42–49.

Vranken, L., & Mathijs, E. (2001, 5–8 August). *The allocative efficiency of land rental markets in transition agriculture.* Paper presented at the American Agricultural Economics Association 2001 annual meeting, Chicago, USA.

Watts, M. J. (1994). Life under contract: Contract farming, agrarian restructuring, and flexible accumulation. In P. D. Little & M. J. Watts (Eds.), *Living under contract: Contract farming and agrarian transformation in sub-Saharan Africa* (pp. 21–77). University of Wisconsin Press.

White, B. (1997). Agro-industry and contract farming in upland West Java. *The Journal of Peasant Studies, 24*(3), 100–136.

Wiboonpongse, A., & Sriboonchitta, S. (2008). Analysis of contract farming in Thailand.*CMU Journal of Science, 4*(3), 361.

Wu, J., & Plantinga, A.J. (2003). The influence of public open space on urban spatial structure. *Journal of Environmental Economics and Management, 46*, 288–309.

Wu, J., (2006). Environmental amenities, urban sprawl, and community characteristics. *Journal of Environmental Economics and Management, 52*, 527–547.

Yaro, J.A., Teye, J.K. and Torvikey, G.D. (2017). Agricultural commercialisation models, agrarian dynamics and local development in Ghana. *Peasant Studies, 44*(3), 538–554.

WEBSITES

https://www.africajuice.com

http://www.fao.org/fileadmin/user_upload/ivc/PDF/Asia/15_Punjabi_potato_contract_farming_for_Pepsi_India_formatted.pdf

www.manage.gov.in/pgdmABM/spice/March2k3.pdf

http://www.businesstoday.in/magazine/cover-story/firm-on-the-farm/story/5847.html

https://www.ccsniam.gov.in/images/research/Dr._K._C._Gummagolmath.pdf

http://www.frontline.in/cover-story/tillers-tale/article4898137.ece

http://apeda.gov.in/apedawebsite/SubHead_Products/Cucumber_and_Gherkins.htm

https://www.thebetterindia.com/47534/hosachiguru-agripreuners-farm-asset-management-bengaluru-andhra-pradesh/

https://yourstory.com/2015/03/hosachiguru-agri-asset-management/

http://panamacorporationltd.com/

https://www.kannadigaworld.com/news/karavali/113391.html

Annexure

Table 1A.1 *Details of Households Selected State and District Wise (No.)*

Name of the State	Contract Households	Lease Households	Sharecropping Households	Non-contract Households	Total Sample Households
AP/Telangana	402	59	0	41	502
Haryana	314	130	8	73	525
Punjab	284	135	1	58	478
Karnataka	408	8	0	93	509
Aggregate	1,408	332	9	265	2,014

Table 1A.2 *The Number of Households Selected and Their Area Operated in Acres*

Farm Size	Contract HH	Acres/ HH	Leasing-in HH	Acres/ HH	Control Group HH	Acres/ HH	Sum Total HH	Acres/ HH
AP								
Marginal	120	1.7	8	2.0	17	1.8	145	1.7
Small	207	3.9	39	3.8	19	3.8	265	3.9
Medium	56	6.9	9	7.1	4	7.1	69	6.9
Large	19	14.8	3	17.7	1	16.0	23	15.2
Aggregate	402	4.2	59	4.8	41	3.6	502	4.2
Haryana								
Marginal	9	2.0	12	1.9	16	1.6	37	1.8
Small	36	4.2	27	4.1	11	4.2	74	4.2
Medium	80	8.1	31	7.4	26	8.1	137	7.9
Large	174	27.8	66	26.1	15	17.9	255	26.8
Aggregate	299	18.9	136	15.3	68	8.1	503	16.5
Punjab								
Marginal	1	2.5	5	2.1	9	1.8	15	1.9
Small	16	4.0	11	3.9	16	4.2	43	4.1
Medium	68	8.3	32	8.0	23	8.0	123	8.2
Large	214	29.9	90	22.2	15	16.6	319	27.1
Aggregate	299	23.5	138	16.7	63	8.2	500	19.7
Karnataka								
Marginal	205	1.7	2	2.3	48	1.8	255	1.7
Small	155	3.8	6	3.7	38	3.7	199	3.7
Medium	41	7.2	0	0.0	6	7.0	47	7.2
Large	7	13.8	0	0.0	1	12.0	8	13.6
Aggregate	408	3.2	8	3.3	93	3.0	509	3.2

Table 1A.3 Tenure of Leasing and Prevailing Rate of Leasing Land

Farm Size	Short-Term lease-in		Rent Paid (₹ per Acre per Year)	Long-Term lease-in		Rent Paid (₹ per Acre per Year)	Duration of Lease (Years)
	Irrigated (Acres per HH)	Unirrigated (Acres per HH)		Irrigated (Acres per HH)	Unirrigated (Acres per HH)		
AP							
Marginal	0.13	0.01	18,154	0.04	0	13,600	2.00
Small	0.55	0.03	15,605	0.14	0.030	10,167	2.61
Medium	0.78	0.16	14,615	0.27	0.000	6,237	3.38
Large	5.24	0.44	12,437	0.00	0.000	0	0
Total	0.67	0.06	14,442	0.12	0.016	9,597	2.62
Haryana							
Marginal	0.57	0	22,588	0	0	0	0
Small	1.43	0	23,196	0	0	0	0
Medium	2.05	0	29,253	0.03	0	5,000	4.00
Large	13.42	0.02	34,531	0.07	0	18,816	9.50
Total	7.61	0.01	33,766	0.05	0	16,413	7.67
Punjab							
Marginal	0.68	0	35,122	0	0	0	0

(Table 1A.3 Continued)

(Table 1A.3 Continued)

Farm Size	Short-Term lease-in			Long-Term lease-in			
	Irrigated (Acres per HH)	Unirrigated (Acres per HH)	Rent Paid (₹ per Acre per Year)	Irrigated (Acres per HH)	Unirrigated (Acres per HH)	Rent Paid (₹ per Acre per Year)	Duration of Lease (Years)
Small	0.59	0	38,784	0	0	0	0
Medium	2.61	0	42,268	0	0	0	0
Large	14.67	0	40,841	0	0	0	0
Total	10.07	0	40,910	0	0	0	0
Karnataka							
Marginal	0.13	0	14,925	0.05	0	8,531	3.91
Small	0.34	0.01	17,460	0.10	0.005	8,837	3.17
Medium	0.34	0.14	12,044	0.17	0	11,458	3.50
Large	1.25	0	18,000	0	0	0	0
Total	0.25	0.02	15,974	0.08	0.002	9,260	3.52

Table 1A.4 Tenure of Leasing-Out and Prevailing Rate of Leasing-Out Land

Farm Size	Short-Term Lease Out			Long-Term Lease Out			Duration of Lease (Years)
	Irrigated (Acres per HH)	Unirrigated (Acres per HH)	Rent Received (₹ per Acre)	Irrigated (Acres per HH)	Unirrigated (Acres per HH)	Rent Received (₹ per Acre)	
AP							
Marginal	0.021	0.005	12,533	0	0	0	0
Small	0.004	0	20,000	0	0	0	0
Medium	0	0	0	0	0	0	0
Large	0	0	0	0	0	0	0
Total	0.008	0.001	14,105	0	0	0	0
Haryana							
Marginal	0.000	0	0	0	0	0	0
Small	0.068	0	15,000	0	0	0	0
Medium	0.069	0	28,421	0	0	0	0
Large	0.139	0	35,296	0	0	0	0
Total	0.099	0	31,960	0	0	0	0
Punjab							
Marginal	0.400	0	33,000	0	0	0	0

(Table 1A.4 Continued)

(Table 1A.4 Continued)

| Farm Size | Short-Term Lease Out | | | Long-Term Lease Out | | | Duration of Lease (Years) |
	Irrigated (Acres per HH)	Unirrigated (Acres per HH)	Rent Received (₹ per Acre)	Irrigated (Acres per HH)	Unirrigated (Acres per HH)	Rent Received (₹ per Acre)	
Small	0.547	0	39,255	0	0	0	0
Medium	0.142	0	35,543	0	0	0	0
Large	0.003	0	40,000	0	0	0	0
Total	0.096	0	37,135	0	0	0	0
Karnataka							
Marginal	0	0	0	0.020	0	15,933	3.33
Small	0	0	0	0.013	0.013	6,500	2.67
Medium	0	0	0	0.085	0	13,333	3.50
Large	0	0	0	0.000	0	0	0
Total	0	0	0	0.023	0.005	11,821	3.13

Annexure 2A.1. Land Leasing Companies

SOME EXAMPLES

Hosachiguru Company

The company established by three directors from engineering background today is reaping money from agriculture. The success of the company lies in good personnel and planning of the company to help investors to reap money from agriculture. The company operates in parts of Karnataka and AP that include in and around Bengaluru, Ananthapur and Hindupur districts. The crops grown by the company include short- to long-duration crops. They are papaya, banana, melon, ginger, pomegranate and timber plants. The company also maintains green houses for healthy seeds and seedlings for the main farm. The company takes 50 per cent of share only in the marketed produce.

Initially, company acquired good-quality land for scientific farming and observed slow growth because of less availability of such lands and even if available, it was at different locations to operate. The company then realized that there were arable lands of landowners who were interested in investing in agriculture but had no time. Such lands were usually less fit for cultivation. Those lands were bought under farming after rigorous manuring and improving the land-health condition.

The company identifies those crops that are commercially attractive, less labour dependent and that suits the soil, procures healthy saplings or seeds, uses technology in place of labourers, adopts scientific farming techniques to maximize productivity and benefit the local environment. The marketing of the produce is also in the hands of the company and it sells the produce at maximum price available.

All that the investors do is to make investments in agriculture and involve in the planning. The investors get to know the day-to-day operations carried in their farms through the online portals they get subscribed with the company. Field supervisors are responsible for on-field operations as well as update the data for the landowners. The model adopted by the company includes planning, mobilizing, farming execution, harvesting and marketing of the produce. Investor's faith in the company lies in the company's transparency in business, expert's service and real-time data availability.

Panama Nature Fresh Private Limited

The company registered and governed by US laws as Panama Corporation Limited is a pioneer today in mineral trading, mining and organic farming. Panama started its subsidiary in India in 2006 in Karnataka at Mangaluru. In order to expand the business in agricultural sector, Panama Nature Fresh Private Limited was established in 2013. The motive of the industry is to reduce post-harvest losses and reduce middlemen chaos.

The company leases land from farmers and cultivates ginger, potato, pomegranate, lettuce, tomato and cucumber for domestic Indian markets. The company had leased 2,800 acres of land in Mangaluru and started cultivating ginger and potato from the year 2013 and by 2018 it expects to cultivate 12,000 ha of land.

Field Fresh Foods Private Limited

It is an integrated food solutions company that delivers high-quality products to consumers. It is a farm-to-fork agri-venture that satisfies the needs of farmers as well the consumers. The company partners with the farmers year-round to ameliorate the farm incomes from 25–30 per cent and increase productivity and impart training and technical knowledge to improve the yield.

Field Fresh has a joint venture with Bharti Enterprises and Del Monte Pacific Limited. Field Fresh offers a range of food and beverage products under the Del Monte Pacific Limited. The company has an Agriculture Centre of Excellence (ACE) at Ludhiana where research and demonstration of crops (baby corn, sweet corn, chillies, snow peas, sugar snaps) is carried out in 300 acres of land under protected conditions and open field cultivation. At ACE, the advanced technologies and best practices are showcased to the partner farmers to increase productivity and farm income in an environmentally sustainable manner. Apart from field demonstrations, the company conducts training and imparts technical knowledge to the farmers. The company partners 5,000 farmers across 8,500 acres in Punjab and Maharashtra to grow vegetables for export to Europe. This has made Field Fresh the number one exporter of baby corn in India with a share of 35 per cent to UK retail market.

Table 3A.1 *Positive and Negative Effects of CF on Labourers*

AP		
Sl No.	Positive Effects	Percentage
1	Wage days have been increased	36.45
2	Income of wage workers has been increased	30.84
3	Regular payment (daily/on the spot)	7.48
4	Interest-free advance	7.48
5	More secure	6.54
6	Company meets costs of accidents	2.80
7	Works hours/time is fixed	2.80
8	Fixed wage rates	1.87
9	Reduction in out migration	0.93
10	Wage earners get their wages irrespective of loss or gain for company	0.93
11	Waste/fallow lands are brought in productive use, thereby providing wage employment for more people	0.93
12	Have information on total-wage days in a season	0.93
Sl No.	Negative Effects	
1	Creates health problems such as allergy, dizziness, vomiting, back pain, etc.	18.75
2	Non-contract farmers have stopped engaging in work as we are working in contract farms	14.58
3	Extract more work by paying less wages	8.33
4	No payment for extra hours of work	8.33
5	No security	6.25
6	Farmers dominate on labourers	6.25
7	Labourers are not allowed to do their personal work without completion of work in farm	4.17
8	Wage rates are on a par with wages paid by farmers	4.17
9	No one is interested in working with small farmers	4.17

10	Delay in payment	2.08
11	Don't allow to work with other farmers	2.08
12	Won't tolerate if we stop working in mid-way	2.08
13	Don't provide advance (at the beginning of the season)	2.08
14	May face health problems in the long run	2.08
15	Work available only for 3–4 months in a year	2.08
16	Contract farmers are very strict and won't allow skipping work	2.08
17	Contract farmers have created a situation where labourers have to bind with them	2.08
18	Land value has gone up	2.08
19	Labour shortage for other farmers	2.08
20	Affects social fertility	2.08
21	Work hours/time is not followed	2.08

Haryana

Sl No.	Positive Effects	
1	We get job easily	72.90
2	Payments are made on time	24.30
3	First aid is taken care of by the firm	1.87
4	Necessary implements are easily available	0.93
	Negative Effects	
1	Workers are underpaid	36.75
2	There is no time limit for work	23.49
3	Work pressure is more	16.87
4	It also creates unemployment	9.04
5	It didn't make any difference	8.43
6	Breach of agreement is easy because of oral agreement	5.42

Punjab

Sl No.	Positive Effects	
1	We get job easily	72.00
2	Payments are made on time	24.00

3	Necessary implements are easily available	1.33
4	Wage workdays have been increased	1.33
5	First aid is taken care of by the firm	1.33
	Negative Effects	
1	Workers are underpaid	41.18
2	There is no time limit of work	26.89
3	Work pressure is more	10.92
4	Breach of agreement is easy because of oral agreement	9.24
5	It also creates unemployment	7.56
6	It didn't make any difference	4.20

Karnataka

Sl No.	Positive Effects	
1	Wage days have been increased	35.77
2	Income of wage workers has been increased	34.15
3	Ensured well being through sufficient work	12.20
4	No tension on availability of work	3.25
5	More secure	2.44
6	Reduction in out migration	2.44
7	Regular payment (daily/on the spot)	1.63
8	Company meets costs of accidents	1.63
9	Works hours/time is fixed	1.63
10	Interest-free advance	0.81
11	Fixed wage rates	0.81
12	Social status has improved	0.81

Sl No.	Negative Effects	
1	Face health problems occasionally—injuries, vomiting, back pains, skin problems, etc.	34.62
2	Extract more work by paying less wages	21.79
3	Allergy, dizziness, etc.	11.54
4	No payment for extra hours of work	8.97
5	Carry heavy loads for long time in a day	7.69

6	No security	2.56
7	Delay in payment	2.56
8	Non-contract farmers have stopped engaging in work as we are working in contract farms	1.28
9	Farmers dominate on labourers	1.28
10	Don't allow to work with other non-contract farmers	1.28
11	Won't tolerate if we stop working in the mid-way	1.28
12	Indiscriminate use of chemicals will affect our health	1.28
13	Don't provide advance (at the beginning of the season)	1.28
14	May face health problems in the long run	1.28
15	Affects social fertility	1.28

Table 3A.2 *Suggestions for Making CF More Beneficial for Labourers*

Sl No.	Suggestions	Percentage
AP (No. of Respondents—50)		
1	Higher wage rates, that is, more than wages paid by regular farmers	26.00
2	Ensure wage employment throughout year	20.00
3	Shelter/shade at work site	20.00
4	Water at the site	18.00
5	Health insurance	14.00
6	Additional payment for extra time worked	10.00
7	More companies need to take up CF and help more people getting wage employment	10.00
8	Health safety measures to be followed (dresses, masks, gloves, etc.)	10.00
9	Transport facilities are to be provided	10.00
10	First aid kit at work site/field	10.00
11	Need PF, ESI[a]	8.00

Sl No.	Suggestions	Percentage
12	Compensation to injured workers	8.00
13	Total costs are to be borne by company in case of accidents	8.00
14	Strict adherence to work time	6.00
15	New crops are to be grown	6.00
16	Pension for wage earners of old age	4.00
17	Companies provide masks and gloves	4.00
18	Companies need to give advance and loans	4.00
19	Adequate time for rest	4.00
20	Health safety and protection	4.00
21	Labourers are to be allowed to attend their personal work, whenever needed	2.00
22	Mid-day meals to be given	2.00
23	Companies should directly work without agents (may be using representatives)	2.00
24	More land to be brought into cultivation	2.00
25	If companies go for more mechanization, wage opportunities my go down	2.00
26	Companies to be established within a village	2.00
27	Processing unit also to be established within a village to help in creating more employment	2.00
28	Reduction in use of pesticides	2.00
Haryana (No. of Respondents—90)		
1	Contract should be in written form	61.11
2	There should be limitation of wage work-hours in a day.	53.33
3	Wage rate should be increased	42.22
4	Payment should be done for overtime work	35.56
5	In a year, at least 11 months of employment should be created	15.56
6	Wages should be more than ₹400 per day	12.22
7	Wage should not be less than ₹350 per day	8.89
8	Wages should follow inflation rate	6.67

Sl No.	Suggestions	Percentage
9	Wage rate should be decided by government	4.44
10	Labourers need to work more	3.33
11	Payment should be done everyday	3.33
12	Contract should be done under the guidance of government	3.33
13	Workers should not be overexploited	2.22
14	Payment should be done in advance	2.22
15	Fare for transport should also be provided	2.22
16	Wage work should be created in our village	2.22
17	Sometimes, wages should be paid by offering grains and vegetables	1.11
18	There should be transparency in wage payments	1.11
19	Some part of land should be given on share-cropping basis	1.11

Punjab (No. of Respondents—83)

Sl No.	Suggestions	Percentage
1	Contract should be in written form	63.86
2	Payment should be done for overtime work	60.24
3	There should be limitation of wage work hours in a day.	56.63
4	Wage rate should be increased	37.35
5	Wage work should be created in our village	13.25
6	In a year, at least 11 months of employment should be created	10.84
7	Payment should be done in advance	3.61
8	Fare for transport should also be provided	3.61
9	Wages should be more than ₹400 per day	3.61
10	Wage should not be less than ₹350 per day	2.41
11	Wage rate should be decided by government	2.41
12	Payment should be done everyday	2.41
13	Sometimes, wages should be paid by offering grains and vegetables	2.41
14	There should be transparency in wage payments	2.41

Sl No.	Suggestions	Percentage
15	Contract should be done under the guidance of government	2.41
16	Workers should not be overexploited	1.20
17	Labourers need to work more	1.20
18	Some part of land should be given on share-cropping basis	1.20
Karnataka (No. of Respondents—51)		
1	Higher wage rates, that is, more than wages paid by regular farmers	39.22
2	Transport facilities are to be provided	37.25
3	Companies need to give advance payment and loans	35.29
4	Ensure wage employment throughout year	23.53
5	Water at the site	21.57
6	Companies should provide masks and gloves	21.57
7	First aid kit at work site/field	19.61
8	Mid-day meals to be given	17.65
9	Shelter/shade at work site	17.65
10	Work hours to be reduced	9.80
11	Health insurance	5.88
12	Additional payment for extra time worked	5.88
13	Health safety measures to be followed (dresses, masks, gloves, etc.)	3.92
14	Strict adherence to work time	3.92
15	Pension for wage earners of old age	1.96
16	Need PF, ESI	1.96
17	More companies need to take up CF and help more people getting wage employment	1.96
18	New crops are to be grown	1.96
19	Companies should directly work without agents (may be using representatives)	1.96
20	Adequate time for rest	1.96
21	Health safety and protection	1.96

Note: Provident fund (PF), Employees' State Insurance (ESI).

About the Authors

Parmod Kumar is Professor, Agricultural Development and Rural Transformation Centre, Institute for Social and Economic Change, Bengaluru, India. Professor Kumar has authored 11 research volumes and published more than 60 research articles in refereed national and international journals. He has published articles in high-impact journals. He is leading several research projects sponsored by the Government of India and various international organizations. He was managing editor of the Journal of Social and Economic Development and is on the editorial board of *Indian Journal of Agricultural Economics*, *Agricultural Situation in India* and the *Indian Journal of Agricultural Marketing*. Professor Kumar was empanelled as visiting professor in economics for deputation to Indian Council for Cultural Relations (ICCR) Chair Abroad by the ICCR, New Delhi. Currently, he is chairing Working Group on crop husbandry, agricultural inputs and, demand and supply projections constituted by the NITI Aayog. Professor Kumar was conferred the International Development Research Centre India Social Science Research Award for his work on the public distribution system. Professor Kumar is guiding 7 PhD research scholars and has been on Doctoral Committee of more than 20 PhD research scholars. His major area of research belongs to agricultural economics, environment economics, rural development and development economics.

Manjunatha A. V. obtained his MSc degree in agricultural economics from University of Agricultural Sciences, Bengaluru, and an international MSc degree in rural development (Erasmus Mundus Fellow) from the University of Ghent, Belgium. He holds a doctoral degree in agricultural economics (DAAD Fellow) from Justus Liebig University, Giessen, Germany. He has completed several state, national and international projects and has been involved in drafting policy documents for the state and central governments. He has published research articles in reputed journals, conferences and leading national newspapers, and books with reputed publishers. His main research areas include Natural Resource Management, agricultural water management, agricultural markets, value chains, impact analysis of developmental programmes, technology adoption, international trade, energy and climate change in agriculture. He served as assistant professor at the Institute for Social and Economic Change, Bengaluru, from July 2012 till August 2019 and from September 2019, he is serving as Director (Evaluation) at Karnataka Evaluation Authority, Planning, Programme Monitoring and Statistics Department, Government of Karnataka.

Suman K. Sourav is a social science researcher who holds a joint masters' degree in rural development from Ghent University in Belgium, Humbolt University in Germany and the University of Pisa in Italy. He had started his education in agricultural sciences at Panjabrao Deshmukh Krishi Vidyapeeth agricultural university in Maharashtra, India. Prior to joining DFG (Deutsche Forschungsgemeinschaft) FOR2432-Project A01 as a doctoral researcher, he worked in a variety of Indian and international research organizations, including Indian Council for Research on International Economic Relations, Institute for Social and Economic Change, The International Water Management Institute, United Nations Economic and Social Commission for Asia and the Pacific, and Precision Agriculture for Development. Suman's PhD study deals with plant growth, water quality, carbon and nutrient flows in rural–urban cropping systems at different spatial scales in Bengaluru. His area of interest mainly lies in sustainable development of agricultural ecosystem in developing countries.

Index

.144|31-34T/22T